VOLUNTEERS AGAINST
CONFLICT

The United Nations University is an organ of the United Nations established by the General Assembly in 1972 to be an international community of scholars engaged in research, advanced training, and the dissemination of knowledge related to the pressing global problems of human survival, development, and welfare. Its activities focus mainly on peace and conflict resolution, development in a changing world, and science and technology in relation to human welfare. The University operates through a worldwide network of research and postgraduate training centres, with its planning and coordinating headquarters in Tokyo.

The United Nations University Press, the publishing division of the UNU, publishes scholarly books and periodicals in the social sciences, humanities, and pure and applied natural sciences related to the University's research.

Volunteers Against Conflict

UNITED NATIONS VOLUNTEERS

In collaboration with the Humanitarianism and War Project of the
Thomas J. Watson Jr. Institute for International Studies, Brown University

**United Nations
University Press**

TOKYO · NEW YORK · PARIS

United Nations University Press
The United Nations University, 53-70, Jingumae 5-chome,
Shibuya-ku, Tokyo 150, Japan
Tel.: (03) 3499-2811   Fax: (03) 3406-7345
Telex: J25442   Cable: UNATUNIV TOKYO

UNU Office in North America
2 United Nations Plaza, Room DC2-1462-70, New York, NY 10017
Tel: (212) 963-6387   Fax: (212) 371-9454   Telex: 422311 UN UI

United Nations University Press is the publishing division of the
United Nations University.

Typeset by Asco Trade Typesetting Limited, Hong Kong
Printed by Permanent Typesetting and Printing Co., Ltd., Hong Kong
Jacket design by Kerkhoven Associates, London

UNUP-923
ISBN 92-808-0923-7
02000 C

To Atsu

CONTENTS

Contents

ILLUSTRATIONS

Illustrations

FOREWORD

THIS BOOK IS a voyage of discovery into what the United Nations has done and is doing against conflict in the world from the perspective of individual UN Volunteers who served in the field. We tend to forget that the world, and the United Nations, are made up of individuals, each with his or her own personal commitment to the cause of world peace. A personal story can often say more than an entire library.

Through these chapters we become part of UN peacekeeping and humanitarian missions. Through the eyes of the volunteers themselves we see the daily realities of life under extremely trying circumstances. We learn of their hopes and fears, their frustrations and successes, as well as the satisfaction derived from their work.

What have these UN Volunteers done? They have organized and observed elections, demobilized ex-combatants and helped them into productive livelihoods, protected and resettled victims of war, and worked on resolving conflicts before they erupt. Reading these accounts, we gain insights into comprehensive efforts to stabilize nations and bring peace. We also understand more about the determination, persistence, and character of those who have volunteered. One cannot but admire the courage and dedication of UN Volunteer specialists working in communities to restore confidence and to bring back opportunities for development.

This perspective balances the pictures of unabated disaster and crises in the world. At a time when the international community celebrates a half-century of the United Nations, the organization has been criticized. However, the UN has, in spite of formidable difficulties, provided humanitarian assistance to threatened populations and successfully aided in the repatriation of millions of refugees and displaced persons in Asia, Africa, and Central America. The UN has promoted democracy by organizing or observing elections in war-torn countries. The UN continues the crucial work of assisting countries to develop their capacities to sustain peace and provide an environment conducive to healthier lives, expanded opportunities, and greater fulfillment. UN Volunteers have lent their talents and dedication to all of these efforts.

The truth these stories bring to bear on the subject describes some unrecognized UN successes, while at the same time it unveils inherent contradictions that UN Volunteers have sometimes faced in the field. Authenticity is part of the attraction of this volume. It is a very human and humane book.

The book also makes it clear that UN peacekeeping and humanitarian missions are only part of the work of the world organization. It has become clear that the international community and the UN cannot afford to implement strategies for peace effectively without simultaneously addressing developmental concerns; the main causes of conflicts are often social and economic.

United Nations Volunteers Programme, a branch of the United Nations Development Programme, is, at its core, a multilateral means of programming and fielding volunteer specialists to assist the developing world. UN Volunteers have been doing this work for 25 years in close conjunction with the United Nations Development Programme. Over the last decade UNV has combined its development work with contributions to UN humanitarian assistance and peacekeeping missions. It seems only natural that UN Volunteers would become involved in the entire spectrum of activities from crisis to sustainable human development.

Peace is more than the absence of war. Sustained development and the healing of societies and nations requires the commitment and staying power of the international community. As UN Volunteers work at the grassroots to reduce conflict, they are also a powerful resource to consolidate peace.

JAMES GUSTAVE SPETH
Administrator
United Nations Development Programme

PREFACE

WE LANDED IN a swirl of dust. 1992: we were behind the lines in Cambodia. A sea of children in the village located next to a Khmer Rouge-controlled area were holding hands with UN Volunteers, waiting for our helicopter. This was a good sign. The volunteers had become part of the village, part of the people. And the people trusted them.

That night there was shooting on the Khmer Rouge side. Yet, the next day UN Volunteers travelled to Khmer-controlled villages, with their "green light," to register voters. Cambodia's elections were being organized by volunteers at the grassroots in the midst of turmoil. These kinds of contradictions are not unknown to UN Volunteers, who face tough assignments in the field, where conflict is the enemy. UN Volunteers have at times voluntarily put themselves on the line to reduce conflict despite the risks involved. We dedicate this volume to UN Volunteer Atsuhito Nakata, who, along with his Cambodian interpreter Lay Sock Phiep, gave his life in the quest for democracy and peace.

Cambodia was the first operation where hundreds of UN Volunteers worked alongside the people who live there to bring hope through democratic elections. UN Volunteers went on to other countries—South Africa, Mozambique, and Haiti—helping to establish freely-elected democratic governments.

But elections are only part of the story. Giving assistance to people in crises, in Rwanda, former Yugoslavia, Somalia, is another part of serving. Helping stave off future violence to promote peace, and creating space for people to develop themselves, is also part of the work against violence.

The experiences UN Volunteers have doing this work can be painful and sometimes frustrating. And these experiences can also be pleasant, even exhilarating, and deeply satisfying. In the end, volunteers who work to make a difference are themselves changed.

We are not only inspired by UN Volunteers—we listen carefully to what they have to say, to learn, and draw lessons for the future. There is so much to learn in the various circumstances in which they serve. An organization should not let that go, but should seek it out, gather it together, and capture the growth. This book is an attempt to do that. Volunteers are not the same after experiencing the field, neither are their national team-mates. In this book they share what they know and one point emerges loud and clear: UN Volunteers receive, just as they give.

Gaining the confidence of people is at the heart of the *Agenda for Peace* of the UN Secretary-General. We at UNV are coming to understand the process of confidence building—both confidence earned and confidence shared—because UN Volunteers have consistently experienced the confidence entrusted in them by the United Nations in operations around the world and by peoples at the grassroots.

These stories demonstrate the value and relevance of the person-to-person exchange in the volunteer experience. Through the eyes of a single volunteer telling his or her personal experience, we can also imagine that it could be any one of us, that we, as individuals like these volunteers, can become directly involved in the tasks to make the world a more secure, safer, and more peaceful place.

It is important that these stories are personal. They combine the facts with the feelings. This combination is as telling as it is unique. We learn more by knowing the reactions of people than from the bare facts of the situation. We can see how ideas on paper are translated into reality in partner countries and communities. This alone can be a source of learning and inspiration for all of us at headquarters, as well as you, the reader.

Running an organization could become a matter of moving paper. We could get lost in the plans, strategies, funding, logistics. I personally benefit from learning about what UN Volunteers are actually doing on a day-to-day basis. This information refreshes, helps us remember why what they are doing is important. The experiences of volunteers feed all of us and tell us much more than a mere collection of words.

That is why I remember from these chapters the smiles on the faces of

Cambodian children, the tattered clothes of Fernando in the demobilization camp in Mozambique, the long dusty roads in South Africa, the old woman in the former Yugoslavia, the compound wall in Somalia, the "roses" in Rwanda.

We thank the United Nations for its faith in UN Volunteers, and the United Nations Development Programme, under whose auspices we serve, for its continued support of these new arenas where volunteers are making their vital contributions. We also thank all of the people who made this book possible. Above all the volunteers themselves, and especially those who took time from their lives to reflect and then write their chapters. We hope you enjoy what they have to say. We thank Diane Conklin, the book project manager, Stephen Kinloch and Gláucia Yoshiura, who diligently worked with her, and the many others who worked alongside them.

The world can be a scary place. Sometimes it seems as if everywhere one looks there is war, conflict, and violence. We can feel insecure, unhappy about the state of the world when we learn nothing but bad news. Yet there are good things happening—and the United Nations organization is part of many of the good things we do not always hear about. This book helps to balance the dreary picture we may too often carry in our heads. It gives us hope and restores our faith that the committed individual is a source of action. To try is perhaps to falter, yet to try is certainly a chance to succeed. Perhaps this is the greatest lesson we can take away from these special UN Volunteer stories.

BRENDA GAEL MCSWEENEY
Executive Co-ordinator
United Nations Volunteers

INTRODUCTION

*Larry Minear and Thomas G. Weiss**

WE ARE PLEASED to introduce *Volunteers Against Conflict*, the fruit of a productive collaboration between the United Nations Volunteers (UNV) Programme in Geneva, Switzerland, and the Humanitarianism and War Project of Brown University's Thomas J. Watson Jr. Institute for International Studies in Providence, Rhode Island.

This volume contains narratives by nine individuals who have worked in zones of armed conflict in the last few years. These chapters are valuable in their own right as accounts by ordinary people of extraordinary experiences on the front lines of history. In addition, they provide a glimpse of the dynamics of major UN initiatives in action and of the difference that concerned individuals can make.

As researchers who have spent the last five years studying the conflicts of the post-Cold War era with an eye to improving the performance of humanitarian organizations,[1] we take pleasure in placing this book before an international readership. Its contents help combat the fatigue and cynicism that often result from the ugly realities of complex emergencies in such places as Somalia, Rwanda, Chechnya, and Bosnia. One cannot fail to be touched by the vivid descriptions of the nine sets of experiences recounted here. In today's climate, the simple fact that the authors volunteered for tough UN missions is in many ways inspirational.

1

This volume is not a systematic description of the experience of the United Nations Volunteers Programme or of the major conflicts in which volunteers have served. Nor is it an academic overview of recent crises, although several of the authors themselves have pursued or are pursuing such studies. Instead, the volume is a series of reflections from a group of international personnel who have shared common experiences on the front lines in zones of armed conflict. While the lens is personal, the experiences are similar to those of UN Volunteers in other operations. Taken together, they represent a composite snapshot of the view from the ground of UN Volunteers in wars and their aftermath.

The management of the United Nations Volunteers Programme is to be complimented for encouraging the publication of this book and for providing the requisite freedom for former and present staff members to express themselves frankly. We envision this volume, which emanates from a year-long process of dialogue between UNV personnel and ourselves, as useful for at least two reasons. First, its users will include persons across the globe considering careers in international service, organizations seeking to equip their personnel to deal with the everyday realities of work in war zones, academics who frequently lack a familiarity with the nitty-gritty of field activities, and the concerned international public upon whose support the United Nations ultimately depends. Second, the spirit of openness and self-criticism may stimulate other organizations struggling with the same issues to encourage a similar reflection process among their own staffs.

The widespread euphoria that accompanied the toppling of the Berlin Wall and the spread of democracy has given way to a more sober assessment of the likelihood of continuing and even rising levels of civil strife. Early optimism has been replaced by a sense of powerlessness generated by a seemingly endless stream of crises confronting an international community overextended by the scale and number of military and humanitarian operations. The need to respond to the multitude of tasks in what are now "multifunctional" operations—combining military, civil administration (including election and human rights monitoring and police support), and humanitarian expertise with an overlay of political negotiations and mediation—is one of the central challenges to the UN system as it begins its next half century.[2]

In the face of this "crisis of crises," it is useful to ponder the first-hand perspectives of this group of volunteers. They deserve to be heard, having devoted a period of their professional lives and applied their personal skills to UN operations. The fact that many are youthful—the average age of the contributors is 34—lends a certain freshness and enthusiasm to their comments. This is the first time that a group of UN Volunteers has written extensively about their experiences in the humanitarian arena. Their personal accounts follow a brief introduction of the UNV Programme, a summary of the chapters themselves, and a sketching out of the themes that emerge and form the basis for our own conclusions to this volume.

THE UN VOLUNTEERS PROGRAMME

The entire international system has been groping with the growing number of armed conflicts and the resulting civilian suffering. The last five years have witnessed a number of institutional experiments, including the widespread resort to using military force (soldiers are now sometimes called the "new humanitarians"); the increased use of non-governmental organizations (NGOs) as subcontractors by governments and UN organizations; the creation of the UN's Department of Humanitarian Affairs (DHA); and debate and implementation of codes of conduct for humanitarian agencies. Even the most established of institutions dealing with internal armed conflicts, the International Committee of the Red Cross (ICRC), is rethinking its unique (that is, Swiss) character. At a time of growing pressure to coordinate activities among international actors more tightly, the ICRC is keeping its distance from the UN in the interests of protecting its neutrality while regularly informing the president of the Security Council about its humanitarian concerns.

As the international community celebrates the fiftieth anniversary of the United Nations, the world organization and all of its components are receiving careful scrutiny. This is perhaps most visible in Washington, D.C., where the 104th Congress is very much on the attack, but it is also true in a more general and global sense as well. In this period of soul-searching, the United Nations Volunteers Programme has itself been involved in institutional adaptation and change. A revitalization is underway to meet the needs of the post-Cold War world. In fact, this volume itself is a healthy reflection of the programme's efforts to come to terms with the challenges of making a difference in complex emergencies.

Established by General Assembly Resolution 2659 (XXV) on 7 December 1970, the United Nations Volunteers Programme was created to foster international development cooperation through the work of volunteers. A subsidiary organ of the United Nations, UNV functions under the overall administration of the United Nations Development Programme (UNDP). More than 70 volunteers are based in UNDP field offices to help administer the United Nations Volunteers Programme under the guidance and supervision of UNDP Resident Representatives. They also recruit UN Volunteers to be fielded in their home countries or internationally.

Most UN Volunteers are provided to assist governments, UN agencies, international financial institutions, UN peacekeeping operations, non-governmental and community-based organizations. Funding comes from a variety of sources. About half is from country and regional funds provided by UNDP. Other significant sources include the regular programme budgets of the UN system, contributions from host governments, special purpose grants by donor governments, and the UNV Special Voluntary Fund.

More than half of all UNV activities are carried out in Africa, a third in Asia and the Pacific, the remainder in the Arab states, the Caribbean, Central and South America, Central and Eastern Europe, the Baltic nations and the Commonwealth of Independent States. About 4,000 men and women from more than 120 countries were posted in 1994. In the last quarter of a century, some 13,000 UN Volunteers have served.

UN Volunteers come from a variety of backgrounds—the recruitment roster includes 130 professional categories under 11 broader headings. They are serving in 125 different countries around the world in four main activities: technical cooperation; community-based initiatives; humanitarian relief and rehabilitation efforts within the UN; and UN operations for peace-building, human rights, and democracy.

Focused initially on development cooperation, the United Nations Volunteers Programme in the late 1980s developed an emphasis on humanitarian assistance. By the early 1990s, UN Volunteers were setting up peace corridors in Angola to allow for the passage of aid convoys. They were administering food assistance in Liberia. They accounted for more than half of the UN field presence in Afghanistan. The Humanitarian Relief Unit (HRU) was established in 1991 (simultaneously with the creation of the UN Department for Humanitarian Affairs) to recruit short-term volunteers. Since then the unit has maintained a roster of standby candidates to meet requests for rapid deployment and has helped to shape UNV policy on complex emergencies.

In recent years, the United Nations Volunteers Programme has become increasingly involved in United Nations peacekeeping operations—first in Cambodia, and later in Mozambique, South Africa, the former Yugoslavia, Somalia, and Rwanda. About 500 people are serving this year in humanitarian assistance efforts in Rwanda, Haiti, the former Yugoslavia, and Angola. Since 1992, more than 1,500 UN Volunteers have worked in emergency relief, reconstruction, rehabilitation, and disaster preparedness in Africa, Asia, and Central America, as well as in the former Soviet republics of Azerbaijan, Tajikistan, Georgia, and Uzbekistan. Today between 10 and 20 per cent of the 4,000 UN Volunteers fielded annually are helping in UN humanitarian relief operations and democratization efforts. A review of recent experience was the subject of a 1994 special consultation, "Between Crisis and Development."[3]

Who are these volunteers? Drawn mainly from the developing countries, they each bring with them on average 10 years of practical working experience. In the humanitarian arena, they are engaged in conflict resolution and prevention, confidence and capacity-building at the community level, rehabilitation of infrastructure, repatriation and reintegration of refugees, food aid monitoring, camp management, human rights promotion and protection, democratization, demobilization of soldiers and reintegration into civilian life, implementation of disaster prevention and preparedness programmes. The accounts in this volume provide a microcosm of such UNV activities.

As in many societies, volunteer contributions to the UN system are special, by virtue both of their modest costs and of their spirit of solidarity and partnership with those in distress. The average annual per capita cost of an international UN Volunteer is about $30,000. Moreover, the comparative advantage among international volunteer-sending agencies derives from the programme's identification with the United Nations and its multilateral character. UNV mobilizes resources from around the world. It benefits from UNDP and the UN system's institutional presence in the field in virtually all developing countries and many other countries in transition.

AN OVERVIEW OF THE CHAPTERS

The volume appropriately begins with Nandini Srinivasan's "Organizing Elections in a Mine Field: The Cambodian Challenge." The UN Transitional Authority in Cambodia (UNTAC) represented in many ways the most ambitious UN undertaking since the UN's controversial efforts in the Congo in the early 1960s. A country traumatized by civil war and genocide, Cambodia was the setting for an influx of over 20,000 outside personnel—military, police, and civilian. Although UNTAC has been analyzed in detail,[4] the story is less well known of how some 465 UN Volunteers serving as District Electoral Supervisors recruited and trained 50,000 Cambodians and how together they organized the registration and voting of millions of citizens. Srinivasan, an Indian national who now is a lecturer at the University of Malawi, helps readers to understand the delicate conditions resulting from insecurity—proven by the death of one Japanese UN Volunteer, to whom this book is dedicated—and the crucial contribution of UN Volunteers to a successful election in May 1993. Although the country has not definitively turned the corner on its conflict, Cambodians have begun a long and difficult road toward reconstruction and peace. The special representative of the Secretary-General in Cambodia, Yasushi Akashi, credited UN Volunteers with having been "the spearhead of consciousness-raising for democracy."

In Chapter 2, Diane Conklin presents "The Politics of Reassurance: International Presence at the Local Level in South Africa." A former journalist with a law degree with whom we worked to produce this volume, she examines efforts by some 200 UN Volunteers that helped to open the door to the first all-race elections in post-apartheid South Africa in April 1994. Deliberately recruited for this delicate assignment from 39 different countries, half of the volunteers were African. They joined observers from governments and NGOs to constitute a large international presence during the transition from white-minority to black-majority democracy. Confronting random violence, one of the major UNV contributions, according to Conklin, was the presence of multiracial teams of volunteers. Their personal witness demonstrated throughout South Africa that cooperation among races was not an abstraction but a reality.

Chapter 3 consists of Gláucia Vaz Yoshiura's "Voting for Peace: Preparing for Post-war Democracy in Mozambique." The author is a Brazilian national with a background in corporate law who is now pursuing doctoral studies after her UNV assignment. Unlike other recent civil wars in which the UN has been active, Mozambique has been the subject of few scholarly analyses.[5] Thus, after 16 years and a million inhabitants displaced by a grisly guerrilla war, a presentation of the role of UN Volunteers in the UN Operation in Mozambique (ONUMOZ) is welcome. The tasks accomplished ranged from voter registration to monitoring political campaigns, from staffing polling booths to counting the results. As elsewhere, UN efforts would have been considerably diminished without the presence of volunteers, especially in outlying areas away from the relative security and comfort of the cities.

UN Volunteers were active in other sectors, as detailed by Henri Valot's "End of the War Machinery: Demobilization in Mozambique." A French national who is also currently pursuing a doctorate, the author examines the contribution of UN Volunteers in assisting the UN military to establish and manage some 50 demobilization assembly areas for the two warring parties to lay down their arms. The transition involved a rough passage for the soldiers, personally and psychologically, as is described in moving personal images. Demobilization has been too often unsuccessful; one need only compare what happened on the other side of the continent in Angola, another former Portuguese colony, to gauge its importance. This chapter points to an ongoing role for UN Volunteers in future UN demobilization efforts.

No other recent humanitarian crisis has proved more unsettling to the international community than the one in the former Yugoslavia.[6] Chapter 5 consists of Benny Ben Otim's "Caught in the Crossfire: Dilemmas of Human Rights Protection in Former Yugoslavia." A former refugee from the earlier wars in his own Uganda, the author, having completed his UNV assignment, continues to work in Zagreb as a staff member of the UN High Commissioner for Refugees. The size and complexity of the problem in the heart of Europe—four million persons depend on international succour for daily survival—present challenges that are not only logistical but substantive in nature.[7] The author provides insights into the painful dilemma faced by UN Volunteers and others who may have helped to foster "ethnic cleansing" by moving refugees rather than leaving them exposed in unsafe "safe areas."

Chapter 6 is Stephen P. Kinloch's "Back from Rwanda: Confronting the Aftermath of Genocide." A dual French and British national also working on his doctorate, the author has served in four war zones as a UN Volunteer. The subject for his analysis is his last assignment as a volunteer in the south-western area of Rwanda initially stabilized by the French through *Opération Turquoise*. Lamenting the inability of the member states of the United Nations to stop the genocide,[8] the author underscores the need to find ways to prevent such carnage in the first place and lends another voice to Sir Brian Urquhart's call for the establishment of a rapid deployment force.

Chapter 7 consists of Anthony C. Nweke's analysis of "Behind the Compound Wall: Volunteerism under Challenge in Somalia." The various military efforts by the international community, both under the auspices of the UN and of a U.S.-led coalition, have done little to overcome Somalia's tragedy.[9] The determined efforts by humanitarians, including the UN Volunteers recounted in this chapter, have unfortunately done little to counteract the sentiment that has emerged since the UN's withdrawal in March 1995 that little can be done by outsiders to rebuild a "failed state."[10] The issues at the interface between military actions and traditional principles of impartiality and neutrality present a conundrum for humanitarians. The UN's pullout from Somalia was an admission that outsiders had come to a dead end. This theme is graphically illustrated by

Nweke in his discussion of the second UN Operation in Somalia (UNO-SOM II). Confined to the official compound, his situation was typical of the plight of the UN as a whole, its operation hostage to the raging clan warfare outside the walls.

Chapter 8 is Masako Yonekawa's "Part of the System: Varieties of Volunteer Support Roles." The author is a Japanese national and sociologist who is still serving as a UN Volunteer in Rwanda, her sixth such assignment. The subtitle of her essay emphasizes the diversity of her postings and the range of contributions by a single individual, and by volunteers more generally, to the work of the UN system in war zones. Whether dealing with insecurity in Cambodia, racial tensions in South Africa, the grinding madness of Liberia's civil war, the isolation of staff in Somalia, or the aftermath of genocide in Tanzania and Rwanda, Yonekawa stresses what has been the key to UNV success and her own personal satisfaction: working with the grassroots and building local capacities.

The final essay is Shantum Seth's "The Art of Building Peace: Artisan Skills for Development and Peace in South Asia." A dual Indian-British national and a UN Volunteer Programme Manager, the author extols the virtues of UN Volunteers employed in what the Secretary-General in his *Agenda for Peace* has called "post-conflict peace-building."[11] In light of the debris from the ongoing humanitarian crises detailed in previous essays and the accumulated costs of conflicts during the Cold War,[12] this essay summarizes positive learning experiences from a series of efforts by UN Volunteers in South Asia to provide an economic basis for communities to get back on their collective feet after bitter wars. It holds before us the continuing challenge of pursuing development in the midst of crises, precisely at the time when the immediacy of suffering seems to overshadow longer-term considerations. Seth's approach recalls the need to approach even emergency assistance from a development perspective.[13] Since the roots of armed conflict often lie in economic inequalities, bringing people together across barriers of caste, religion, and national borders suggests an example of grassroots methods of preventing conflict in the first place.

SOME RECURRING ISSUES

The conflicts treated in this volume, and others raging across the world, vary enormously. The geopolitical context must be taken into account in interpreting the value and limitations of contributions by UN Volunteers and others in providing assistance. Some conflicts that raged during the

Cold War have benefited from its passing—for example, the struggles in Central America, Cambodia, the Middle East, Mozambique, and South Africa. Yet in Afghanistan and Angola, conflicts fueled by superpower rivalry have taken on a life of their own. East-West rivalries dampened strife in the Balkans and the former Soviet Union for decades. More recently, however, shooting wars have erupted in nine of the 53 member states of the Organization for Security and Cooperation in Europe (OSCE). In some settings with virtually no direct links to earlier superpower rivalry—for example, in Liberia, the Sudan, and Sri Lanka—seething ethnic, political, and religious tensions continue to boil. While it is inappropriate to take refuge in the scholarly shelter that every conflict is unique and generalizations are impossible, it is important to be aware of the limits of analysis across the vastly differing terrains.

There is also a fundamental difficulty in evaluating recent UN operations. In examining the UN Volunteers Programme and other such international efforts, we confront the ambiguity of "success" and "failure." Have efforts in the former Yugoslavia been successful because they saved lives and avoided a wider conflict in Europe, or a failure because the international community has not stood up to aggression, genocide, and the forced movement of peoples? Were short-term efforts in Somalia successful because death rates dropped in 1993, or a failure because the billions spent did not prevent a reversion to banditry and chaos in 1995? Were efforts in Cambodia a short-term success because Cambodians went to the polls and permitted the return of King Norodom Sihanouk, or a long-term failure because the Khmer Rouge remain poised to return to civil war? Were efforts in El Salvador successful because peace was negotiated and elections held, or a failure because the root causes of the civil war remain in the form of unequal land distribution and limited participation in decision-making? Without greater precision about the expectations of comprehensive operations, analysts can agree on the facts and differ in their evaluations about the utility of a particular operation.

Whatever the differences among conflicts and the difficulties in establishing criteria for success and failure, the volunteer experiences recounted in these pages illustrate the struggle of UN Volunteers with the same fundamental issues of policy and practice which currently preoccupy the broader international community. They have encountered in microcosm the practical dilemmas which have given the broader humanitarian effort pause. Their reflections constitute a rich vein of experience that should be mined for answers to general policy queries such as the following:

1. What types of outside assistance and involvement are the most effec-

tive—or the least effective—in international responses to humanitarian emergencies?

2. What is the proper balance between and among humanitarian, political/diplomatic, and military interventions in responding to conflicts?
3. In crisis situations in which states and governments have failed to meet human needs and protect human rights, should the international community be prepared to step in on a temporary basis?
4. Without significant disarmament of belligerents and enhanced measures to slow the international arms trade, is the world simply on a treadmill in assistance efforts in war zones?
5. With dwindling resources and growing crises, what should be the relative priority of responding to "loud" emergencies (such as wars) as against "silent" emergencies (chronic impoverishment or disenfranchisement)? Should belligerents be left alone to slug it out until a situation is "ripe" for outside mediation and assistance?

The answers to these questions—"dilemmas" would be a better description since the choices are rarely clear or easy—vary from person to person and from country to country. However, many of the perspectives offered in this volume about humanitarian initiatives and the roles of the United Nations are remarkably similar to those formulated over the years by other analysts as well.[14]

Emerging from these chapters are also a number of more specific questions as UN Volunteers seek to interpret their own experiences. These include the following:

1. What types of professionals and personalities are best suited to work in complex emergencies? What types of briefings are necessary before posting such international personnel? How may their experiences help to shape future programme planning? How may a cadre of professionals with multiple country experience be developed and utilized?
2. How much bureaucratic inertia is "normal" and "inevitable" in massive international responses to major emergencies? How much of the impatience with UN procedures and administration is justifiable, and how much is simply the idealistic reaction of newcomers to international humanitarian action?
3. How important are links to community groups? To what extent are such connections feasible for outsiders not steeped in local cultures?
4. What is the value of personal witness and lifestyle in a war zone?
5. What is "volunteerism?" What types of differences, if any, in salaries, benefits, and responsibilities are justifiable for different types of assignments in war zones? Should differences between UN Volunteers and regular UN staff be based on productivity, experience, results, or job titles?

In the light of the nine accounts that follow, we will examine some of these and related issues in the concluding chapter.

NOTES

* Codirectors of the Humanitarianism and War Project at Brown University's Thomas J. Watson Jr. Institute for International Studies. Larry Minear has worked on humanitarian and development issues since 1972 on behalf of non-governmental agencies and has served as a consultant to UN and U.S. government organizations. Thomas G. Weiss has written extensively about international security and organizations in addition to having held a number of UN posts. He is now associate director of the Watson Institute and executive director of the Academic Council on the UN System.

1. For an overview of some of our findings and recommendations, see *Mercy Under Fire: War and the Global Humanitarian Community*. Boulder: Westview, 1995.

2. See Weiss, Thomas G., ed. *The United Nations and Civil Wars*. Boulder: Lynne Rienner, 1995.

3. For a summary of the discussions, see " 'Between Crisis and Development': Volunteer Roles and UNV's Contribution," Summary of Discussions, 4th UNV Special Consultation, October 20–21, 1994.

4. See, for example, Ratner, Steven R. *The New UN Peacekeeping*. New York: St. Martin's, 1995; Findlay, Trevor. *Cambodia: The Legacy and Lesson of UNTAC*. SIPRI Research Report No. 9. Oxford: Oxford University Press, 1995; Heininger, Janet E. *Peacekeeping in Transition: The United Nations in Cambodia*. New York: Twentieth Century Fund, 1994; and Chopra, Jarat. *UN Transition in Cambodia*. Occasional Paper #15. Providence: Watson Institute, 1993.

5. One exception is Hume, Cameron. *Ending Mozambique's War*. Washington: U.S. Institute of Peace, 1994.

6. See, for example, Minear, Larry (team leader), Jeffrey Clark, Roberta Cohen, Dennis Gallagher, Iain Guest, and Thomas G. Weiss. *Humanitarian Action in the Former Yugoslavia: The UN's Role, 1991–1993*. Occasional Paper #18. Providence: Watson Institute, 1994; Rieff, David. *Slaughterhouse: Bosnia and the Failure of the West*. New York: Simon & Schuster, 1995; Ullman, Richard H., ed. *The World and Yugoslavia's Wars*. New York: 1996 forthcoming; and Woodward, Susan L. *Balkan Tragedy: Chaos and Dissolution After the Cold War*. Washington: Brookings Institution, 1995.

7. For an elaboration of the problems of protecting the human rights of refugees and the internally displaced, see Human Rights Watch. *Lost Agenda: Human Rights and U.N. Field Operations*. New York: Human Rights Watch, 1993; and *Human Rights Watch World Report 1995*. New York: Human Rights Watch, 1994.

8. See, for example, Destexhe, Alain. *Rwanda: Essai sur le génocide*. Brussels: Editions Complexe, 1994; Brauman, Rony. *Devant le Mal: Rwanda, un génocide en direct*. Paris: Arléa, 1994; Minear, Larry and Philippe Guillot. *Soldiers to the Rescue: Humanitarian Lessons from Rwanda*. Paris: Organisation for Economic Co-operation and Development, 1995 forthcoming; and Omaar, Rakiya and Alex de Waal. *Rwanda: Death, Despair and Defiance*. London: African Rights, 1994.

9. See, for example, Herbst, Jeffrey and Walter Clarke, eds. *Revisiting Somalia: The Lessons of U.S./U.N. Intervention*. Boulder: Lynne Rienner, 1996 forthcoming; Sommer, John G. *Hope Restored? Humanitarian Aid in Somalia 1990–1994*. Washington: Refugee Policy Group, 1994; Allard, Kenneth. *Somalia Operations: Lessons Learned* Washington: National Defense University, 1995; Sahnoun, Mohamed. *Somalia: Missed Opportunities*. Washington: U.S. Institute of Peace, 1994; and Chopra, Jarat, Åge Eknes, and Toralv Nordbø. *Fighting for Hope in Somalia*. Peacekeeping and Multi-

national Operations Paper No. 6. Oslo: Norwegian Institute of International Affairs, 1995).
10. Helman Gerald B. and Steven R. Ratner. "Saving Failed States." *Foreign Policy* 89 (winter 1992–93): pp. 3–20.
11. Boutros-Ghali, Boutros. *An Agenda for Peace*. New York: United Nations, 1992.
12. For a discussion and cost estimate, see Lake, Anthony E., ed. *After the Wars: Reconstruction in Afghanistan, Indochina, Central America, Southern Africa, and the Horn of Africa*. Washington: Overseas Development Council, 1990.
13. See Anderson Mary B., and Peter J. Woodrow. *Rising from Ashes: Development Strategies at Times of Disaster*. Boulder: Westview, 1989; Anderson, Mary B. "Development and Prevention of Humanitarian Emergencies." In: Weiss Thomas G., and Larry Minear, eds. *Humanitarianism Across Borders: Sustaining Civilians in Times of War*. Boulder: Lynne Rienner, 1993, pp. 23–38; and Stiefel, Matthias. *UNDP in Conflicts and Disasters: An Overview Report of the "Continuum Project."* Geneva: Graduate Institute of International Studies, May 1994.
14. See Weiss, Thomas G., and Leon Gordenker, eds. *NGOs, the UN, and Global Governance*. Boulder: Lynne Rienner, 1996 forthcoming.

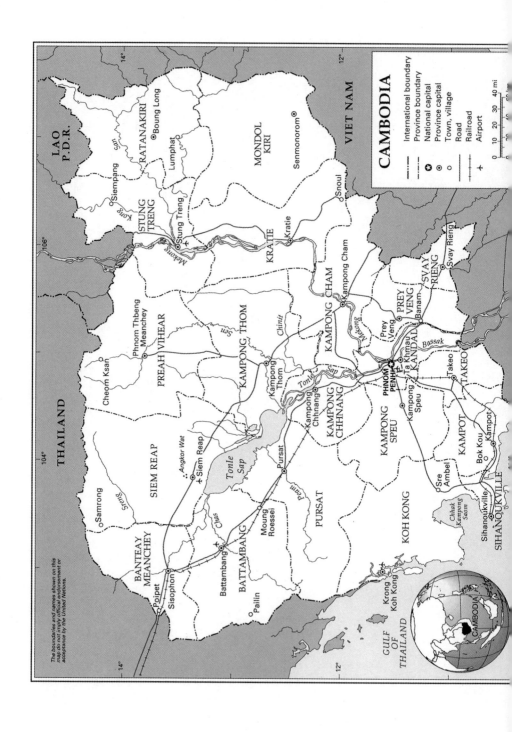

1

ORGANIZING ELECTIONS IN A MINE FIELD: THE CAMBODIAN CHALLENGE

Nandini Srinivasan

THERE WERE NO sounds of exploding mines or gunfire, nor evidence of any physical threat at the time of my arrival in Phnom Penh mid-1992, nearly a year before the elections slated for May 1993. On the contrary, the main streets were alive with the roar of congested traffic, four-wheel drive cars, cycle rickshaws, moto taxis. Large billboards advertised the local Tiger beer; restaurants were doing business all around the city. The old central market, where shoppers could buy anything from bananas to 24 carat gold, was buzzing with activity from morning to evening. On the surface, everything seemed peaceful.

The Cambodians appeared at first to the casual observer as innocent, warm-hearted, and friendly people. A closer look, however, combined with serious conversations with them, quickly revealed unseen tensions and anxieties, as well as their resilient, confident, and courageous nature. Their revelations were terrifying and pathetic. Almost each one had a story about the loss of a dear one; stories surfaced of torture and brutal

Nandini Srinivasan is an Indian national born in 1961. Presently a lecturer in social sciences at the University of Malawi, she served as a UN Volunteer District Electoral Supervisor, who also worked in human rights within the United Nations Transitional Authority in Cambodia from July 1992 to June 1993. She holds a Ph.D. in International Relations from the University of Bombay.

treatment at the hands of the former Khmer Rouge regime. But it was not easy to get a Cambodian to speak. One could read fear in Cambodian faces, fear of Pol Pot, the Khmer Rouge leader who overthrew the government in 1975 and engineered millions of deaths, fear of mines, fear of many unknown things. Therefore, to get a Cambodian to trust and to talk required patience, understanding, and compassion. In spite of what they had gone through, the Cambodian people still had hope, which was now placed in an apparently straightforward project: holding democratic elections. They looked to the international community for the means that they expected would ensure their future peace and prosperity.

Organizing elections in a country where invisible mines, both underground and psychological, could blow up during any step and stage of the process, meant Cambodia was going to be a real challenge. This challenge extended to the Cambodians themselves and to everyone serving with the United Nations Transitional Authority in Cambodia (UNTAC), especially for the United Nations Volunteers charged with organizing elections at the local level.

I served as a UN Volunteer in Cambodia for one year. Out of that experience I learned about the Cambodian people, their way of life, and their aspirations for the future. I also learned about organizing elections and conducting civic and human rights education within a United Nations mission. In this chapter, I will describe the role the UN Volunteers played in the electoral process in Cambodia within the complex UNTAC operation.

A MASSIVE OPERATION IN A FRAGILE CONTEXT

After centuries of foreign interference, and many brushes with near-disintegration, Cambodia by the early 1990s had survived its difficult history and one of the most horrible and systematic genocides of modern times.[1] The country was the victim of the East-West Cold War game, and a battleground for outside ideological and political currents, the economic ambitions of Thailand, and the demographic pressures of Vietnam. Cambodia was indeed a traumatized country.[2]

Since 1979, when the Pol Pot regime was overthrown by the Vietnamese troops, Cambodia had been under constant UN purview, leading to several initiatives by the UN Secretary-General. After decades of conflict, the conditions for the signing of a peace agreement began to materialize in the 1980s. The less active role of the former Soviet Union in world affairs, the converging commercial interests of China and Vietnam, and the charismatic figure of Cambodia's Prince Norodom Sihanouk set the framework that would make possible the launching of an active United Nations operation in Cambodia. The process of dialogue and negotiation gathered momentum in the late 1980s and led to the first face-to-face talks between all four Cambodian factions[3] at the Jakarta Informal Meeting in Indonesia in July 1988, followed by a second meeting in February 1989. A general understanding emerged from the discussions that an international control mechanism should help supervise any agreement reached by the factions.[4]

The four Cambodian factions, along with 19 countries, participated in the month-long Paris Peace Conference held in July 1989 at the initiative of the French government. Following additional meetings in 1990,[5] a second session of the Paris Peace Conference took place in October 1991. These efforts finally culminated in a 1991 peace plan, known generally as the Paris Peace Agreements.[6]

The peace plan also recognized an enhanced UN role in Cambodia and anticipated the establishment of UNTAC, which UN Secretary-General Boutros Boutros-Ghali called "[m]assive in size, comprehensive in scope and precise in its mandate...."[7] UNTAC was the result of a very special confluence of events in international relations, and it was specifically designed for the complexity of the Cambodian situation.[8] UNTAC was composed of both civilian and military components. These components were designed to further the national security of Cambodia during the transitional period, which spanned the time between the Paris Peace Agreement and the completion of free and fair elections.[9]

The UNTAC mandate was comprehensive, and it provided for seven components, covering civil administration, military matters, civil police (CIVPOL), human rights, elections, rehabilitation, and repatriation.[10] The electoral component, in which UN Volunteers served, was charged with organizing the electoral process, developing a framework of laws and regulations to govern the elections, and undertaking large-scale civic education and training for the local Cambodian electoral staff. Among other duties, the military component was responsible for disarming the factions, which was necessary for the peaceful conduct of the elections. This meant finding and confiscating caches of weapons and military supplies throughout Cambodia, assisting with mine clearance, and teaching the Cambodian people about the millions of mines that remained in the ground.[11]

THE FORWARD LINE

The largest number of UNTAC civilian staff was concentrated in the electoral component, which included the 465 UN Volunteers District Electoral Supervisors deployed in 172 districts of the 18 provinces of the country.[12]

Stationed around the country, including some of the most remote areas, UN Volunteer specialists constituted the forward line of the UN electoral presence throughout Cambodia. "They were the spearhead of consciousness-raising for democracy," wrote Yasushi Akashi, Special Representative of the Secretary-General in Cambodia.[13] Coming from 65 countries,[14] with diverse academic and professional backgrounds, the volunteers had the distinction of being the only arm of UNTAC to live and work continuously in local communities. UNV District Electoral Supervisors were the heart of the electoral component.

Our role in Cambodia demanded intense community involvement, since we conducted the electoral organizational process at the village level. We also carried out a massive education campaign to inform Cambodians about the elections, slated for May 1993, and democratic principles. In this work we were assisted by the 50,000 Cambodians whom we recruited, trained, and deployed throughout the districts.

On arrival in Cambodia, we underwent a six-week intensive training in the Khmer language and culture, organized by the UNV Support Unit,[15] before we were deployed to our respective districts. The training acquainted us with local traditions, the Khmer language, and the basics of Khmer culture, and helped us greatly in the field. Over and above the instruction on language and culture, the most valuable aspect of our training was in the informal interaction between the UN Volunteers and our Cambodian teachers, young men and women who, while not formally trained as teachers, shared with us their experiences and opened our eyes to the untold miseries they or their families had suffered.

UN Volunteers was the only arm of UNTAC that benefited from an extensive training programme. This training period also provided a time for our own orientation and our transition into living for a year among the people in remote districts of the country. By receiving training and time to adjust, we avoided many of the potential pitfalls of being sent into the field too early. Volunteers also learned informally about the ways of the people through sidewalk conversations and everyday contact during these weeks of training in the capital city.

PAVING THE WAY: REGISTRATION OF VOTERS

We proceeded to our respective districts with mixed feelings of excitement and enthusiasm, and anxiety and fear since no district was free from the threat of violence. Once in the districts, UN Volunteers in teams of two found appropriate locations, and established district electoral offices and living quarters, usually near our offices. This work was done in consultation with CIVPOL at the district level, the provincial military component, and commune chiefs.

Reaching some districts was very tough due to prevailing bad road conditions and the ever-present possibility of land mines. In some areas the only way to move was by helicopter or boat. Visiting districts was also difficult due to the varying road conditions from province to province, and among districts within provinces. For instance, one UN Volunteer recounted that a trip that should have taken 13 hours took 64, and included such rigors as "killing two cars, crossing three rivers and cutting a giant tree."

The first and the most effective message conveyed to the local people was that we UN Volunteers, as part of the UNTAC staff, were going to live with them in their villages for the ensuing months and work towards holding free and fair elections. Communicating this plan alone made for the beginnings of a healthy, warm, personal relationship with the people. In this manner, UN Volunteers slowly and steadily built up local support and established communications at the grassroots, complementing the work of the various UNTAC components.

An important step at the early stages of district election organization was the recruitment and training of Cambodian staff to work with UN Volunteers in registration and civic education teams. UN Volunteers also recruited local interpreters who worked hand-in-hand with us. Recruitment of Cambodians was a useful exercise in itself. It gave us the opportunity to get to know the young people in the country, and to discover their own assessments and expectations from UNTAC. They were proud to be part of UNTAC and were eager to perform their tasks. This became obvious in their level of commitment to UNTAC's objectives and their corresponding high level of performance. They were instrumental in establishing effective communications between UN Volunteers and the local people. In a short time, our Cambodian colleagues functioned as our eyes and ears.

Phnom Penh and the nearby provinces of Kandal and Takaeo became scenes of immediate success during the early phase of voter registration, which began in October 1992. More than 27,000 Cambodians registered in 22 sites in the capital city alone during the first week of registration. In Mundulkiri ("Middle of the Mountains" in Khmer), however, geographical conditions required an extra effort from UN Volunteers, if all the population was to be registered. UN Volunteers traveled the mountainous terrain by traversing narrow jungle roads and crossing almost impassable rivers, in search of some 21,000 people, mostly non-Khmer, who lived in 87 villages scattered throughout the province.

In other provinces such as in Kampong Thom, Kampong Cham, Kampong Speu, and Siem Reap, the situation was even more difficult. These provinces prepared for registration under the most tense conditions. The Khmer Rouge faction, which had participated in the Paris Peace Conference and signed the Peace Agreements, did not abide by them and soon started to boycott the electoral process.[16] The lack of cooperation by this major faction in the elections resulted in high levels of violence and increased security problems for the UN, including its volunteers.

A helicopter carrying UN Volunteers to Varin in the Khmer Rouge-controlled Siem Reap district was fired on, wounding a volunteer in the leg. Registration in the district was abandoned. Meanwhile, in the Svay Leau district, the electoral office and UN Volunteers' house was shelled, preventing further registration activity at that site. As a result, other means were devised to reach the voters, including wholesale transporting of people from this district to an adjoining one where they could register.

In Kampong Thom province, in the centre of the country, the UN Volunteers were operating in areas partly controlled by the Khmer Rouge. To register the voters, UN Volunteers had to devise complicated strategies in coordination with the CIVPOL, the military component, and the civil administration, while they were under direct threat of attack and shelling.[17]

Yet, on the whole, the first phase of the electoral process got underway remarkably well throughout the country. The corresponding repatriation of 350,000 Cambodians living in the refugee camps along the Thai-Cambodian border was being carried out successfully, although the process was painfully slow and difficult. This was the first large repatriation operation of its kind in the history of the United Nations High Commissioner for Refugees (UNHCR), the lead agency in charge of coordinating repatriation. To accommodate the late arrivals, the voter registration period was extended to register the returning refugees.

CIVIC EDUCATION: THE SEEDS OF THE FUTURE

Any assessment of UNTAC's performance must include the element of mutual trust and confidence that was built between the population and UNTAC, despite the serious ups and downs in the process of holding elections. A significant factor responsible for the overwhelming response of Cambodians to the electoral operation was, in fact, the manner and extent to which civic education was carried out.

From the day of our arrival in the districts, we established our presence in the community and opened a direct channel for communication. Every informal meeting with villagers, monks, local chiefs, and others was an opportunity to pass on valuable information, to guide them in a particular direction, and to get a feeling for their expectations and own responses. Conducting civic education sessions in coordination with the commune chiefs, generally at the Buddhist temples, was a major activity for us, both before registration and until the general elections.

A wide range of educational material was produced by UNTAC. Pamphlets, posters, books, and audio and video cassettes explained in detail the election process.[18] The Cambodians welcomed this information and were particularly interested in the democratic experience of other countries. Eager to rid themselves of the nightmare of the totalitarian regime, Cambodians reacted favorably to new information; their excitement was clear from their responses. During civic education sessions, Cambodians described to us their fearful and gloomy past, the deaths of those they loved. In listening to these personal histories and tragic stories, we became temporary members of families where, in the act of communicating understanding, language differences were no longer a barrier.

In some districts UN Volunteers supplemented the UNTAC civic education materials with their own ideas. For example, in one province the volunteers found a way to use theatre to promote registration, which was very well received by the villagers and people living in communes. Generally, the civic education sessions felt like social gatherings where men, women, and children gathered in large numbers, delighted to see the television screens and so many new people around them. Balloons and candies were often distributed to children, adding to the festive air.

Civic education was not confined to information pertaining to elections. It also covered a wide range of issues on the process of democratization, and general information on human rights. UN Volunteers regularly assisted provincial human rights officers in disseminating human rights

Passing the word: civic education conducted in the remote Ratanakiri province by a UNV District Electoral Supervisor and local Cambodian staff. Photo: UN Photo 18612I/J. Isaac

materials because civic education was also an integral part of the activity of the human rights component of UNTAC.

The Buddhist monks also played an important role as a focal point in the civic education programmes in coordination with us, often lending the use of their temples to UN Volunteers for the purpose of ongoing education gatherings, registration, and polling. The Grand Patriarch Tep Vong, Cambodia's spiritual leader, organized mobile meditation teams to visit locations throughout the country for two months leading up to the election, carrying the message of peace. Consequently, UN Volunteers found common ground with Cambodia's religious community, which, while it shared enthusiasm for the goals of UNTAC, remained neutral during the election campaign.

The earlier experiences of genocide, occupation, and totalitarian government in Cambodia meant that the civic education campaign organized and taught by UN Volunteers became more than simply a matter of a national civics class. It was a seed of democratic principle that volunteers hope will flourish beyond the time of the elections and into the future as the country evolves into a true democracy.

The job of conducting education sessions, initially done by UN Volunteers, was eventually passed to the local staff under UNV guidance to enhance the "Cambodianness" of the electoral process and Cambodian ownership of the elections. The Cambodian civic education teams and interpreters became eloquent advocates of democracy, and expressed confidence in the process as they carried the message of free and fair elections in their own language to the people. The educational materials they used paved the way for healthy discussions at the end of each presentation. "Civic education," a UN Volunteer pointed out, "was a human resource building operation too, not insignificant in a country like Cambodia." In these large gatherings, our Cambodian counterparts also emphasized the all-important principle of secrecy of the vote.

During the anxious and stressful final weeks before the elections, UN Volunteers traveled extensively in their districts to emphasize the secrecy of the ballot. It was repeated, through all possible aids, including visual and written materials, that "your vote is your secret." One volunteer, describing this process, said, "We pointed out at least a hundred times in each session, that nobody, not the Khmer Rouge, not Hun Sen (at that time the prime minister), nor his State of Cambodia Police, nor anybody else would ever know whom they voted for, if they didn't tell anyone. And the miracle happened: the Cambodians believed us."[19]

UN Volunteer specialists also trained the local polling staff and party

Getting to the people: a UNV District Electoral Supervisor and a UN Civilian Police officer crossing the Mekong River, Cambodia, 1992. Photo: UNV/ Kathleen Graf

agents in a detailed and systematic way. At the end of the elections the performance of the Cambodian polling staff was highly commended.

MY OWN EXPERIENCE

While living in Cambodia, I discovered that the Cambodians have a fascination for Indian films, songs, and, especially, for Indian movie stars. I learned this through my own experiences traveling to the districts in my Indian saree. The villagers thought I was going to sing and dance for them! Instead, I taught them about elections and learned about their own society.

One aspect of the Cambodian society I found striking was the status and role of women. Women played the lead role in business, as well as in the family, due to the tragic Pol Pot era, when so many men died. Even as they played a dynamic social role, the Cambodian women preserved their culture, dignity, and morale. Women political candidates also appeared to be competent and confident.

After my initial training, I was deployed to the northern province of Siem Reap as the District Electoral Supervisor for Banteay Srey. Once I and my teammate had completed the preliminary findings on our area, I was called to the provincial headquarters and remained there until the end of the mission.

My new duties included conducting civic education programmes in coordination with all UN Volunteers province-wide, coordinating with the human rights component on human rights education programmes, compiling weekly reports submitted by volunteers throughout the province, and gathering information on the activities of the political parties. I was also a member of the Committee on Complaints and Compliance, which dealt with reported violations of electoral laws and abuses of human rights. On election day, I was the International Polling Station Observer in the district of Puok in Siem Reap province.

During the first six months, I mainly worked on civic education and human rights programmes. These were designed for specific groups, such as schoolteachers, judicial staffs, and the police. I conducted a 12-session course on human rights for secondary school teachers and the staff of the provincial court. At the end of the course certificates were awarded. It was fascinating for me to conduct these courses, and to find out that most civil and political rights seemed new and strange to the people. For example, the concept of the right to form trade unions sounded not only strange, but also unacceptable to the judicial staffs, including the judges.

In the later period before the elections, as both political activities and the corresponding violence increased, the work of the Committee on Complaints and Compliance also increased. I represented the electoral component on the committee, and as such was a part of ongoing investigations. I also frequently communicated with political party officials regarding their campaigns, complaints, and the general climate of political activity.

THE DEMOCRATIC CHALLENGE

The security and the political situation became volatile in some provinces as preparations continued for the final, hectic phase of our mission, the elections. This deteriorating situation, however, did not prevent Cambodian society from becoming gradually accustomed to the idea of democracy and to developing its own democratic mechanisms, starting with the creation of a pluralist system of parties. Political parties with platforms and ideologies officially registered themselves. At the national level there were 20 of them. Yet, for practical or security reasons, only seven or eight parties opened offices in the provinces.

There were four main political parties. The Cambodian People's Party (CPP) was the ruling political party of the State of Cambodia. Just a week before the Paris Peace Conference, this party abandoned its Communist-based policies and officially adopted the principles of multiparty democracy and free economy. The United National Front for an Independent, Neutral, Peaceful and Cooperative Cambodia (FUNCINPEC), founded in 1981 by Prince Norodom Sihanouk, was originally a liberation front aimed at ending the Vietnamese occupation of Cambodia. It transformed itself into a political party in 1992. The Khmer People's National Liberation Front (KPNLF), which had first emerged in 1979, turned into the Buddhist Liberal Democratic Party (BLDP). This was one of the several groups fighting against the Khmer Rouge rule; after the signing of the Paris Peace Agreements, this group also transformed itself into a political party. The Liberal Democratic Party (LDP), formerly KPNLAF, a non-Communist resistance army, was Cambodia's oldest political party; it re-established itself in 1992. These main political parties, along with the smaller ones that registered, were eager to carry out their campaign activities. The people were also looking forward to participating in these meetings and being introduced to their potential leaders.

Unfortunately, an environment where parties could exercise their right to propagate their viewpoints and campaign freely did not come about in Cambodia. The concept that all political parties enjoy an equal right to campaign did not reach the party workers and their followers. They continued to act on the assumption that competition in elections presupposed physical fighting, including attacks and assaults against rival party workers and disruptions of their meetings. The ruling Cambodian People's Party was the greatest violator of democratic norms during this period. It exercised its high-handedness by openly using the state-controlled Cambodian People's Armed Forces (CPAF) and the State of Cambodia Police for political activities.

Government officials, secondary school teachers, and others were forced to campaign for the CPP. Public buildings were used as party offices. The aspirations of other parties were frustrated by continual attacks. Cambodian army soldiers also resorted to plundering the villages and creating a reign of terror. Probably fueled by the suspicion and fear that other parties enjoyed greater public sympathy and support, the CPP resorted to confiscating voters' registration cards. Rumors were spread that those who had no cards could not vote, or that the identification number of the confiscated cards was recorded and that their votes would not be secret.

Meanwhile, complaints from individuals and political parties were piling up at the UNTAC provincial offices. At UNTAC Phnom Penh headquarters, a Complaints and Compliance Unit was set up to look into the most serious cases and conduct investigations. At the provincial level, a committee composed of several UNTAC components was set up to deal with complaints. This committee held regular meetings with the local army and police chiefs, and sought their cooperation in conducting impartial enquiries.

The work of these committees was extremely slow and hazardous because of the well-known and particular role of the army and the police as tools of the ruling party. Moreover, in the interest of the security of the victims, it was not possible to reveal identities of victims. Neither was it possible in most cases to establish the identity of the offenders.

The UNTAC staff closely watched these gross violations of democratic norms and the sufferings of the villagers. The UN Volunteers offices were flooded with complaints and grievances from the people. They demanded justice from the UN Volunteers, to whom they could pour out their hearts. Most of the time we felt absolutely helpless. The promise of securing a "neutral" or "free and fair" political environment seemed meaningless.

To counter the growing fears, UN Volunteers stepped up the campaign to boost the morale of the people. We accelerated civic education programmes, particularly regarding the "tendered" ballot, a system whereby Cambodians could vote even without their registration cards, provided they had registered previously. We emphasized to future voters that even if their voter cards had been illegally confiscated, they could still vote and their vote would be secret.

THE SECURITY DILEMMA

A very destabilizing factor for us as UN Volunteers in the field was the contrast between the expected democratic character of the elections and the physically dangerous environment in which its preparation was taking place. Demobilization and disarmament, which should have been completed before the beginning of the election period, were abandoned.[20]

Security conditions, which kept fluctuating, were therefore obviously a matter of great concern for UN Volunteers. And as UN Special Representative Yasushi Akashi described it later, there was also the "... nagging question among Volunteers, particularly from the Western countries, as to the validity of elections held in an atmosphere of insecurity and the threat to freedom of expression or movement."[21]

Overall, the situation was becoming increasingly tense, particularly in the strategic provinces of Kampong Thom, Battambang, and Siem Reap. Violent incidents such as blowing up of bridges, exchanges of artillery fire between the two factions, and all-night shelling multiplied. In several districts UN Volunteers spent long nights in bunkers. In Kampong Thom province, two important bridges on national Route 6 linking Phnom Penh to the north and a smaller bridge on Route 21 were blown up on 13 October 1992. UN Volunteers in some parts of this province heard constant shellings at night. They expressed a need for clear information about the security situation, especially during these tense periods. In my Siem Reap province, the districts of Varin and Svay Leau controlled by the Khmer Rouge were totally inaccessible.

Political violence coupled with escalating military activity threatened the conducting of elections on schedule. Two of the major political parties expressed their dissatisfaction with UNTAC. One of the two was the Cambodian People's Party, which was itself repeatedly challenged by UNTAC for misconduct, crimes, and violations of human rights. The CPP did not find UNTAC to be a supporter and defender of the government, which it probably had expected, and it started to openly criticize the operation.

The FUNCINPEC was gravely concerned by the murders of its party workers. In December 1992, Prince Sihanouk issued a statement saying that he could not "... stay without reacting when confronted with the multiplication of political terrorist acts and the continuation, with absolute impunity, of crimes with political motivation."[22] He also said that the UN Transitional Authority in Cambodia was apparently incapable of stopping the violence, and threatened to stop working with UNTAC and the government of Cambodia if they could not maintain peace in the country.[23]

The Khmer Rouge engaged in ongoing attempts to destabilize the country. One of its methods was the slaughter of the Vietnamese in Cambodia. One evening in March 1993, a band of gunmen attacked a floating village of sleeping Vietnamese fisherman in the north of Tonle Sap Lake. Thirty-five people were killed and 24 others were injured. Two weeks later, in another floating village, eight more Vietnamese were murdered.[24]

Starting in early 1993, the movements of UN Volunteers and local staff within the districts for education and preparation of polling had to be curtailed because of the danger. The general sentiment was that UNTAC had failed in its basic task of securing an environment conducive to the elections. It was embarrassing for us as UN Volunteers to explain the ideas of freedom of expression and political assembly, and at the same time to helplessly watch the gross violations of basic human rights.

There was another problem connected to the deteriorating security situation. During the recruitment of the local polling staff, thousands of candidates thronged to the district offices seeking to be hired by UNTAC. UN Volunteers even discovered that Cambodian People's army soldiers and local policemen had appeared at the exam to qualify as polling officials, which was forbidden under electoral rules, and had passed the exam before it was discovered that they were soldiers and policemen. Some of the Cambodians who were not recruited expressed their disappointment and anger at the UN Volunteer recruiting officials. Several UN Volunteers received threatening messages.

In sensitive provinces, we UN Volunteers frequently faced intimidation and threats from the very people who initially welcomed us with warmth and friendliness. Suddenly they turned indifferent and even hostile. The Cambodian staff were also victims of intimidation. The same staff who at one time had taken so much pride in being part of UNTAC now had to conceal their identity cards. In spite of this, these Cambodians continued to perform their duties with the same spirit and enthusiasm, even as deteriorating conditions led to UNTAC, CIVPOL, and military casualties in ambushes or mine explosions.

These frustrations and anxieties crystallized in the tragic murder on 8 April 1993 of Atsuhito Nakata, UN District Electoral supervisor, and his Cambodian colleague, Lay Sok Phiep, in Kampong Thom. The volunteers of that province had repeatedly expressed concerns about their own safety, since the province had long been a site of cease-fire violations and political violence. Following the death of our Japanese colleague, 10 out of 16 UN Volunteers in the province of Kampong Thom decided to leave the mission because of dejection, anger, and fear for their own lives. UN Volunteers in Khmer Rouge-controlled areas in other provinces almost had to give up their districts, as in Svay Leu and Varin, or operate in a very cautious and restrained way.

With elections drawing closer, we volunteers found we could no longer inject optimism into the scene as we had in the initial period of our assignment. As of April 1993, one UN Volunteer had been wounded in ambush, one had been injured by an exploding mine, one had been bitten by a poisonous snake, and one had been murdered. All these incidents occurred while the UN Volunteers were performing their duties. About 25 per cent of the UN Volunteers suffered from one kind of illness or another, including malaria and dengue fever. The longer the UN Volunteers were in the country, the greater were the risks to their own personal security. We pressed for improved security arrangements and a review of the prospects for free and fair elections.

An emergency two-day security workshop was held in mid-April 1993 in response to the mass discontent, fear, and anxiety among UN Volunteers about the deteriorating security situation and the absence of a neutral political environment. Chaired by the UN Volunteers deputy executive coordinator and attended by all UNV district electoral supervisors and senior UNTAC staff in Phnom Penh, the meeting's objective was to determine the security conditions in the provinces and to address security issues through measures to be adopted and implemented. As a result, Force Commander Lieutenant-General J.M. Sanderson promised to increase the military response to the needs of the electoral component as we got closer to the elections. He emphasized the need for more coordination and cooperation between electoral and military personnel.

In the security meeting the UN Volunteers were asked by UNTAC officials not to show the same enthusiasm and vigor as during the registration period. We also were asked to restrict our activities, and not to venture in areas that we felt were not safe without CIVPOL or military escort. Special Representative of the Secretary-General Akashi and Lieutenant-General Sanderson asserted that if the election did not take place as scheduled, it would never happen. The probability of war breaking out if elections were canceled in May was reasonably high, they said.[25]

Despite the lack of clear assurances that their safety could be guaranteed, a large majority of the UN Volunteers returned to their districts, ready to stay until the task was accomplished. One UN Volunteer from a high-risk area was heard to say: "We have worked for this so long and we would like to see some fruitful results." Out of the 465 district electoral supervisors, 60 decided not to go back to their districts. Some of those had faced serious difficulties and life-threatening situations; others were simply skeptical or discouraged.

The feeling of security or insecurity among the UN Volunteers depended heavily on the level of communication and confidence between the electoral and the military components in the provinces. For instance, in Kampong Thom province, the UN Volunteers stated that they doubted the ability of the Indonesian battalion to protect them effectively, especially after an Indonesian battalion camp had been overrun in late March 1993 by undisciplined government soldiers trying to steal radios.

In contrast, in the province of Siem Reap the security conditions were even worse than those in Kampong Thom, but a major difference was the confidence the UN Volunteers had in the Bangladesh battalion. Chief Electoral Officer Professor Reginald Austin agreed that "there is a high level of confidence in the military in Siem Reap even though it is actually a much more disturbed place than Kampong Thom."[26]

Fortunately, the situation by the end of April and early May 1993 was relatively quiet. It was, however, the uneasy calm before the storm. Following a brief respite, a final and severe challenge to UNTAC's ability to hold elections on time came in the form of surprise attacks by the Khmer Rouge as it made its last effort to sabotage the elections. It attacked four of the provinces, one after another.[27]

In the very early hours of 3 May 1993, shelling and firing began in Siem Reap, the province where I worked. It was countered by firing from the state army. Cross-fire continued for nearly six hours before the Khmer Rouge army retreated. Once again, an uneasy calm descended over the country, and continued until the day of the general elections.

Contrary to all expectations, the Cambodian elections were held peacefully at the end of May. They were a great victory for the Cambodians, for UNTAC, and for the UN Volunteers. More than 4 million Cambodians, representing 89.6 per cent of the registered voters, cast their ballots at the 1,400 fixed polling stations or at the 200 mobile stations in remote or dangerous areas.[28]

SHORTCOMINGS AND SUCCESSES

Taking part in the 24,000-person UNTAC operation, against heavy odds, in setting up the democratic process in Cambodia was an extraordinary experience. This was my first mission and it proved to be not only highly challenging but also very rewarding personally. I particularly enjoyed the civic education sessions in the villages and communes. For each one of the UN Volunteer specialists serving in Cambodia, and especially for those deployed in sensitive provinces, the mission was a test of confidence, tolerance, and determination.

Above all, the major requirements towards making a satisfactory contribution in any operation are commitment and faith in the objective of the operation. Granted an enormous amount of responsibility, we UN Volunteers performed our duties under physically demanding conditions, and were constantly vulnerable to reactions of those around us.

However, at the end of the day, we UN Volunteers felt that it had been worth all the trouble. The large turnout of voters in long queues on 23 May brushed aside all fears and vividly demonstrated to all of us the reason we had stayed on. The success of the Cambodian election was also a personal achievement for everyone in UNTAC.

Serving with UNTAC in the field required a great deal of adaptability and flexibility. Often the situations in the districts were not fully understood and appreciated at the provincial headquarters and the national capital. Therefore, decisions taken at higher levels frequently did not reflect local requirements. This often led to frustration and dejection. An UNTAC official who worked as a provincial human rights officer and later became UNTAC special prosecutor in Phnom Penh went so far as to say that people at the provincial headquarters or national capital give "... ridiculous orders which sometimes just have to be disobeyed because they are not safe...."[29]

Functioning between these two influences—the on-the-ground reality and the official policy—also required special qualities. Adaptability was essential to manage the physical and social conditions, but it was also necessary to respect the local traditions and cultures in order to earn the cooperation and friendship of the people. In Cambodia, for instance, women have a strong sense of proper dress, and the society did not approve of short dresses. Most UN Volunteers respected this tradition and dressed accordingly.

Though UN Volunteers had the capacity and dedication to carry out their responsibilities, the level of success in achieving the desired results and overcoming the dangers depended greatly on the ability of each UN Volunteer to establish and maintain good working relationships with people from other UNTAC components. A greater understanding of each other's backgrounds, combined with more efforts at tolerance, could have furthered mutual cooperation and cordiality.

CIVPOL's presence at the district level added support and assistance in the vital areas of transportation and logistics. UN Volunteers confidence was increased by district-level meetings with local police and army representatives to exchange views on security issues. The provincial level military component kept a close watch and an obvious presence in the provinces. Within the provinces, UN Volunteer specialists stayed in constant communication with each other through hand radio and car radio sets. In some provinces, the provincial electoral officer called for a weekly meeting of all UN Volunteers at the provincial headquarters.

A major difficulty we UN Volunteers faced within UNTAC was our relationship with the CIVPOL. The civilian police force was drawn from different ranks and nations, and there were great variations in their conduct and performance. There were, in fact, many instances in which the CIVPOL's negligence towards their duty or outright misconduct could have put the lives of UNTAC personnel, and especially of UN Volunteers, in danger. These cases of negligence or misconduct also could have had a disastrous effect on UNTAC's image in the eyes of the local population.[30] In several districts, UN Volunteers who worked closely with the CIVPOL were obliged to express their disapproval and disappointment.

One of the shortcomings of this operation was the lack of coordination and effective communication between UNTAC components. Each UNTAC component (e.g. military, CIVPOL, electoral, etc.) tightly safeguarded its operational jurisdiction and authority. This hampered the cordiality between the components. For example, there could have been improved coordination between the UNTAC electoral and human rights components, since public education was an integral part of both. Unfortunately, coordination between these two components did not improve. In some provinces, it was purely through the individual initiatives of the UN Volunteers that human rights education—normally in the purview of the human rights component—was carried out by the electoral staff.

Some other negative aspects of UNTAC operation, especially social problems such as prostitution, emerged out of relations with the local population. For example, in some instances of attacks on UNTAC police residences by the local uniformed officials, the motive turned out to be UNTAC police officers relations with local women. The United Nations Research Institute for Social Development (UNRISD) held a workshop in April 1993 on "The Social Consequences of the Peace Process in Cambodia," which recommended stricter guidelines governing recruitment, briefing, and training of peacekeeping personnel.[31]

UN personnel involved with peacekeeping and electoral duties could have also become involved with post-conflict community development work and thus become a part of the rehabilitation and reconstruction process. Some of the UN Volunteers had a strong desire to continue their work in this direction. We wanted to train and educate the local population on a variety of issues, such as sanitation and deforestation. Our year-long acquaintance with Cambodia produced a very clear idea of local needs and requirements. Unfortunately, as a general rule, this did not happen. After the elections, most UN Volunteer specialists were repatriated.

CONCLUSION

"Nothing the UN has ever done can match this operation," said UN Secretary-General Boutros Boutros-Ghali just before Cambodia's elections.[32] UNTAC was the first comprehensive peacekeeping operation undertaken by the UN in a member state. Despite the difficulties, UNTAC's success ultimately was seen as a demonstration of the ability of the United Nations to organize elections.

UN Volunteers played a central role in achieving this task. The operation placed great demands on us. In addition to professional and educational qualifications and experience in our respective fields, our tasks required the non-quantitative qualities of courage and determination to live under circumstances where even the basic necessities of life were not always adequately secured. In addition, what made UN Volunteers different from other components was our daily contact with the population, which was our own distinct advantage.

Civic education was a significant factor in dispelling the fear that gripped Cambodia. As a fellow UN Volunteer summed it up, "The voters had fears. Fear of being killed, fear of being isolated, fear of losing face, fear of being seen as a cynic and fear of being declared renegade.... Our strongest weapon to root out the fear in voters was the provision of secrecy of the ballot." The success of the civic education programme represented a crucial contribution in the final victory of the ballot box in May 1993.

Credit also goes to the military chief and his component for showing great restraint throughout the operation. UNTAC maintained its position as a peacekeeping force, and did not change into a peace enforcing force, despite numerous requests for more forceful action against the Khmer Rouge because of its non-compliance with the Paris Agreements.[33] The Cambodian experience demonstrated the effectiveness of establishing a mass presence of international and local staff all over the country. The presence of three parallel UNTAC components, military, civilian police, and electoral, contributed significantly in building confidence in the country.

For UNTAC the election of the Constitutional Assembly[34] by the people was the end of the operation, but for Cambodia it represented the beginning of a process of consolidating democracy, whose roots are still fragile. In order to ensure political stability, the Cambodian political parties need to grasp the proper meaning of political campaigning. The Cambodian people already have demonstrated continued faith in, and commitment to, the democratic system.

It was the inability of UNTAC to compel the Khmer Rouge into compliance with the Paris Peace Agreements, coupled with that faction's controlling 5 to 10 per cent of the territory, that threatens to disturb the peace and tranquility of the nation. But the Khmer Rouge is no longer a force with a popular base and international support. Cambodia's new democracy and rehabilitation efforts have worked, and are working, to neutralize this warring faction.[35] Cambodia today is open for foreign investment to rebuild its economy and to continue the process of reconstruction. The seeds of hope have been planted where there was fear, and new ideas have been introduced where there was isolation. The mine field is now a more level playing field that needs continued international support to sustain the progress that has been made.

NOTES

1. For more information on the history of Cambodia, see Kaonn, Vandy. *Cambodge: 1940–1991, ou la politique sans les Cambodgiens*. Paris: L'Harmattan, 1993, pp. 1–157.
2. Randall, Stephen J. "Peacekeeping in the Post-Cold War Era: The United Nations and the 1993 Cambodian Elections." *Behind the Headlines* 51 (Spring 1994), no. 3: 1–16.
3. The four Cambodian warring factions that were parties to the negotiations were the Peoples's Republic of Kampuchea (PRK), currently called the Government of the State of Cambodia, and represented by Hun Sen; the United National Front for an Independent, Neutral, Peaceful and Cooperative Cambodia (FUNCIPEC), led by Prince Norodom Sihanouk; the Khmer People's National Liberation Front (KPNLF), led by Son Sann; and the Party of Democratic Kampuchea (PDK), also known as the Khmer Rouge, led by Khieu Samphan.
4. "Towards Peace in Cambodia." *United Nations Focus*. UN Doc. DPI/1091–September 1990–3M.
5. Additional meetings were held among the four Cambodian factions in Jakarta in February 1990 and in Tokyo in June 1990.
6. *Letter dated 30 October 1991 from France and Indonesia transmitting, as representatives of the Co-Chairmen of the Paris Conference on Cambodia, the full text of agreements signed in Paris, 23 October 1991, by the States participating in the Conference*, 30 October 1991, UN Doc. A/46/608-S/23177. For a historical and negotiating background, as well as a legal analysis of the Paris Peace Agreements, see Ratner, Steven R. "The Cambodia Settlement Agreements." *American Journal of International Law* 87 (January 1993), no. 1: 1–41. The Paris Peace Agreements consisted of a Final Act and three agreement instruments: Agreement on a Comprehensive Political Settlement of the Cambodian Conflict; Agreement concerning the Sovereignty, Independence, Territorial Integrity and Inviolability, Neutrality and National Unity of Cambodia; and the Declaration on the Rehabilitation and Reconstruction of Cambodia.
7. *The United Nations and Cambodia 1991–1995*, The United Nations Blue Books Series II. New York: United Nations Department of Public Information, 1995, pp. 1–351. This collection of United Nations documents, with an introduction by UN Secretary-General Boutros Boutros-Ghali, provides a comprehensive record of the Organization's efforts in Cambodia.
8. Doyle, Michael W. and Nishkala Suntharalingam. "The UN in Cambodia: Lessons for Complex Peacekeeping." *International Peacekeeping* 1 (Summer 1994), no. 2: 117–147.

9. The Agreement on a Comprehensive Settlement of the Cambodian Conflict provided *inter alia* for the creation of a Supreme National Council (SNC) composed of the four Cambodian factions as the legitimate source of authority in Cambodia. Throughout the transitional period, SNC acted as the center of national internal unity and sovereignty, while at the same time it represented Cambodia to the outside world.

10. The Security Council, approving the *Report of the Secretary-General on Cambodia containing his proposed implementation plan for UNTAC,* 19 February 1992, UN Doc. S/23613, authorized the establishment of UNTAC in Resolution 745, 28 February 1992, UN Doc. S/RES/745/1992, for a period not to exceed 18 months.

11. The duties of the military, civil administration, civilian police, human rights, repatriation, and rehabilitation components were as follows: the military component was charged with the verification of the withdrawal of foreign forces, along with their arms and equipment, and the supervision of the cease-fire. Its tasks also included demobilization, weapons control, and monitoring the cessation of outside military assistance. The civil administration component was responsible for the direct supervision and control over the state of Cambodia administrative agencies, in order to ensure a neutral political environment for the conduct of the elections. This allowed for an unprecedented involvement of the UN in a country's administration. The civilian police component (CIVPOL) was designed to ensure effective and impartial maintenance of law and order as well as the protection of human rights and fundamental freedoms. The human rights component concentrated on encouraging the ratification of international human rights instruments and on organizing an extensive campaign of human rights education. Refugees were the responsibility of the repatriation component. Rehabilitation of the country fell to the rehabilitation component, which focused on the maintenance and support of basic infrastructure, institutions, utilities, and other essential services as well as urgent humanitarian needs.

12. There were a total of 674 UN Volunteers serving in Cambodia in different specialties. See Whitcomb, Giles M. and Kanni Wignaraja. *Collaboration Between United Nations Transitional Authority in Cambodia (UNTAC) and United Nations Volunteers (UNV).* Evaluation 1 April–15 May 1993. Geneva: United Nations Volunteers, 1993, pp. 1–72.

13. Akashi, Yasushi. "The Challenge of Peacekeeping in Cambodia." *International Peacekeeping* 1 (Summer 1994), no. 2: 206.

14. Whitcomb and Wignaraja, *Collaboration Between,* p. 62.

15. Whitcomb and Wignaraja, *Collaboration Between,* p. 22.

16. The Khmer Rouge refused to canton, disarm, and demobilize its forces, and ultimately resumed hostilities, alleging that the Paris Peace Agreements were not being implemented properly. According to this faction, Vietnamese troops remained in Cambodia and the State of Cambodia had not surrendered power to the Supreme National Council. See Ratner, Steven. "The United Nations Operation in Cambodia and the New Peacekeeping." In Daniel Warner, ed. *New Dimensions of Peacekeeping.* Dordrecht: Martinus Nijhoff, 1995, p. 49.

17. For instance, the first UNV/DES team to register Cambodians in a Khmer Rouge area was successful thanks to the valuable support of CIVPOL and the local administration and to the distribution of rice to the people by UN Volunteers. By doing this, the UNV/DES team prevented a violent Khmer Rouge response, since it would not seem right in the view of the people to use violence against the people who were helping them.

18. The Training, Education and Communications Division of UNTAC was responsible for producing these materials.

19. *Free Choice—Electoral Component Newsletter, UNTAC*—Information and Communication Division, 30 April 1993. Besides reviewing the overall situation in all districts, this internal newsletter described the UN Volunteers' tasks and achievements, and functioned as a vehicle of UN Volunteers' opinions.

20. Ratner, "The United Nations Operation in Cambodia," p. 49.

21. Akashi, "The Challenge of Peacekeeping in Cambodia," p. 206.

22. *The Bangkok Post*, 15 December 1992.
23. *The Bangkok Post*, 15 December 1992.
24. "Voter Registration a Success—Cease-fire Violations Continue." Cambodia, *UN Chronicle* (June 1993): 24–25.
25. "Free Choice."
26. "Free Choice."
27. Akashi, "The Challenge of Peacekeeping in Cambodia," p. 204.
28. "Cambodia Election Results." *United Nations Focus: Cambodia* UN Doc. DPI/1389–July 1993–5M.
29. Interview conducted for the Australian radio programme Background Briefing (Cambodia), The Talk of Australia (ABC Radio tapes, no date), cited in Peter Utting, ed. *Between Hope and Insecurity: The Social Consequences of the Cambodian Peace Process.* Geneva: UNRISD, 1994, p. 30.
30. The fact that the quality and qualification of the civilian police sent by UN member states were uneven was recognized by Special Representative of the Secretary-General Yasushi Akashi and was recalled in overall assessments of UNTAC. See Akashi, "The Challenge of Peacekeeping in Cambodia," p. 214; and Ratner, "The United Nations Operation in Cambodia," p. 55.
31. Utting, *Between Hope and Insecurity*, pp. 1–241.
32. Statement made by UN Secretary-General in April 1993 and cited in "The 'Second Generation'—Cambodia elections 'free & fair' but challenges remain"—UN Peace-keeping, *UN Chronicle* (September 1993): 32.
33. See Lieutenant General J.M. Sanderson, *International Humanitarian Law and the Role of Military Establishments*, Speech to Australian Red Cross Regional Conference. Australian Defence Studies Centre, Camberra, December 1994.
34. With 45.47 per cent of the votes, FUNCIPEC of Prince Norodom Sihanouk won 58 seats in the 120-seat Constitutional Assembly, while CPP, led by Hun Sen, won 51 seats. The promulgation of the new Constitution took place on 24 September 1993. Accordingly, a constitutional monarchy was established and Prince Sihanouk was elected King of Cambodia (he holds the throne, but not the power). Prince Hanariddh and Hun Sen were elected as first and second prime ministers. See "UNTAC mandate ends—New Constitution, Government welcomed"—Cambodia, *UN Chronicle* (December 1993): 16–18.
35. Neou, Kassie. "Don't Squander Progress in Cambodia." *Herald Tribune* (3 March 1995): Editorial Page.

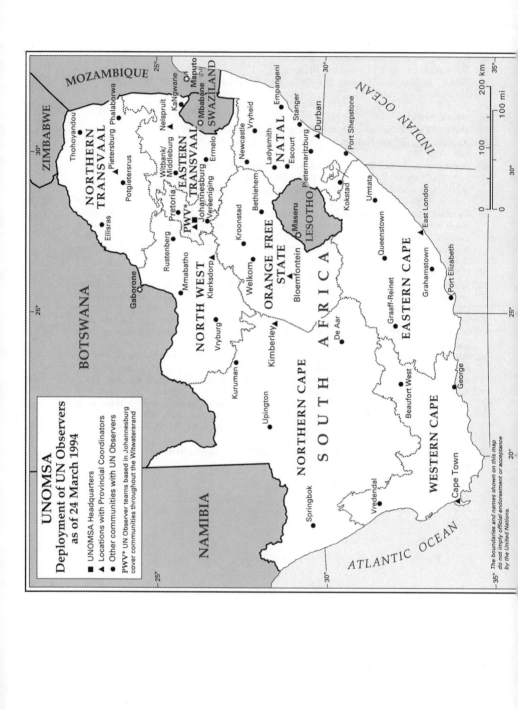

UNOMSA
Deployment of UN Observers
as of 24 March 1994

■ UNOMSA Headquarters
▲ Locations with Provincial Coordinators
● Other communities with UN Observers

PWV* UN Observer teams based in Johannesburg
cover communities throughout the Witwatersrand

ZIMBABWE

MOZAMBIQUE

BOTSWANA

NAMIBIA

NORTHERN TRANSVAEL

Thohoyandou
Ellisras
Phalaborwa
Pietersburg
Potgietersrus
Thabazimbi

EASTERN TRANSVAAL

Nelspruit
KaNgwane
Maputo
Mbabane
SWAZILAND

Witbank/
Middleburg
Ermelo
Vryheid

PWV*
Pretoria
Johannesburg
Vereeniging

Rustenberg
Mmabatho
Klerksdorp

NORTH WEST

Vryburg
Kimberley
Kuruman

NORTHERN CAPE

Upington

Springbok

Vredendal

WESTERN CAPE

Cape Town

ATLANTIC OCEAN

Kroonstad
Welkom
Bethlehem

ORANGE FREE
STATE

Bloemfontein
De Aar

Newcastle
Ladysmith
Escourt

NATAL

Pietermaritzburg
LESOTHO
Maseru

E.C.
Kokstad
Umtata

EASTERN CAPE

Queenstown
Graaff-Reinet
Grahamstown

Beaufort West

George
Port Elizabeth

East London

Empangeni
Stanger
Durban
Port Shepstone

INDIAN OCEAN

SOUTH AFRICA

Gaborone

35° The boundaries and names shown on this map
do not imply official endorsement or acceptance
by the United Nations.

0   100   200 km
0   100 mi

25°   30°   35°

25°

30°

2

THE POLITICS OF REASSURANCE: INTERNATIONAL PRESENCE AT THE LOCAL LEVEL IN SOUTH AFRICA

Diane Conklin

THE FOUR-WHEEL drive pickup truck entered the rural village from the main road and stopped. The view out the windshield was typical of the villages in this homeland area of the Far North Transvaal: round daub-and-wattle thatched roof huts, each enclosed by a stockade-type fence, one or two large trees, a few stray chickens crossing the proverbial dusty road. It was a place devoid of young men and inhabited mostly by women, children, and the old. Where was the voting station?

My South African companion slowly rolled down the truck's window. Hot, dry air whooshed into the air-conditioned cab as the big motor laboured harder to keep us cool. She spoke to a woman busy hanging out her wash in the yard of the first hut. She spoke to her in their own language, the Sotho tongue, for a few minutes. The woman, a white scarf piled on her head, occasionally peeked beyond my companion to look at me in the driver's seat, a blue United Nations cap on my head. She said something while indicating me with her chin, and then smiled at my companion's reply. Once directions were secured, the window was rolled up,

Diane Conklin, a USA national born in 1947, holds a law degree from the University of Wyoming. A former journalist, she participated in the United Nations Observer Mission in South Africa as a UN Volunteer Observation Support Officer from March to May 1994 before becoming the Programme Manager of the project which produced this volume.

and the truck began moving in the right direction, I asked, "What did she say?" "She said she is afraid if she sees white people here. I told her you were here as a friend."

The two words "South Africa" evoke powerful images. The country is a unique historical site where an enshrined, legitimized, and brutally enforced view of the superiority of one race over all others met head-on with an equally long-term resistance to that view. The result was the transformation of society to one that would begin operating by the present-day axiom: all people are created equal.

Through that confrontation, which was carried out over a very long period of time and which entered the limelight of world attention only recently, the views of the past ultimately lost all of their political meaning and credibility. Since there was nowhere for the majority of the 6 million whites living in South Africa to go, peace was made with the real majority of South Africa, the 33 million indigenous black people,[1] who had suffered the long experience of exclusion and indignity, known in its most recent manifestation as "apartheid."[2] It was in this sea change, a prerequisite to the country's subsequent political transition, that the magic celebrated by the world in April 1994 lies.

Along with hundreds of other United Nations Volunteers, I was privileged to serve as an Observation Support Officer in the United Nations Observer Mission in South Africa (UNOMSA) during the final phase leading up to the elections. From my deployment in the Far Northern Transvaal, I was able to witness and to be part of this truly extraordinary historical event. It was, above all, an experience of inspiration. Our task in South Africa was to map out and inspect the thousands of voting stations across the country, and to observe the entire gamut of political activity, including the voting and counting of ballots. But what we observed was richer than any set of defined tasks. What we saw was a miracle.

THE HISTORICAL LEGACY

The practice of separation of the races was deeply rooted in South African history, beginning with the landing of the Dutch at the Cape of Good Hope in the middle of the seventeenth century. Frontier wars expanded white settlements from the Cape eastward. In the mid-1800s, the Boers, South Africans of Dutch descent, began an inland trek in protest against the abolition of slavery. This movement led to the establishment of the Orange Free State and the Transvaal.[3]

The powerful Zulu kingdom was then destroyed in a series of wars with

Symbol of apartheid: segregated stands in the old South Africa. Photo: UN/DPI Photo 177913/H. Vassal

the Boers and the British. The Xhosa tribe also suffered the same fate. Soon after, the diamonds and gold of South Africa attracted mining enterprises that needed tens of thousands of men to work the diamond mines of Kimberly and the deep gold mines of Johannesburg. The development of race codes designed to control the supply and behaviour of cheap black labour in the cities resulted in early forms of segregation.[4]

What came to be known as the African National Congress (ANC) was formed in 1912 to oppose the impending land act. Nevertheless, the 1913 Natives Land Act was passed relegating all black South Africans to 10 per cent of the land in "reserve" areas, and apportioning the other 90 per cent exclusively for whites. As a result of the act, the indigenous black population became aliens in South Africa, a country that, for all practical purposes, now belonged to whites.[5]

The National Party came to power in 1948. Racial segregation had existed before World War II, but now it became an official state policy. Mixed marriages were forbidden and interracial sex was made illegal. The Group Areas Act restricted the ability of blacks to live in urban areas, often splitting families; the Separate Amenities Act segregated all public facilities; a Bantu Authorities system was set up to break down the black majority into separate tribal "nations";[6] and black education was limited to non-professional training. Under the Population Registration Act, blacks were made to carry the hated passbook at all times and were prohibited from remaining in white areas without specific permission. Only whites could vote or run for public office.

The horrific result of the residential separation of blacks from whites was growth of black townships, where people were housed in overcrowded conditions and on a temporary basis, since black ownership of the land was prohibited. All-male hostels were built to house thousands of black labourers shipped from the countryside. Restrictions blocked townships from benefiting from the development of normal business: no banks, clothing stores, or supermarkets were allowed. Squatter camps sprang up where thousands of people built makeshift shelters, only to have them repeatedly bulldozed. Hundreds of thousands of black South Africans were forcibly removed to so-called homelands set up inside the boundaries of South Africa and established for the purpose of confining blacks; four of these later were declared "independent" states[7] in an attempt to lend an air of legitimacy to the apartheid system.

A handful of educated resistance leaders, including Nelson Mandela, formed the ANC Youth League, and led the Defiance Campaign of the 1950s. In 1955, the Freedom Charter, which declared that "South Africa belongs to all of its people, black and white,"[8] was adopted by a host of organizations.

The traditional non-violent approach of the ANC was changed by the 1960 Sharpeville Massacre of protesters demonstrating against the pass laws. Following the Sharpeville Massacre, the ANC, the Pan African Congress (PAC), and the South African Communist Party were banned, and armed resistance got underway. After leading the underground ANC for one year, Nelson Mandela was arrested in 1962. In 1964, following the infamous Rivonia trial, he was sentenced to life imprisonment on Robben Island.[9]

In the mid-1980s, after the government set up yet another way to divide people by means of a three-house Parliament for whites, Coloureds, and Indians, totally excluding black South Africans,[10] the country erupted into terrible violence. A state of emergency declared in 1986 was to last through the rest of the decade.

The situation in South Africa also had major consequences beyond its borders. Externally, the policies of apartheid during its existence influenced the whole of southern Africa. The South African government's deliberate attempts to support governments favourable to its regime or to destabilize those in opposition resulted in massive negative effects abroad.[11]

Internal economic pressures exacerbated by external trade sanctions and a credit freeze, as well as continued domestic violence, led to the 1989 election of Frederick W. de Klerk to the presidency and the beginning of the official process of transition to a non-racial democracy.[12] The various parties in South Africa, including the government and the ANC, decided that year to commit themselves to a negotiated political settlement of the conflict in the country.

The changes in South Africa following former President de Klerk's unprecedented 1990 "Rubicon" speech to the Parliament were seismic.[13] Bans were lifted from political parties, the state of emergency lifted, and in February 1990 Nelson Mandela was released after 27 years of imprisonment. In June 1991, the legislative pillars of apartheid—the Land Act, the Group Areas Act, and the Population Registration Act—were repealed.

In September 1991, the National Peace Accord was signed by the ANC, the Inkatha Freedom Party (IFP), the South African Government, and 16 other signatories.[14] The accord established the National Peace Committee, the National Peace Secretariat, Regional and Local Peace Committees, and the Goldstone Commission, whose task was to investigate and expose the reasons for violence. These structures worked against the background of constant violence (sometimes identified with the security force or political parties and sometimes not) which wreaked havoc in South Africa. Later, black-on-black violence became a serious threat to the process of national healing.[15]

In December 1991, the first formal talks on the transition to majority rule began with the Convention for a Democratic South Africa (CODESA I and II). However, after the massacre of 40 people in the Boipatong township in June 1992,[16] the ANC pulled out of CODESA, broke off bilateral negotiations with the government, and called on the international community to monitor the violence. But ongoing informal talks between the government and the ANC led in March 1993 to the convening of the Multi-Party Negotiating Council (MPNC), which adopted a number of constitutional principles and institutions to guide South Africa during a transitional period to last until April 1999.[17] This included the establishment of the Transitional Executive Council (TEC) to run the country until the April 1994 elections. On 3 June 1993, the date for the first democratic elections was provisionally set for 27 April 1994; in that year Frederick de Klerk and Nelson Mandela shared the Nobel Peace Prize.

UNV IN SOUTH AFRICA WITH THE UN

The United Nations had been involved in a campaign against apartheid for more than four decades.[18] Many long debates in the General Assembly and other bodies, such as the Commission on Human Rights, dealt with the situation in South Africa with the resulting Security Council votes calling for economic sanctions against the country.[19]

During this time the UN maintained a confrontational stance towards the apartheid system. However, once the winds of change had finally and radically altered the situation and negotiations between the representatives of the government and the majority population were underway, the United Nations moved away from the position of confronting to one of assisting the ongoing transition to a democratic society, as did the rest of the international community.

UNOMSA was the immediate result of Security Council resolution 765 in 1992.[20] This was a new exercise in preventive diplomacy outlined in the Secretary-General's proposals in "An Agenda for Peace,"[21] and it called for greater use of fact-finding and preventive diplomacy by the UN in coordination with other international organizations.[22]

The observer mission itself was established under Security Council resolution 772 of August 1992.[23] The first contingent of UN observers, made up of regular UN staff, arrived in South Africa in mid-September 1992 and were deployed mainly in Johannesburg, to cover the Witswatersrand/Vaal region, and in Durban, covering Kwa Zulu/Natal. Ninety per cent of the political violence had occurred in these two areas.[24] Gradually the numbers of UNOMSA observers grew, and by September 1993, 100 of these were deployed throughout all regions to attend mass gatherings and other forms of political activity. Later the number of UNOMSA observers was further increased,[25] and these observers were joined in March 1994 by 200 UN Volunteer specialists.

At the request of the Transitional Executive Council, the mandate of UNOMSA was expanded early in 1994 by Security Council resolution 894[26] to include UN observation of the planned April elections. This expanded mandate called for the UN to engage in a wide variety of tasks in connection with the upcoming elections, including those in the purview of United Nations Volunteers.[27]

I arrived in South Africa on 12 March 1994 knowing that I would live and work in a possibly volatile environment for the next two months. Before leaving home, I was asked by friends and relatives who were alarmed at television news reports on the situation in the country if I was afraid to go there. I said I believed the vast majority of South Africans were not violent and were living peacefully. However, once in South Africa, I learned more about fear.

As a whole, the UN Volunteer specialists serving in South Africa were experienced and professional, and most had advanced education and degrees. Our average age was 38 years old; we came from 39 countries; more than 50 per cent of us were from Africa,[28] deliberately recruited for this mission. We set our own multiracial example as we converged on the Riverside Sun Hotel in the Johannesburg suburb of Vanderbijlpark.

UNV established a Programming and Administrative Support Unit (PASU) at the UNOMSA headquarters that supported us in the field. During an intensive week-long UNV-organized orientation, the most extensive briefing of its type conducted on site, we heard presentations on the current situation from the South African Defense Force,[29] the South African Police, and UNOMSA personnel. It was an important learning experience and was crucial to our understanding the mandate of UNOMSA and our own specific terms of reference, as well as our general role as representatives of the United Nations in the field.

Meanwhile, we read daily of the random shootings and violence that plagued the country. People at a bus stop killed from a passing car; train passengers shot at by an unseen sniper; continued violence in the townships, where ANC and the Inkatha Freedom Party, the Zulu cultural organization transformed into a political party by Chief Mangosuthu Buthelezi, were battling for political dominance.

The Johannesburg area and Natal were hit worst by clashes between IFP and ANC supporters, but there were other unrelated incidents of violence reported from around the country before our deployment. This included the explosive televised violence in the BophuthaTswana homeland, which occurred during our first week in South Africa, when Afrikaanse Weerstandsbeweging (AWB),[30] an organization of extreme rightists, drove into the area in an organized convoy, killing bystanders, and, in turn, was routed. It was a dramatic example of the collapse of the apartheid structures no longer propped up by the central government in Pretoria and which now had begun to fall as the way to new government opened. It was a bloody end, resulting in both black and white deaths, and was symptomatic of the tremendous tensions in the country.

Fear accompanied our understanding of the situation, and each volunteer had to face it. Would we become victims of the upheaval around us? Would we be wounded or killed? There was fear, but the overwhelming feeling of the group was that of determination. I felt the fear myself, but as we left the hotel to be deployed I realized that my fear could be used to make me more careful, and to thereby lessen my chances of becoming a victim of the violence.

UN Volunteers were deployed to the nine newly-created electoral provinces of South Africa; the group I was with went to the Far Northern Transvaal. Working under the supervision of UNOMSA provincial coordinators, UN Volunteers were eventually dispersed to various parts of the provinces, serving in mixed teams with UNOMSA staff. We were integrated into UNOMSA, rolled into the final operations of the mission. This was important because it meant that UN Volunteer specialists stood on equal ground with the international UN staff, and from this position we could influence, as well as carry out, UNOMSA activities in the field. The integration of volunteers into these mixed teams was an implicit recognition of our ability to serve in an extremely sensitive mission that required the constant exercise of professional judgment.

UNOMSA also coordinated the efforts of more than 1,600 International Election Observers (IEOs), who would arrive shortly before the elections to join us in observing the voting. In addition, UNOMSA was also responsible for coordinating observers from the Organization of African Unity, European Union, and the Commonwealth.

Once we were deployed, our first responsibility was to map the location of the voting stations for the international observers. The situation called for an all-out effort to verify in fact what had been theoretically promised by the newly created Independent Electoral Commission (IEC).[31] Since this was the first all-race election in South Africa, it meant that the majority of newly enfranchised voters had never voted before. It also meant that an entire structure of elections for a vast and often illiterate population had to be organized by the IEC. The voters living in both the congested townships and in the deep rural areas had to be provided a safe place where they could cast their ballots.

The Far Northern Transvaal, the northernmost province of South Africa, was known as a deeply conservative place consisting of white farming communities and towns separated from black homeland areas and townships. The population of about 2.7 million was 97 per cent black, 3 per cent white. Huge farms with thousands of farm labourers dominated the province in the west. In the north, east, and south, the black "independent state" of Venda and the two "self-governing" black homeland areas, Gazankulu and Lebowa, with divided and noncontiguous borders, were surrounded by an area dotted with white towns and farms. The white mining community of Phalaborwa,[32] with a population of about 8,000, was located on the extreme eastern edge of the province, bordering Kruger National Park. This was my final destination. Politically, the province was dominated by the ANC.

Our UN Volunteers group was deployed in late March from the provincial seat in Pietersburg to Phalaborwa. The stark contrast between the neat white town of Phalaborwa, with shops and supermarkets lining its paved streets and lush residential areas of large, well-maintained houses, and the dirt streets, the occasional tiny shops, and the small frame homes of the crowded black township of Namakgale, was our first introduction to the appearance of apartheid. Underlying these physical differences were the great gaps in understanding between the two very differently situated groups.

While other areas of South Africa were experiencing escalating violence between supporters of different political parties along with the ever-present random violence,[33] in our area resistance arose in the form of disenchanted whites who wanted no part in the elections. They were attempting to devise the option of their own "volkstaat"[34] (state) where they would continue to live insulated from the influences of a majority government. The signs of this discontent were plain to see. Shortly after I arrived in Phalaborwa in late March, a large banner was unfurled at the overpass bridge with the word "Volkstaat" emblazoned on it in red. "Volkstaat" messages in bold reflector-paint letters appeared on the pavement of major street intersections at the edges of the town.

Following the UN Volunteers arrival in Phalaborwa, three teams of volunteers and UNOMSA staff ranged outward into the rural and heavily populated homelands, as well as to the local black township of Namakgale, with an estimated population of 40,000, located 12 kilometres west of Phalaborwa. It was a large territory to be covered by six people in three vehicles. Each of the more than 300 voting stations in our area had to be checked, and the preparation time between the calling for elections and the elections themselves was short for the amount of work to be done.

In the Transvaal the IEC was very slow in organizing. When we arrived in Phalaborwa, a mere 40 days before the election, preparations for the election were non-existent. Moreover, the final lists of voting stations were not available, so we used provisional lists to begin our work. There were no maps available for the rural homeland areas and even tourist maps were in short supply, so we copied the one good tourist map we had and set up a schedule and routes to begin the process.

The mapping of the voting stations, usually located in rural schools, was often a test of endurance. Finding the voting stations and inspecting them to check their security and neutral location meant travelling long distances, day after day, into rural areas where no UN presence had ever been before. Except for the white towns, the entire area is distinctive for its lack of signposts and identification of streets. The anonymity of the rural homeland villages was also related to the fact that on most South African maps there was no indication of where the many millions of black South Africans lived. Townships were often designated simply as "locations" by both black and white alike, and there were no indications on the maps of major areas of population density. It was as if the people who lived there did not exist.[35]

I "adopted" the Gazankulu homeland. While we were always supposed to work in teams of two, our numbers were scarce and the territory was large, so we would often work individually with a local person to map the voting stations. In order to locate the villages in the remote corners of the Gazankulu homeland, I asked the appointed IEC District Electoral Officer (DEO)[36] to help me, and he graciously travelled with me for 10-hour days to visit the voting stations. Later, when time was very short and he was needed at the office, he arranged for his assistants to act as guides.

Due to the long distances between voting stations in the homelands, we used trip metres to record directions, which meant recording every turn and fork in the road from one voting station to the next. The mapping directions, which were to be used by the incoming international observers, were then compiled into reports describing the area generally and listing the IEC officials. In addition to mapping the voting stations, we also observed Local Peace Committee meetings and political party rallies, voter education carried out by political parties and even private businesses, as well as the issuance of temporary voting cards (TVCs). It was estimated that millions of people did not possess the identification necessary to qualify to vote. In our area that translated to thousands who walked many miles or took long bus rides to stationary TVC issuing centres, or who were visited in their villages by mobile TVC teams.

I followed the progress of the TVC-issuing station in Gazankulu, which was often painfully slow. Long lines of people waited all day to get their cards, sometimes returning to their villages without success. The facilities were overwhelmed by the demand and it seemed as if many people would not be able to vote because they had no identification. I spoke with the

Phalaborwa Home Affairs office and the Gazankulu district electoral officer about the situation and suggested extending the use of the mobile TVC trucks to Saturday hours and lengthening their scheduled use, which was to end a week before the election. I was reassured that the scheduled use of the mobile teams would be extended and that at least one truck would be sent to Gazankulu. But a problem still remained for remote areas because the truck would be useless in many villages lacking electricity to power the truck's computers. A report to the provincial officer in Pietersburg noted the difficulties of issuing thousands of cards in a very short period of time. This report was then forwarded to UNOMSA in Johannesburg to alert UN officials of this reality in the field.

THE EXERCISE OF NEUTRALITY

When we first arrived in Phalaborwa we met with the local branches of the South African Defence Force, the South African police, Phalaborwa elected officials, and leaders in the Namakgale township, to gather information to assess the local situation. These meetings preceded others we would have later with the Gazankulu Local Peace Committee. It was not always easy to maintain the mandate of simply observing and not getting overly involved. Each encounter with the ongoing process presented its own challenge. For example, four of us attended one of the organizational meetings of the Local Peace Committee in Gazankulu. This so-called self-governing homeland was home to more than 200,000 people.[37] The structures of the Gazankulu "government" had been paid for by the South African government, which built a complex of buildings to house a bureaucracy, headed by a Council of Ministers and a Chief Minister.

We were ushered into an auditorium of one of these buildings to observe the formation of the committee, composed of the major political parties, the South African Police, church leaders, and others. During our visit the temporary chairman abruptly relinquished his position and turned to us, four diverse people hailing from India, The Gambia, Russia, and the United States, indicating that we should conduct the meeting.

It was a difficult moment. While we were there to support the process, we were not there to lead it. We resolved the problem by giving some advice, and then we gently reminded those present that we were observers and encouraged them to continue the process they had already started. At first there was some reluctance on the people's part to take back the gavel. It was as if the internationals should tell the group what to do. If we did not, why were we there? But eventually the group went back to work, nominating and then voting for their leadership. We were given, in the end, the task of verifying the vote.

Questions of the neutral observer role also came up during a meeting with local ANC activists in the township of Namakgale. Sitting together around a long table, formal introductions completed, we were asked, "What is the UN doing in South Africa anyway? Why aren't you peace-keepers, soldiers rather than civilians?" Again we explained our observing role. Ours was a parallel track to the official efforts of the people of South Africa themselves and our observation was intended to support the transition underway. While the questioner was somewhat mollified, the answers were not totally well received.

Voting started on 26 April and was originally supposed to end two days later, but was extended an extra day due to the lack of voting materials in some areas, including our own. It was a source of great joy to see black and white voters standing peacefully together for the first time, to register their voice through the ballot. Moreover, on the election days the violence throughout the country had miraculously stopped.

As nearly 20 million South Africans voted,[38] UN Volunteers joined the recently arrived International Election Observers to observe the voting. On the first day of voting, my election observer partner, a member of the Dutch Parliament, and I saw at one station a line of elderly women standing in the hot sun.

"Hello, mother," we heard, the local greeting of respect. The woman addressed took her identity card slowly from a small purse which hung from a leather strap around her neck. She placed her hands under the ultraviolet lamp. Her hard, labour-worn hands were covered with an invisible ink that would not wash off more than a week, a procedure to assure no person would vote more than once. A national ballot paper was handed to her as she moved toward the two-sided voting booth. She made her mark and then dropped her ballot into the ballot box. She then repeated the entire sequence for the regional elections. She had just voted for the first time in her life.

UN Volunteers also observed the counting process, which was slow and laborious. I first observed the counting in Namakgale. Later I visited parts of Lebowa, where the voting had been delayed by the late arrival of ballots, delivered finally by a South African Defence Force army helicopter. The product of an election with paper ballots is many metal ballot boxes, sealed and delivered to the counting station. Teams of counters appointed by the IEC first undertook the time-consuming task of reconciling their records and then finally opened the ballot boxes.

It struck me, as I watched the groups assembled in a large hall in

New times: Nelson Mandela casting his ballot in the country's first all-racial election in which he became President of South Africa. Photo: UN photo 186830/ C. Sattleberger

Namakgale slowly organize, that there was a kind of deliberate but pleasant reluctance to open the ballot boxes. Individuals would finger the metal wire wrapped around them and carefully examine the tags. The boxes were almost ritually touched. These boxes, it seemed, were presents under a psychological Christmas tree. One wants to open them immediately, but then one wants to wait to prolong the happiness of receiving gifts.

Eventually the boxes were opened and each ballot paper was individually held up for all—UN Volunteers, IEC election monitors, political party agents—to see. After many days of counting around the country, the process was completed and the election was declared "sufficiently free and fair" by the IEC.[39] Nelson Mandela became the first black president of South Africa.

THE VALUE OF THE INTERNATIONAL PRESENCE

Our assignment required that all UN Volunteers quickly and comprehensively adopt a friendly, impartial stance toward all South Africans we met. While the neutrality of our position was sometimes perplexing to South Africans, regardless of their race or political point of view, it yielded the greatest rewards in the trust we built up with the people we encountered. This kind of moment-to-moment diplomacy is at the heart of an international approach that touches people directly and becomes involved in their lives.

In this approach, distances between people are broken down and mutual respect can be the reward. The exchange of knowledge about each other is key to its success, and the small things, rather than the grand ideas, emerge as the most important. This approach is also one of the most challenging that can be undertaken. Even when it occurs under spelt-out terms of reference and very real rules, including an emphasis on neutrality, listening rather than talking, and careful assessment of what is observed, it also requires exercising professional judgment.

The major lesson learned in South Africa was that, fundamentally, it was simply our presence that reassured. This was the real benefit of the UNV/UNOMSA teams on the ground, in combination with well-defined tasks that would take us to the farthest reaches of the land. Another important lesson was that this delicate work of mingling with populations undergoing democratic transition in trying circumstances can be undertaken successfully and enhanced by the presence of volunteers. UN Volunteers took time from our work and travelled the long distance to South

Africa, interrupting our regular lives and schedules, to assist. We were there because we wanted to make a contribution at this important time. I think this was recognized by the people we talked to. The fact that we were volunteers was important because it represented a commitment by people from other countries to volunteer their efforts towards South Africa's own process. This motivation, a personal desire on our part to help which South Africans may not have even realized existed, was infectious and contributed to overall good relations between ourselves and the South Africans we met.

The by-product of the segregated and separated life of South Africa was an insular society that was not used to outside contact, especially in the rural areas of the country. The impact of international observers would be felt strongly by local people under any conditions. Under the conditions in South Africa, which by their very nature heightened differences and drew distinctions, the impact of multinational, multiracial teams of observers was exponentially increased.

There were small and large responses to our presence. Before our deployment in Phalaborwa, walking down the street shoulder-to-shoulder in Pietersburg with a fellow UN Volunteer from The Gambia on the important task of buying a radio so that we could get the news, was in its own way our simple introduction to the society of Pietersburg, and it did not go unnoticed. We, the observers, were observed. A white woman and a black man walking and talking together may not be so unusual in Johannesburg or Durban or Capetown. However, it was not so usual in the Far Northern Transvaal.

From that moment on, it was evident to me that our own conduct was as important as the duties we were assigned; in fact, it was pre-eminent. Our behaviour in both formal and informal circumstances was monitored by South Africans who were watching us to see if they could trust us, and ultimately if they could trust the UN, the election process, and the ongoing change. By our actions, we could give them either reasons to believe in us and in the process, or impressions that could lead to skepticism, cynicism, and disillusionment.

Our work in South Africa also broke down assumed stereotypes. Travelling together with the District Electoral Officer in the deep rural vastness of the Gazankulu homeland was greeted with incorrect assumptions. The first was that he worked for me; the second, asked of him at a small storefront where we stopped for something to drink, was whether I was his wife. People were surprised at the sight of a white woman with a blue hat and vest and a black man dressed in a suit despite the heat. He explained in the local language that I was with an organization called the United Nations, and was there to help with the elections. This news was usually greeted with a smile.

Understanding the effects of systemic racism also teaches us that we all have a lot to learn about how we perceive relations between people of different colours, as well as people of different sexes. The similarities between a racist attitude and a sexist attitude struck me in South Africa because both rely on stereotyping. I met many South African women and men who were aware that freedom and dignity involves not only the issue of race, but of sex. The awareness of sexism in a society coming to terms with racism was another hopeful South African sign.

It was apparent that the long isolation of South Africans, both white and black, was being broken in the course of this election transition. There was as much curiosity on the part of the local people about us as there was on our part about them and their perceptions of the process they were going through. As we went about our work we represented for the South Africans living symbols of the United Nations. We were at the grassroots, working, eating, refueling our vehicles, buying groceries, mapping voting stations, observing political rallies and meetings of the Local Peace Committees.[40] We represented proof of an international presence that reached into the daily lives of South Africans for a brief but watershed moment in time.

There was little if any initial understanding by local people of either the United Nations or what we were doing there. There was, however, the inevitable attention we would attract whenever we went into the villages and towns, sometimes encircled by curious children, at other times quietly observed from a distant kraal. While we explained our presence and role numerous times, the bald fact that new people were popping up all over the place by itself indicated something was happening. The action of our arrival underscored the transition taking place; this presence as much as anything that was said made for relaxation of tensions and anxieties. After meeting our entire UNV/UNOMSA team, a local community leader from Namakgale told me, "Now I know the elections will happen." In the white community, shopkeepers and others whom we met on our own rounds of personal chores would ask where we were from and why we were here. We would explain and then sometimes hear, as a woman behind the counter of a Phalaborwa bakery stated, "It's good you are here."

We also represented the international community that had formerly shunned South Africa, and that local people knew about only through the media, if at all. The general reaction of the white South Africans I met was that of friendliness. Some individuals genuinely wanted to help us, thereby aligning themselves with the changes occurring around them. This was particularly true of the South African Defence Force (SADF) colonel who ran the base next to Phalaborwa, and of officers from the South African Police Force, who took pains to inform us of needed security information and to aid us in our work. It was also clear that even if some white South Africans we met had reservations, and expressed them to us, they still seemed determined to go forward with the process. There was an apparent effort on the part of some people to put away the past, and a subtle apologetic attitude pervaded some conversations. This attitude was actually the material for a humorous book published in South Africa, where the reader was given an example of how to fill out your official apology form.[41]

Among black South Africans I met, reactions varied. There was a noticeable reserve by some political activists who had been involved in the struggle for many years, and who would not be convinced of change until it was a tangible reality. On the whole though, a warm welcome was extended to us in villages and townships, and we sensed that we were trusted, that people were glad we were there. A black South African lawyer from Lebowa talked about the wrongs of the past without anger. A white mine executive from Phalaborwa described what he saw as the country's main need, to right the wrongs of the past. Both looked to a brighter future for the country.

Individual contacts between ordinary people are much more powerful than is generally understood. Cross-fertilization and mutual understanding are enhanced by contact. In their reports back to UNV Geneva headquarters, many UN Volunteers remarked on the positive interactions they had with the people of South Africa, the friends they made, and the understanding they gained.[42] This was one of the most important aspects of the generally acknowledged accomplishment they felt at the end of the mission.

A point of crucial importance in South Africa was the presence of African UN Volunteers, who smoothed the contact with the black South African community for their other colleagues, and made for a much richer experience.[43] The experience in South Africa also taught UN Volunteers about each other. One of my teammates was from Zimbabwe. When the South African Defence Force helicopter brought the ballots to an area in Lebowa after we had waited there for many hours, I was elated but his reaction was different. He remembered when SADF helicopters had hovered menacingly over his own village compound where his family was confined for some time during Zimbabwe's independence struggle.

Though we both witnessed this means now used for entirely different ends, his memories lingered.

A great deal of concrete work was performed by UN Volunteers in the context of bringing various political actors together to solve mutual problems, to reduce violence, and to improve working relationships.[44] In addition to their own general knowledge and educational backgrounds, UN Volunteers brought specific experience. Seventy of the UN Volunteers serving in South Africa also had served in Cambodia,[45] where UN Volunteers organized the elections at the grassroots level. While South Africa was a very different mission, their experience in Cambodia was useful.

The community contact by UN Volunteers contributed toward the building of confidence of South Africans. Our presence at the local level in informal settings was often the most meaningful. For example, the long road between the white town of Phalaborwa and Giyani, the capital of the Gazankulu homeland, meant time lost in visiting the widely dispersed voting stations in the homeland. So, working this time together with a UNV partner, we decided to stay the night but there was literally no room at the inn.

We were immediately taken into the homes of South Africans, he to the son of a chief, I to the home of the District Electoral Officer, where we sat at their tables, ate their food, and talked together. This was probably the reason why there was a phone call to me from my host's relatives, who wanted to simply greet me and perhaps to make sure that it was true that someone from the UN really was there. We experienced this kind of informal exchange over and over, with invitations to white and black South African homes where we served as informal catalysts simply by being there.

The exchange occurred also in more formal settings, in meetings with the SADF, the South African Police, and the local elected officials. Our meetings with the South African Defence Force colonel and some members of his staff lead to invitations to a Friday drink. Executives of a local mining concern in Phalaborwa invited us to attend a barbecue, a multiracial event in which black and white South Africans joined our UN team to eat and carry on casual talk, this in one of the most conservative areas of South Africa.

These gatherings provided unique opportunities to gauge the temperature of change, and to promote a very difficult process by engaging with people. It was obvious that South Africans were undergoing a kind of traumatic conversion condensed into a very short period of time. All sides needed reassurance, which was given in the most simple gestures of listening, observing, and lending our presence as we worked and relaxed alongside them. Moreover, these hard-won contacts and friendly relations between UN Volunteers and South Africans spanned the society, from an Afrikaanse Weerstandsbeweging member to a black youth in a township, from meetings with officials to everyday interaction with the people in their communities.

These gatherings were also symptomatic of the times, in which a great ice block of pain and remembrance was slowly thawing and giving way to a new vision of the country. There were signs, however, that the new vision did not work for everyone. The Phalaborwa mayor, for instance, said he was literally "going fishing" in Mozambique during the elections. A white policeman, who stopped me on the roadside checkpoint outside a black homeland area, told me that after the elections he was "going to go to heaven."

FEEDBACK FROM THE FIELD

Security was a major problem for UN Volunteers in the troubled townships in and around Johannesburg. In the Natal region, poor security conditions due to deteriorating relations between the ANC and IFP resulted in a late start in identifying the voting stations. In some areas, UN Volunteers entered the townships only with a police escort and in armoured vehicles. The increased violence in Johannesburg weeks before the elections during the mass march of IFP supporters, which resulted in dozens killed and many more wounded,[46] and the bombings downtown and at the airport,[47] were extreme examples of the security risk working in South Africa entailed.

In the Far Northern Transvaal, we could have been victims of violence and no one in the UN would have known about it before it was too late. This was due to the inadequacy of communication equipment; because of their short range, the distributed radios were useless. In my area, there were no radios at all. In future operations where violence can strike, UN Volunteers and others must be provided with adequate communication systems.

Regarding the logistics of election observation, the deployment of the international election observers immediately before the elections and the early departure of some of them made for some inefficiency. In fact, the international election observers left our area at the most crucial time, when the ballots were being counted. Observing the counting became the sole responsibility of the UN Volunteers who, along with UNOMSA staff, took upon themselves the mammoth task, often working 16-hour days or more to reach the counting stations, even if only briefly, to reassure people that the UN was still working alongside them.

Another problem in our area was that the painstaking work we had done in mapping out the voting stations was wasted because cars provided to the international election observers were not equipped with trip metres. While it had been suggested that we create maps, this turned out to be impractical because of the long distances between stations and the many turns and twists in the rural roads. The international election observers eventually called on the police to guide them.

Some of the UN Volunteers felt that the time spent in South Africa was too short, that we should have been deployed for at least another month before the elections in order to capitalize on the heavy dose of learning that we absorbed at the start of this short mission. In addition, some UN Volunteers may have been willing to stay and assist in other transition projects, informed by their extensive and valuable contact with the local population. The contribution that UN Volunteers bring to UN efforts may be squandered if this resource is not recognized for what it is: a powerful alliance at the grassroots by and for people of the country with the United Nations.

Some problems occurred within teams of UN Volunteers and UN personnel on short-term contracts. These kinds of frictions have not been unknown in other missions where UN Volunteers work closely with UN staff. This problem has its roots in what I call the monetization of assistance. It can be traced to the incorrect but traditional point of view that the work of those paid very highly is worth more. This distinction between volunteers and others is an unkind one and it cuts deeply. There is no rational reason to discriminate against a qualified person who works as much out of a sense of spirit of service and personal growth as for monetary payment. This problem can and should be remedied with more information about the high quality of UN Volunteers selected for these types of missions and their equally high motivation. More knowledge about volunteers could lead to more mutual respect between UN international personnel and their UN Volunteer partners, and in many practical suggestions to improve future operations.

CONCLUSION

An important outcome of this type of mission is the mutual learning that goes on during the experience. UN Volunteers actively worked to reassure South Africans, to lessen violence, increase general understanding, and spread knowledge about the UN itself. Also, every UN Volunteer comes away enriched by the experience. Volunteers learned from South Africans of every colour and belief.

This kind of learning is transmitted from the mission itself as volunteers carry their experiences back to their families and friends, to their academic institutions, and to their own governments. A real but perhaps unseen benefit of UN Volunteers' participation in electoral missions is the spread of democratic ideals. What UN Volunteers learned helps increase awareness and inform debate at the everyday level when an individual UN Volunteer's experience becomes part of a community experience.

Today, when I describe South Africa to my family, friends, and colleagues, I tell them it is one of the most hopeful countries in the world. I say it could be one of the best examples of harmony between races and the attainment of understanding so necessary to heal the wounds of racism, ethnic division, xenophobia, and isolationism that we see growing in the world. For as South Africa once went away from the world, some of the world now seems poised to move away from the principles upon which the new South Africa is based.

The process of reassurance and support by the world community for South Africa is not over. This support includes needed foreign investment, which will reflect the level of confidence the country enjoys internationally. This kind of support is vital to overcoming the past and fulfilling promises made to the people for a better life. The news out of South Africa more than a year later, despite reported problems and contradictions, does not disappoint us. The news continues to report the positive changes taking place there, and the hope the world holds for the country. South Africa represents the best of our collective aspirations, and ironically, today South Africa reassures us.

NOTES

1. South Africa's total population is 43,931,000. The population is 75 per cent black, 14 per cent white, 9 per cent coloured, and 3 per cent Indian. *The World Almanac and Book of Facts 1995*. Mahwah, N.J.: Funk & Wagnalls, 1994, pp. 819–820.
2. Apartheid is defined as an official policy of racial segregation promulgated in the Republic of South Africa with a view to promoting and maintaining white ascendancy. (Afrikaans, "apartness": apart, separate, from the French *à part*). *The American Heritage Dictionary of the English Language*. Boston: American Heritage Publishing Co., Inc. and Houghton Mifflin Company, 1975, p. 60.
3. A good analysis of South African history and its effect on the modern sociology of this nation can be found in Sparks, Allister. *The Mind of South Africa*. London: Mandarin, 1993, pp. 1–428. Link between the Great Trek and the abolition of slavery is described on page 105.

4. Sparks, *The Mind of South Africa*, pp. 119–124 and pp. 132–134.
5. Sparks, *The Mind of South Africa*, pp. 136–141.
6. In 1959 the government passed acts providing the eventual creation of several Bantu nations or Bantustans on 13 per cent of the country's land area, though most black leaders opposed the plan.
7. Four homelands, Transkei, Ciskei, Venda, and Bophuthaswana, were declared independent in the 1970s. The six other homelands were Gazankulu, Lebowa, KwaNdebele, Kangwane, KwaZulu, and Qwaqwa. See *The United Nations and Apartheid, 1948–1994*, United Nations Blue Book Series. New York: United Nations Department of Public Information, 1994, pp. 31–32.
8. Sparks, *The Mind of South Africa*, pp. 239–241.
9. In the years immediately following the arrest and imprisonment of Mandela and the exile or arrest of members of the ANC and other resistance movements, the struggle against apartheid cooled, only to be re-ignited a decade later. In 1976 the students of Soweto, in response to an order that half of all instruction in the township schools be conducted in Afrikaans, the simplified Dutch official language of the Afrikaners, rose up in rebellion. At least 600 persons, mostly blacks, were killed in the 1976 riots protesting apartheid. Black Consciousness Movement leader Stephen Biko died in detention in 1977.
10. This unsuccessful attempt to "reform" apartheid was largely boycotted by the newly enfranchised non-white voters and was recognized for what it was by the United Nations. On 15 November 1983 the United Nations General Assembly rejected the tricameral Parliament established under apartheid as "an insidious manoeuvre by the racist minority regime of South Africa to further entrench White minority rule and apartheid." See UN Doc. A/RES/38/11.
11. South Africa sought to destabilize Mozambique (see G. Yoshiura, this volume), Angola, and Zimbabwe, and it occupied Namibia, in contravention of UN Security Council Resolution 435 (1978). See *The United Nations and Apartheid, 1948–1994*, pp. 32–35.
12. It was originally anticipated that De Klerk would lead a slow process of democratization while trying to maintain as much power as possible in the hands of whites through the legal installation of the concept of "group rights." After his election he told foreign diplomats, "Don't expect me to negotiate myself out of power." See Sparks, *The Mind of South Africa*, pp. 370–371.
13. In this speech delivered during the opening of Parliament on 2 February 1990, President De Klerk lifted bans on the ANC, South African Communist Party, Umkhonto we Sizwe (Spear of the Nation guerilla arm of the ANC), Pan African Congress (PAC) and Black Consciousness. The speech has been described "as one of the great leaps of faith in the annals of political leadership.... Here was the Rubicon [former President] Botha had balked at crossing." Sparks, *The Mind of South Africa*, p. 398.
14. *The United Nations and Apartheid, 1948–1994*, p. 97.
15. Political violence, including repeated hostilities between hostel dwellers and their surrounding communities, attacks on commuter trains and minibus taxis, and attacks on squatter settlements and isolated rural kraals, left at least 10,000 South Africans dead between 1990 and 1993, nearly all of them black. "South Africa, United Nations Observer Mission in South Africa (UNOMSA)." *United Nations Focus* (August 1993): 1–2.
16. A band of marauders swept through the township of Boipatong on 17 June 1992, killing some 40 blacks and prompting the ANC to temporarily break off constitutional talks with the white minority government.
17. The Multi-Party Negotiating Council created the Independent Electoral Commission and first proposed the 27 April voting date. It adopted the constitutional principles and the Bill of Rights to be contained in the interim constitution. *The United Nations and Apartheid*, pp. 111–113.
18. The first General Assembly resolution condemning apartheid was passed on 12 September 1952. UN Doc. A/RES/2183.

19. The General Assembly has passed over 200 resolutions concerning South Africa and apartheid, while the Security Council issued over 30 resolutions. A listing of these and some selected documents can be found in *The United Nations and Apartheid*, pp. 175–204.
20. UN Doc. S/RES/765 (1992), 16 July 1992. For an explanation of UNOMSA's role see presentation by King, Angela. "The Role of International Observer Missions in South Africa." (August 1993): 3.
21. *An Agenda for Peace, Preventive Diplomacy, Peacemaking, and Peacekeeping*, Report of the Secretary-General pursuant to the Statement adopted by the Summit Meeting of the Security Council on 31 January 1992, UN Doc. S/24111–A/47/227, 17 June 1992.
22. "South Africa, United Nations Observer Mission in South Africa (UNOMSA)," p. 1.
23. UN Doc. S/RES/772 (1992), 17 August 1992.
24. *Report of the Secretary-General concerning arrangement for United Nations monitoring of the electoral process in South Africa and coordination of activities of internal observers*, UN Doc. A/48/845–S/1994/16, 10 January 1994, paragraph 42.
25. UNOMSA fielded a total of 500 observers—200 UN Volunteers and 300 through regular channels. *UNV Support Unit End of Mission Report* (May 1994): 2.
26. UN Doc. S/RES/894 (1994), 14 January 1994.
27. Collaboration in South Africa between the UN and UNV was established in a Memorandum of Understanding in February 1994. This memorandum called for 200 UN Volunteers to serve as Observation Support Officers for the upcoming national elections and laid out the Terms of Reference for the UN Volunteers. The Terms of Reference spelled out the assignments of the UN Volunteers and included identifying the location of polling stations; noting road conditions; establishing contact with polling station officers, Independent Electoral Commission monitors, political party agents, and other relevant authorities; reinforcing peace activities during the last phase of the electoral campaign; observing rallies and other political events; visiting voting stations and recording events observed on election days; and observing the transportation and security of electoral materials, the counting of ballots, and the review of disputed ballots in the period following the elections. The duties specified in this document for UNV Observation Support Officers are almost identical to those specified for the UNOMSA Electoral Division staff. See *Report of the Secretary General on the Question of South Africa*. UN Doc. S/1994/16–A/48/845, 10 January 1994, paragraph 57.
28. *UNV Support Unit End of Mission Report*, May 1994, 2. Fifty-five per cent of the UN Volunteers recruited for the mission in South Africa were from 15 African nations. The number of UN Volunteers from each was Kenya, 15; Nigeria, 13; Uganda, 11; Tanzania, 10; Zambia, 8; Malawi, 8; Liberia, The Gambia, Zimbabwe, Ghana, 6 each; Sierra Leone, 5; Ethiopia, 2; Tunisia, 1; Benin, 1; Mauritius, 1.
29. The South African Defence Force (SADF) was renamed the National Defence Force (NDF) after the elections. The new body incorporated regional (ex-homeland) militias, as well as former guerilla groups such as the ANC's Umkhonto we Sizwe (Spear of the Nation).
30. The Afrikaanse Weerstandsbeweging (AWB) was formed in 1976 under the leadership of Eugene Terre Blanche and six others. A paramilitary group organized to create independent "Volkstaats" with structures similar to the Boer republics, some AWB members have been arrested in connection with terrorist activities. See Harber, Anton and Barbara Ludman, eds., *The Weekly Mail and Guardian's A-Z of South African Politics*. London: Penguin, 1994, pp. 166–169.
31. The Independent Electoral Commission (IEC) was created by an act of the South African Legislature (Act 202, *The Electoral Act*, chap. 2) "[t]o administer, organize, supervise, and conduct free and fair elections" and "[t]o promote the conditions for free and fair elections." The IEC was made up of both national and international political figures.
32. The Phalaborwa area has been extensively mined for the last thousand years and, until the coming of whites, this was done by the people who gave the town its name. The

Phalaborwa were Sotho-speaking miners and metal workers who compensated for their poor agricultural conditions by trading in metal goods. See, for instance, Cameron, Trewhella and S. B. Spies, eds., *A New Illustrated History of South Africa*. Johannesburg: Southern Book Publishers, 1992, p. 43.

33. For an in-depth analysis of the problem of violence in South Africa, see du Toit, Andre. *Understanding South African Political Violence: A New Problematic?* Geneva: UNRISD/ DP43, 1993, pp. 1–30.
34. The formation of politically independent regions was permitted under amendments to the South African Constitution (*Negotiating Council meeting of 21 February 1994*; revised Chapter 11A). The autonomy of these regions would have to be approved by the South African government.
35. See *The Two South Africas*. Braamfontein: Human Rights Commission, 1992, pp. 1–30. This detailed report graphically shows the lack of mapping to indicate where South Africa's majority black population lives.
36. The IEC Act (*South African Government Gazette*, V344, No. 15506) specifies 374 electoral districts in South Africa, each covered by a District Electoral Officer (DEO). The DEOs were responsible for the preparation and conduct of the polling.
37. This figure was provided by Gazankulu officials and taken from 1991 census figures produced in Pretoria.
38. The ANC took 62.7 per cent of the national vote; the National Party 20.4 per cent; and the IFP received 10.5 per cent. See *The United Nations and Apartheid*, p. 125.
39. *Statement by the Spokesman for Secretary-General Boutros Boutros-Ghali applauding the election process in South Africa*, UN Press Release SG/SM/5282–SAF/176, 6 May 1994.
40. I was one of three UN Volunteers who observed one of the largest and most peaceful gatherings to take place. We were, as far as we could tell, the single UN presence at this event. The occasion was the Easter Sunday gathering of the Zionist Christian Church in Moria where more than 2 million church members received world attention since then-President De Klerk, Nelson Mandela, and Chief Mangosuthu Buthelezi of the Inkatha Freedom Party all attended. The picture flashed around the world of these three men leaving church together. The image was important because of the very real enmity between the ANC and Inkatha, which was being blamed for the increasing violence in Natal and Johannesburg areas. The long and painful process of negotiations between the two and the government concerning the inclusion of Inkatha in the elections, which Buthelezi had threatened to boycott, dramatically culminated in a last-minute agreement ensuring IFP's participation. Rolls of IFP stickers poured out of printing presses both in South Africa and abroad. These were attached to the pre-printed ballot papers at the voting stations. But on that Easter Sunday the issue was still not resolved and therefore the presence of these three men together was significant and produced hope that an understanding could be worked out. The Moria meeting was also singular for the incredible display of organization and peacefulness that South Africa hungered for during this tense time. It was moments such as these, in contrast to the ongoing violence in the country, that signaled the hopefulness that would later become the common currency during the days of voting, when the violence stopped.
41. Silber, Gus. *It Takes Two to Toiy-Toiy*. London: Penguin, 1991.
42. In the *UNV Reports on Service, UNOMSA, R.S.A.* a consistent theme running through the comments by UN Volunteers on their experience in South Africa concerns the positive interactions with the people there and the contribution these interactions made to help further the transition process. As one volunteer stated: "We were able to make contact with and interact with people from all walks of life in South Africa and make a very positive contribution to the peace process of this country at a turning point in its history." UN Volunteers also were rewarded personally and were glad for the experience. "It was the most important single event in my working life. I thank UNV-Geneva for making me a part of a historic process," one volunteer said.

43. UNV was asked by the UN in New York to have persons of African origin constitute at least 45 per cent of volunteers fielded, UNV fulfilled the request by decentralizing identification through reliance on United Nations Development Programme country offices in Africa.
44. For example, UN Volunteer Abebe Hankore, deployed in the violent and unstable Alexandria township, reported on the frequent clashes between the ANC Youth League and the IFP Youth Brigade, which regularly disrupted activities in the township. "We realized," he said, "that unless the youth leaders at grassroots level were convinced they should negotiate a cease-fire and cooperate with each other towards their country's common goal of democracy, decisions at the ministerial level would be ineffective." Hankore was able to facilitate meetings between the youth leaders, which led to a lessening of violence. "It was not during the formal meetings that any compromise was achieved; that was reached informally, between meetings." Cooperation between antagonists in the community allowed normal activities to resume; people could do their grocery shopping and conduct their personal business without constant fear of attack. The late entry of IFP into the elections stilled the violence and allowed free and fair elections to take place there. *UNV News* (June 1994), no. 66: 21.
45. *UNV Support Unit End of Mission Report*, 2.
46. Shooting broke out during a March 1994 mass march of IFP supporters through the center of Johannesburg. This and other violence elsewhere in the city left 53 dead and more than 250 wounded. *Report of the Secretary-General on the Question of South Africa*, UN Doc. S/1994/717, 16 June 1994, 1.
47. A string of bomb attacks, beginning with the 24 April car-bomb explosion near the ANC headquarters, left 21 dead and 200 injured throughout the country. There were no fatalities from the Johannesburg Airport bombing. *Report of the Secretary-General on the Question of South Africa*, UN Doc. S/1994/717, 16 June 1994, 7.

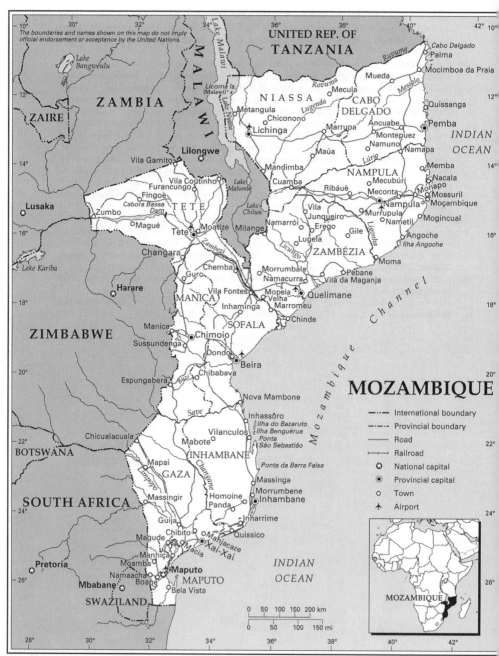

MAP NO. 3706   UNITED NATIONS
NOVEMBER 1992

3

VOTING FOR PEACE: PREPARING FOR POST-WAR DEMOCRACY IN MOZAMBIQUE

Gláucia Vaz Yoshiura

ON A BEAUTIFUL Sunday in mid-1994, a *Mulunga*—the commonly used expression in Mozambique to designate female whites—was with some 15 Mozambicans patiently waiting on Inhassoro beach for a small sailing boat that was approaching the shore. Like everyone else, she wanted to purchase some fresh squid. As soon as the fisherman, an old man, left his boat and started wading towards the beach, everyone could see that he had caught only a few squid and some fish. The Mulunga soon realized that among so many customers it would be nearly impossible for her to buy even one small squid, but she was determined to try. When the fisherman reached the group, however, and before the Mulunga could say anything in Portuguese, the people started yelling at him in *Chitsua*, the local dialect. Seeing this, the Mulunga knew she would not stand a chance at buying some scarce squid. However, a few minutes later, and to the Mulunga's surprise, the fisherman walked over to her and handed

Gláucia Vaz Yoshiura, a Brazilian national born in 1967 and a lawyer graduated from the University of São Paulo, served as a UN Volunteer District Electoral Officer in the United Nations Operation in Mozambique from May to November 1994. An international relations doctoral candidate at the Graduate Institute of International Studies in Geneva, she is presently serving as a UN Volunteer Humanitarian Assistance Officer within the United Nations Angola Verification Mission.

her the few squid he held in his hands. In fact, the local people had been discussing among themselves and with the fisherman who should have the squid; they decided that the Mulunga was the one who should be allowed to purchase them, and so she did, paying the local price.

This is one of the many experiences of its kind that the Mulunga would have during her six months' stay among the Mozambican people, assisting in the establishment of democracy as a United Nations Volunteer. It reveals the gentle nature of Mozambicans, which continuously encouraged not only this particular *Mulunga* but many other international workers to carry on their varieties of field work under the harsh living conditions of rural Mozambique.

Away from the big cities, such as Maputo, the capital, or Beira, lies the real Mozambique. In thousands of villages, huts made of straw and reed or clay stand in stark contrast to the few abandoned and ruined colonial buildings, constructed in the distinctive Portuguese style. Infrastructure such as running water or electricity is non-existent. Eighty-five per cent of the Mozambican people live in these rural areas, which were most affected by the long war carried out by the guerilla movement Mozambique National Resistance (RENAMO) against the Mozambican government.

The nearly 16 years of war completely disrupted the social and economic life of Mozambique. Approximately 1 million people died and 4.5 million out of the total of 16 million inhabitants became either refugees in neighbouring countries or internally displaced persons.[1] One-third of the population was threatened with starvation and only a quarter of the people had access to safe drinking water and sanitation. Mozambican life had long been organized around a land-based subsistence economy. Once the people were separated from their land, they became dependent on foreign aid and on imports. For example, Mozambicans depended on aid imports for 90 per cent of their cereal needs. The health and educational systems throughout the country were also badly damaged. Hospitals and schools had either been closed down or were in extremely poor condition, lacking basic human and material resources.[2]

After more than two years of negotiations, the government and RENAMO were finally able to reach the October 1992 General Agreement of Mozambique,[3] which led to the cease-fire, demobilization, recognition of political parties, and the country's first multiparty elections. Since the supervision and monitoring of these provisions were to become the responsibility of the United Nations, the UN Security Council established the United Nations Operation in Mozambique (ONUMOZ), a comprehensive, "second-generation"[4] peacekeeping operation. With many new dimensions—political, humanitarian, electoral—post-Cold War peacekeeping operations have called upon the services of international civilian professionals, including United Nations Volunteers.

I was one of the 100 UN Volunteer specialists working with the electoral arm of ONUMOZ. Altogether, 278 UN Volunteers from 56 countries, ranging from 24 to 60 years of age, served with ONUMOZ, with the United Nations Development Programme (UNDP), or with other collaborating agencies, such as the International Organization for Migration (IOM). Within ONUMOZ, UN Volunteers undertook a variety of tasks: demobilizing soldiers, coordinating humanitarian assistance, monitoring the electoral process, and providing technical assistance for organizing the elections.

Serving as a UN Volunteer was, above all, an exchange in which UN Volunteers could, as in my own case, be a part of the democratization efforts of a country, and also learn about its people and share with them their culture and traditions. As a former corporate lawyer working in international banking and capital markets, the exchange with Mozambicans was for me at the heart a very different and extremely rewarding experience.

MOZAMBIQUE BETWEEN WAR AND PEACE

Mozambique won its independence from Portugal in 1975 after a decade of guerilla struggle led by the Mozambique Liberation Front (FRELIMO). The struggle for independence started in 1962 when FRELIMO was founded in Tanzania. Under the leadership of Eduardo Mondlane and, after his assassination in 1969, of Samora Machel, FRELIMO gradually succeeded in extending the independence movement from the northern province of Cabo Delgado to other Mozambican provinces. When the military regime of Antonio Salazar in Portugal came to an end with the Lisbon coup of 1974, the way was finally opened for Mozambican independence. FRELIMO dominated the transitional government, and took office in June 1975 in the newly independent Mozambique, which joined the United Nations later that year.

Only two years after independence, however, Mozambique found itself caught in a punishing regional conflict.[5] Its neighbours—first Rhodesia and then the apartheid regime of South Africa—deliberately worked to destabilize the FRELIMO government. In the 1970s, the whole of southern Africa was disrupted by Rhodesia's war of liberation. Because Mozambique supported the Zimbabwean liberation movements struggling against the Rhodesian government,[6] Rhodesia was instrumental in helping to form RENAMO, a guerilla movement originally created to monitor and disrupt the activities of the Zimbabwean African National Union (ZANU) rebels operating against Rhodesia from Mozambique.[7]

When the Zimbabwean liberation movements finally came to power in 1980, RENAMO's financing was transferred to South Africa. By supporting RENAMO and other guerilla movements in the region, the South African apartheid regime deliberately sought to weaken Mozambique, Angola, and other southern African countries by disrupting transport and other economic links among these black-ruled states. Through this policy South Africa hoped to stop its neighbouring countries from supporting the anti-apartheid movement and to maintain its hegemonic power in the region.

At this point RENAMO began referring to itself as a liberation movement fighting on behalf of Mozambicans against FRELIMO.[8] It gathered support among groups that had profound reasons for discontent with the government. Three main groups can be identified:[9] traditional tribal chiefs who had been stripped of their political power by FRELIMO;[10] people who resented interference with some traditional practices largely prohibited by FRELIMO; and people who opposed FRELIMO's agricultural policies, such as confiscation or forced "villagization."

In the 1980s, RENAMO dominated the country, occupying all but 2 of Mozambique's 11 provinces. In a war aimed at dismantling FRELIMO's achievements, RENAMO's targets were invariably health and educational facilities, and the people who staffed them. But it was RENAMO's frequent attacks on rural villages across the country that caused the deepest social and economic disruptions throughout Mozambique, doing harm to millions of people.

In 1984, the FRELIMO government took the unprecedented step of joining South Africa in the Nkomati Accord,[11] in which both states agreed to refrain from interfering in each other's internal affairs. Mozambique agreed to refuse entry of African National Congress's (ANC) exiles; South Africa agreed to stop supporting RENAMO. However, within the context of the Cold War, financial aid from the United States and even from South Africa continued to reach RENAMO, enabling the guerilla movement to carry on its fight against Mozambique's Marxist-Leninist government, which, in turn, received support from the former Soviet Union. By the end of the decade the war had spread even more.

It was not until the demise of the Cold War and the dismantling of the apartheid regime in South Africa in the early 1990s that peace negotiations in Mozambique gathered momentum. Democratic reforms led to a new constitution in 1990 and two years later Mozambican President Joaquim Chissano and RENAMO leader Afonso Dhalakama finally signed the General Peace Agreement of Mozambique, which the United Nations was requested to supervise and monitor.

ONUMOZ AND THE ELECTIONS

The UN Security Council had established ONUMOZ in December 1992 for a period of ten months,[12] but delays in the implementation of the General Peace Agreement resulted in an extension of the mandate through December 1994, when the new government took office.[13] The mission was one of most comprehensive peacekeeping operations ever undertaken by the UN.[14] The sheer size of Mozambique, an extensive area of 800,000 square kilometres, along with the lack of infrastructure and communications meant that ONUMOZ needed to contribute massive human and material resources to accomplish its mandate and also required the establishment of a large organizational and administrative structure to run the mission.

To do its job, ONUMOZ included five distinct components: political, military, humanitarian, electoral, and police.[15] Through these components, ONUMOZ fulfilled the tasks provided in the agreement,[16] including verification of the cease-fire, demobilization, coordination of humanitarian assistance operations, monitoring police activities, and providing technical assistance to and monitoring of the elections.

Most of the civilian field work required by the mission was done by UN Volunteers. One hundred ten UN Volunteer specialists, serving with the Technical Unit for Demobilization or with IOM, helped demobilize approximately 80,000 soldiers.[17] Together with military observers, they set up assembly areas, assisted demobilization, and arranged transportation of former soldiers to their villages. These UN Volunteers performed their tasks under tough conditions, often without proper sanitation, running water, and electricity, in an extremely tense and sometimes violent atmosphere.

In the humanitarian component, my other UN Volunteer colleagues served with the United Nations Office for Humanitarian Assistance Coordination (UNOHAC) in coordinating and monitoring humanitarian assistance operations, in particular those relating to the social and economic reintegration of returned refugees, internally displaced persons, demobilized military personnel and the local population. They evaluated food and water source needs, and existing health and educational units throughout the country. They also served as liaisons with donors and 70 international non-governmental organizations (NGOs) operating in Mozambique. Within the electoral component, 150 UN Volunteers assisted and monitored the entire electoral process.

Under the General Peace Agreement, the Mozambican people were responsible for organizing the first multiparty elections in their country. The ONUMOZ electoral component was designed to monitor the elections, while a UNDP Electoral Technical Assistance Project—kept strictly separate from the monitoring activities of the ONUMOZ Electoral Division—was responsible for the technical end. Fifty UN Volunteer specialists, although not directly responsible for the organization of the elections, were integrated into the Mozambican national and provincial Electoral Commissions and their respective Technical Secretariats for the Administration of the Elections,[18] where they provided technical assistance and logistical support for election organization.

To adequately monitor the elections, a ONUMOZ Electoral Division was created and divided into national, provincial, and district levels.[19] We UN Volunteers worked in teams in the districts under the supervision of provincial coordinators.[20] UN international personnel filled the top posts of the Electoral Division and were based in the national or provincial capitals. The 100 electoral officers deployed to the districts were all UN Volunteers. Together with the civilian police (CIVPOL), UN Volunteers were the only UN presence actually working in the district capitals and villages, responsible for covering the entire country. Our job, to assist the Electoral Division in accomplishing its work, was huge.[21]

UN VOLUNTEERS FACILITATING THE DEMOCRATIZATION PROCESS

My English teammate and I formed one of the 50 UN Volunteer teams working at the district level. Posted in Inhassoro, a small town located on the beautiful northern cost of Inhambane Province, we were assigned to two of the most remote districts of Inhambane, Inhassoro and Govuro. Although a road existed between the ONUMOZ provincial headquarters and our post, the road conditions were so poor that a 350-kilometre trip to our district capital took more than six hours. We had to maneuver our four-wheel drive truck onto dirt tracks on either side of the road to avoid large areas of destroyed asphalt. Evidence of the recent war was always present; we passed burned-out buses and trucks on the roadside where they were left after being attacked, evidence of the grisly past of guerilla

war. Reaching Nova Mambone, the Govuro district capital some 110 kilometres north of our post, was even more demanding due to the enormous
holes along the sandy dirt track.

Upon arrival our first contact was with members of the District Electoral Commissions—known by its Portuguese acronym as CDEs—and
members of the district Technical Secretariats for the Administration of
the Elections—known as STAEs. At that time I knew little about these
elderly men, who occupied the key positions within the CDEs and
STAEs, or about the young men who were constantly questioning me
about life outside Mozambique, a country they seemed to realize had
stopped in time.

As our contact grew closer, I found they were all well-respected citizens of the community, such as the school principal, teachers, staff members of the local administration, "rich" farmers. These Mozambican colleagues of ours revealed to us how proud they were to be in charge of
the organization of the first elections of their country. Ahead of them
was an enormous task—registering voters, organizing the polling and
counting the ballots—activities that, in addition to the political campaigning, we would observe, verify, and monitor.[22]

Registration of Voters

During the registration period, June through September 1994,[23] my
teammate and I regularly visited the 20 registration posts in our two districts. To cover all of them on a weekly basis, we travelled to at least
four posts a day. This meant journeys of more than nine hours, most of
them driving on barely visible "roads," which often were no more than
narrow and dusty tracks cutting across forests and savannas.

We travelled only on roads known to be free of land mines because of
the estimated 2 million anti-personnel and anti-tank mines in Mozambique, some dating back to the colonial period.[24] Almost every Mozambican I met had a story to tell about a mine incident: a child who was hurt
while playing out in the bush, a pregnant woman who stepped on a mine
while chopping wood. From these personal tragedies, the local people
knew which areas were dangerous. We often relied on their information
to reach our registration posts, while trying to avoid tracks that had not
been used recently.

During these visits, I saw how enthusiastic Mozambicans were about
the peace and democratization process of their country. In the first
months of the registration period, the posts were often lively, crowded
with young and old, men and women, the latter wearing colourful *capula-*

nas[25] and carrying their babies. They sometimes had walked more than 20 kilometres to reach the registration posts closest to their villages. Upon arrival, they would sit on the ground under the shadow of a large mango or cashew tree, patiently waiting hour upon hour for their turn to register.

While talking one day to an old man waiting to be registered, I discovered he had walked some 15 kilometres to reach the registration post. I asked how he had walked such a long distance. He replied that it took him a long time to arrive and that he had been obliged to sit down by the side of the track many times to take a rest. When I asked him why he had made such a great effort to register, he answered that Mozambique was changing into a peaceful country and that, although he was very old, he wanted to keep up with the new times.

Before being identified and issued the all-important voter card that would enable Mozambicans to exercise their right to vote, CDE civic educators would give them more detailed information about the presidential and legislative elections scheduled for October. These young, brave civic educators walked from village to village, without their promised bicycles, to explain to the people in their own dialects the importance of registering to vote.

Mozambicans who registered voters in Inhassoro and Govuro, and throughout the country, were called brigade members. These teams of educated young men and women, often accompanied by their children, left their homes and families to do the registration work. I witnessed the exceptional job they did under the harsh working and living conditions. Registration in Colonato had to be carried out in the open air, subject to the capriciousness of the weather, since no shelter, not even a hut, was available. In Mabime, they slept on handmade straw mats laid on the dusty ground of old, shared huts. Their working day meal consisted of corn meal and dried fish delivered by the CDE. Even when they were not paid for months, they did not abandon their posts.

Villagers living near the registration posts were sensitive to brigade members' efforts: out of the bush a village woman carried to them a bucket of water from a recently restored well; a man offered them some freshly hunted game—wild chickens, a gazelle, some birds. These small acts to support the brigade members' work mirrored the larger reality: Mozambicans were engaged together in a giant effort to make the elections possible. They were working hard for what democracy might bring them—continued peace.

The CDE and STAE, responsible for the organization of the elections in the districts, faced major logistical problems throughout the whole electoral process. Funding to feed brigade members, as well as transportation and communication, was inadequate. It was due to the contribution of some CDE and STAE members, who provided food for the brigades and fuel for a small truck, that just half of the registration posts in the Inhassoro district were open upon our arrival.

However, since many people were returning home without registering, we realized that an extra effort had to be made to open the remaining posts. CDE and STAE members managed to obtain more food supplies for the brigade members and we helped by transporting them. After a few days of combined work, all registration posts had been opened in Inhassoro and my teammate and I had established friendly relations with some 30 brigade members while driving them to their destinations.

The Govuro district faced the same type of logistical problems although the electoral authorities managed to deploy all the brigade members within the first week of the registration period. Again, this was possible thanks to the help of some community members and political parties. Sometimes, though, the help got in the way. Because no other transportation was available, the STAE used a RENAMO truck to transport brigade members. As a result, the local people at the remote registration post in Jofane, knowing the brigade members arrived in a RENAMO truck, initially refused to register. Only after careful explanations of why the truck had to be used and reassurances about the impartiality of brigade members and the National Electoral Commission by the president of CDE did the people begin to show up to register for their voter cards.

In both districts, it was clear that we were witnessing the birth of a unified effort by people of different political convictions to attain a common goal. In the Inhassoro district, the simple fact that government and RENAMO members both contributed their own private resources so that the registration posts could be opened was evidence of the ongoing social and political transformation in Mozambique. In Jofane itself, where the truck incident highlighted the underlying tensions, people had begun to realize that it was finally possible for two old enemies to cooperate in achieving their shared dream. For whole communities, holding elections as part of democratization to achieve expected peace can only be characterized as "revolutionary."

The Political Campaign

Due to the several extensions of the registration period, the official political campaign did not begin until late September 1994. During this phase of the electoral process my teammate and I began to maintain closer contact with political party members. As international observers, we could not get as close to them as we had been with members of the District Electoral Commissions because we had to maintain our principles of impartiality, independence, and objectivity.[26] Since the District Electoral Commissions were also impartial bodies composed of representatives of various political parties, our close cooperation with these commissions was not perceived as partiality towards one party or another. Concerning political parties themselves, the situation was more delicate. We were required to allocate our time equally among all of them and to never show any preference towards one or another. After all, we international observers had been invited by the Mozambican government and RENAMO—who were deeply and reciprocally mistrustful—to ensure the highest degree of impartiality in the elections.[27]

In our two districts, only the two major parties, FRELIMO and RENAMO, were able to systematically carry out their political campaigns. FRELIMO was very active in both districts, while RENAMO was more active in the Govuro district. The smaller political parties and coalitions, a total of 14,[28] faced difficulties in getting organized in the districts. Only a few were able to open offices and send district delegates. Their electoral campaign in the form of rallies and public meetings was almost non-existent.

Together with CIVPOL officers, I attended several public meetings held by political parties in the small villages of my districts. The first one, in Chitsotso, was remarkable. We arrived mid-morning at the community meeting place—a large tree. A well-dressed woman, a FRELIMO representative, was speaking in the local dialect to about 100 people, including the village secretary, traditional village chief, teachers, nurses, and the villagers themselves. The audience, very organized and orderly, was listening attentively. Women—the vast majority of the group—were on the right side of the speaker sitting on the ground with their children, while the few men sat to the left on wooden benches.

During her speech, the political party representative briefly explained the party programme and performed what was called "civic education," consisting of teaching people how to vote. She talked about the importance of the voter card, explained how to fill out the ballot paper, how to fold the ballot paper, and so on. The event became festive at the end, when the speaker taught party songs to the assembled group, which picked them up quickly and sang them with the great beauty of African voices. To close the meeting, a few T-shirts, posters, and flags were distributed, while villagers competed to get the electoral materials.

Public meetings like this were held in both Inhassoro and Govuro and were the main instrument used by political parties to carry out their electoral campaign throughout the rural areas country-wide, where the vast majority of the population lived. Political campaign events following the "Western" mold were held only in provincial capitals and in the country capital, as well as in the largest cities.

During the electoral campaign period my teammate and I also observed the CDE and STAE preparations for the voting, which involved identifying the required number and possible location of the polling stations as well as recruiting and training the staff. In doing so I realized that, although limited by the Electoral Division's mandate, I was in a position to contribute more generally to organizing elections.

Even though UN Volunteer District Electoral Officers (DEOs) were observers, I was not prevented from giving useful advice to the district electoral authorities, which was more or less welcome depending on the degree of confidence that had been established. In my two districts, members of the CDE and STAE found it difficult to foresee some of the steps that should have been taken to prepare for the polling, due to lack of experience concerning electoral matters. I suggested to the STAE directors of our two districts that they think about the necessary number of polling stations in their districts and the number of people to be recruited and trained to operate those polling stations. I also suggested that they compile all the information in a chart and send it as a report to the Provincial Electoral Commission.

Surprisingly, a few weeks later the Inhassoro STAE Director told me and my teammate how much the provincial electoral authorities in Inhambane had appreciated my initiative. He said they were going to suggest this method to all other districts in the province. So my suggestion, provoking the STAE directors' reflection and initiative, ended up reaching higher levels and had the advantage, coming from the bottom to the top, of being more in tune with the realities in the field.

Polling

During voting in the October elections most UNV district electoral officers did not work as observers but as trouble-shooters. We helped staff our post 24-hours a day, receiving and relaying information transmitted by the provincial headquarters and by the international electoral observers (IEOs)[29] deployed in our districts. We also did liaison work with CDEs/STAEs on electoral matters. Additionally, we assisted the IEOs in emergencies.

Everywhere in the country, elections could be held thanks to the huge

Choosing her future: a Mozambican woman voting at a rural polling station in Catembe. Photo: UN photo 186910/ P. Sudhakaran

efforts that had already been made and to the continuing cooperation of those involved—the provincial and district commission members, STAE members, and UN Volunteers serving with United Nations Development Programme. Yet, two days before polling, money for feeding and transporting the station staff was not forthcoming. The Inhassoro and Govuro STAE members told us they wanted to send their representatives to the provincial capital to obtain the funds. However, if they were to depend on the only public transportation available—a bus from Beira to Maputo once a day they would never return in time.

I drove to Inhambane, once more, to get the money so the polling station staff could be deployed on time. In Inhambane, at the Provincial Electoral Commission, we joined other STAE representatives from various districts who were crowding the entrance of the building. We were informed that a check had arrived from Maputo. However, because it was a large check, the provincial STAE was having problems cashing it. Because of this problem, we could not return to Inhassoro until the next day, the evening before the elections would start.

It was around 6 p.m. the next day when we arrived in Inhassoro. After quickly splitting the funds among the polling station staff, STAE started deploying them. This meant those posted in the most remote parts of the district would be arriving at their destinations in the middle of the night. I still needed to go to Nova Mambone. After a four-hour trip and a flat tire—the third since we started our journey to Inhambane—we finally arrived in Nova Mambone late at night in a borrowed truck.

As our truck lights lit up the CDE building, I saw some of our STAE colleagues and dozens of polling station staff gathered around a huge truck. Some of them were busy in the dark trying to repair their own tire! I left my truck lights on so they could see to work. The director of the CDE emerged from the crowd to welcome me happily. He said they were all waiting for the money to deploy the polling station staff and would have a long night of work ahead.

Logistical problems of this nature were eventually surmounted, and all the polling stations opened on time in our districts. But the real excitement was to come when the voting started. Voters overflowed the Vuca station that first day of voting, spilling out onto the road. I slowed my truck as I passed them, marveling that after six months of preparations the voting day had finally arrived!

The polling, however, took place in a very tense atmosphere. Just hours before the beginning of the first day of polling, RENAMO leader Afonso Dhalakama surprised the whole country with his announcement that his political party was boycotting the elections. He alleged that the National

Life in the field: a UN Volunteer about to board an ONUMOZ helicopter during the elections in Niassa Province, Mozambique. Photo: C. Valenzuela

Electoral Commission had failed in achieving the necessary conditions to hold the elections. Nevertheless, in my districts, people continued to stream into the polling stations *en masse*, even in RENAMO-controlled areas. Radio reports told the same story around the country; we were witnessing a country-wide demonstration for a new Mozambique.

On the second day of voting, after a strong appeal from the international community and especially for Mozambique's neighbouring countries, Dhalakama revoked his decision and RENAMO officially re-entered the election. To ensure all citizens could vote, the National Electoral Commission decided to extend the polling to a third day.

Counting

Due to communications difficulties faced by the electoral authorities, the counting did not take place uniformly at all polling stations. A few polling stations located in remote areas, whose members were unaware of the extension of the polling to a third day, started counting according to the original schedule. The majority, however, started the counting on 30 October, after the third day of voting. Observed by the IEOs, the counting in Inhassoro, Govuro, and the rural areas country-wide was done during daylight hours since electricity was not available. Once counting was completed, all result cards were sent to a tabulation centre at the Provincial Electoral Commission in Inhambane.

I was asked to travel to the provincial capital to observe the counting in the tabulation centre. The contrast was tremendous. The tabulation centre was equipped with modern computers and printers operated by Mozambican staff trained in Maputo. Yet the system was far from trouble-free. As soon as tabulations were fed into the programme, approximately 80 per cent of the cards were rejected. The cards had not been uniformly filled out by polling station members and had to be manually corrected one by one, an extremely slow process.

After two weeks of work, the provincial results could finally be sent to the National Electoral Commission in Maputo. The commission formally announced on November 18 that President Chissano had won the presidential elections with 53.3 per cent of the vote. His party, FRELIMO, took 129 seats of the Legislative Assembly's total 250 seats. RENAMO took 109 seats, and 12 seats went to *Uniã o Democrática*.[30] Aldo Ajello, Special Representative of the Secretary-General, then issued a statement based on the reports of the UN observers, declaring the elections free and fair.[31]

A Bridge of Trust

Communication and transportation were difficult for the CDE and STAE during the entire electoral process, if they existed at all. Ironically, UNV district electoral officers could visit registration posts and polling stations on a more regular basis than the electoral authorities themselves could. Therefore, my teammate and I unintentionally ended up functioning as a bridge between the actual registration posts and the authorities. We often found ourselves delivering instructions from electoral authorities to brigade members, and messages and requests from brigade members to district electoral authorities; we were the missing communications link they needed. The same pattern emerged during polling.

As time went by, we even drove CDE and STAE officials to the registration posts so they could give proper assistance to brigade members in carrying out their voter registration task. We also regularly helped the electoral authorities distribute sorely needed food, water, and other items to the brigade members. These kinds of activities informally and effectively contributed to solid professional and friendly relationships between us UN Volunteers and CDE and STAE representatives from the time of our arrival.

Our active participation during the registration period turned slowly into the most efficient trust-creating mechanism. Instead of being perceived as observers, which is generally equated with inspectors—the people who are going to point out the irregularities to superiors—we were more often seen as the people who could help them do a better job. I felt rewarded whenever I visited the CDE, STAE, and brigade members. The STAE director of Inhassoro and Govuro and other electoral authorities frequently welcomed me and my colleague with a big smile and even complained when we took too long to visit them. They repeatedly came to us for help to solve problems.

Our assistance was perceived as beneficial to everyone involved. My teammate and I were able to produce reliable reports, since we had easy access to the needed information. The CDE and STAE members, who were often unsure of themselves since it was the first time they had conducted an election, also benefited from our work because our suggestions enabled them to do their jobs more efficiently.

BECOMING A UN VOLUNTEER: A MOST REWARDING EXPERIENCE

Serving as a UN Volunteer District Electoral Officer within ONUMOZ was a challenge for me. It was also an opportunity to contribute to the historic democratization of a country, a democratization that helped bring peace to a people who had suffered badly. After having lived and worked in Mozambique for six months, I feel, however, that I received much more than I gave. My experience as a UN Volunteer—and I believe that being a UN Volunteer made the whole difference—was a most rewarding one, both at personal and professional levels.

At the personal level, I learned more about life and about myself. After years of drafting contracts, preparing legal opinions for international banks, and writing academic essays, I finally had the chance to be close to a people who were struggling but who taught me a way to happiness. With Mozambicans, I could recover what I call the essence of life: people and their well-being are what really matter. Interestingly, well-being is not necessarily, or solely, material progress. I was not raised in a materialistic way, but after experiencing life in Mozambique I understood that we really do not need much to live and be happy. What we need is the chance to survive, to work, to develop our abilities to the fullest possible extent. We all have a right to our own human dignity.

In Mozambique, I also learned more about my ability to adapt to challenge. I deliberately intended to find out what my reactions would be, not just in difficult situations, but also in completely different contexts, such as working in a remote village in the bush of Inhambane province. Having grown up in a large Brazilian city, accustomed to the luxuries of modern life, my capacity to adapt greatly surprised me.

Since routine did not exist for me in Mozambique and each day was completely different from the one before, I was regularly exposed to difficult and new situations, like getting lost near mined areas or getting stuck in the middle of nowhere with flat tires. These experiences helped me realize that there was always a way out if I managed to keep calm and positive. After all, nothing could be worse than the past tragedies my Mozambican friends were constantly telling me about, such as massacres, rape, kidnapping. Most important, I learned that difficulties I faced were small in comparison.

At the professional level, working as a UN Volunteer helped me redefine some career goals. Before going to Mozambique, I had returned to graduate school and had completed a master's dissertation on the legal aspects of international banking cooperation. I had planned to continue in this field. In Mozambique, I had the opportunity to see how UN peacekeeping operations—a microcosm of the United Nations—are organized and managed in the field. After returning from Mozambique, I am interested now in researching the state-building aspects of UN peacekeeping operations. Now I can hardly picture myself working for an international organization in New York or Washington, as I had dreamt for so long. Instead, I feel much more inclined to go back to Africa and work more with people at the grassroots.

But who were these UN Volunteer specialists and what made them different from other ONUMOZ professionals? Since UN Volunteers in Mozambique regularly had to cope with the harsh living and working conditions in the field, we necessarily had to be adventurous people, but with a well-developed sense of responsibility and commitment in carrying out our tasks.

Since we were observed far more than we could observe, whether on duty or off duty, anything in our behaviour, such as the way we talked or the way we drove our cars, was immediately associated by Mozambicans with the UN. I will never forget the Mozambican children on the sides of the roads as they shouted "ONUMOZ" whenever we passed, reminding us constantly of why we were in Mozambique. This spontaneous attitude of Mozambicans showed that we all needed to act in a discreet and polite way in whatever we did, to gain the respect of the people and to preserve the good image of the UN.

UN Volunteers also needed an advanced degree of initiative, coupled with some extra imagination and creativity. Since we were on our own in the field, and since communication and transportation were not always available, oftentimes we could rely only on ourselves. This meant taking the necessary steps every day to improve our overall security. For instance, due to the problem of land mines, we constantly made decisions based on local information whether or not to use certain dirt tracks. There was also the risk of malaria or other endemic diseases, which infect thousands each year. Innovation was necessary to find simple and appropriate solutions for these kinds of day-to-day problems that we faced.

Above all, UN Volunteers serving with ONUMOZ cared about the Mozambican people. Living and working in the communities throughout the country, we were moved not by the will to give orders but rather to exchange information, whether it be learning and teaching a foreign language, traditions, or new skills. The scale of responsibilities did not trouble the volunteers. We just hoped to facilitate the coming of peace and democracy in Mozambique, because volunteers held the firm belief that Mozambicans could do it themselves!

UN VOLUNTEERS WITHIN ONUMOZ

One of the most interesting things about working in a UN peacekeeping operation was to observe the UN's own field operations. What struck me as soon as I arrived at ONUMOZ he adquarters in Maputo was the huge administrative machine supporting the peacekeeping operation. In fact, ONUMOZ's main headquarters in Maputo was in a fairly large hotel building of some 10 floors, which housed all the various parts of the ONUMOZ machinery.[32]

The decisionmaking process in heavy administrative structures in general consumes an enormous amount of time. Unfortunately, ONUMOZ was not an exception to that rule. For example, getting an extra spare tire from ONUMOZ cost us more energy and time than the energy and time actually required to do our job (we never succeeded even though we were on the road several times with two flat tires). We had to struggle to be able to work!

In addition, a reasonable radio communications network between either the CIVPOL post and our electoral truck or between the CIVPOL post and our provincial headquarters was not functioning properly until immediately before the polling. In other words, we worked more than five months under harsh conditions without the communications support we needed for our security. And UNV district electoral officers received instructions from the Electoral Division in Maputo about our role as polling trouble-shooting teams after the polling was finished! Fortunately, we UN Volunteers and our coordinators were able to figure out what our role should be.

In general, we UN Volunteers had good relationships with our coordinators within the electoral component and with international personnel working in the support areas. The military component—the Uruguayan Battalion in the Province of Inhambane—also provided us with overall support and security. However, within ONUMOZ, most of our contacts were with the civilian police.

UNV district electoral officers were required to work closely with CIVPOL for security reasons during all phases of the electoral process. My teammate and I had the opportunity to develop a friendly and cooperative relationship with some of the CIVPOLs working in our districts. We often exchanged information and combined our visits to registration posts or political party meetings. Unfortunately not all CIVPOLs were as motivated as most UN Volunteers were about our assignment in Mozambique. Some seemed uninterested in Mozambicans and in the democratization unfolding before them. This was a cause of difficulties some of us faced in undertaking joint tasks with them.

Actually, when talking to CIVPOLs I found out that some of them had decided to become international civilian police with ONUMOZ for financial reasons—high allowances—or because they saw in it a good opportunity for career advancement. Due to the importance of their work in the field, it would have been better if CIVPOLs had been more appropriately motivated and trained to accomplish their tasks. It would have also been beneficial if they had been more interested generally in getting closer to the people. Recruitment at the national and international levels that stresses the importance of the CIVPOL tasks could address this discrepancy.

One area of relative conflict within ONUMOZ at the provincial level was between the temporary professional staff and the longer term international staff who were working as field service administrators. Because they were permanent and because they were in charge of the support areas that needed to work properly, field service administrators tended to concentrate more power within the organization than temporary professionals did. Even though we all worked to achieve a common goal, temporary professionals and UN Volunteers ended up being overly dependent on international staff to perform well. This hierarchy of power, informally established within the organization, was extremely frustrating to temporary professionals and even more so to UN Volunteers.

Concerning the relationship between UN Volunteers and the UN international personnel, UN Volunteers sometimes felt that some international staff mistakenly perceived us as being on the bottom of the UN career ladder and tended to devalue our role. In general, UN staff did not work under the demanding living conditions of the field, with both its challenges and rewards. It would be useful if an awareness and information campaign about UN Volunteers and their important contributions could be developed and directed especially to career staff.

In fact, reflecting on my experience working within ONUMOZ, I saw UN Volunteers demonstrating not only high professionalism in carrying out their work, but also a conspicuous sense of solidarity and motivation. My teammate and I, for instance, often worked long hours and during weekends because we wanted to, as did many other UN Volunteers serving throughout the country. Aldo Ajello, Special Representative of the Secretary-General in Mozambique, commented on the performance of UN Volunteer specialists in Mozambique by stating, "If I would run another mission, I would ask immediately for volunteers."[33]

I believe that UN Volunteers worked well in the field due to a strong desire to undertake the necessary adaptation, even to the extent of learning local languages. A sense of solidarity developed between UN Volunteers and Mozambicans. Since we worked very close to the people, we could see what their needs were; we soon realized that even the little things we did seemed to be very meaningful to them.

Enjoying considerable freedom in planning our daily and weekly activities, we often could fit some extra voluntary work into our schedules to help with needs that would suddenly emerge. Interestingly, this informal support we gave, such as helping a registration post to become operational, produced results almost immediately, and this was extremely gratifying. However, we sometimes felt that this sense of initiative was not welcomed by our coordinators. We were even advised not to get involved in local problems, such as food distribution and transportation. Therefore, it seems that some clarification on the role of UN Volunteers would be useful so that volunteers can feel more at ease when performing extra voluntary work.

Finally, the quality of adaptation meant that UN Volunteers tended to soften the indirect negative impact that large UN peacekeeping operations imposed on the economic and social life of the country. UN Volunteers, who were generally prepared to face difficult living conditions, adapted well to the local lifestyles, if they did not actually become temporarily integrated. This is important because foreign lifestyles, ostentatious when compared with local standards, might cause undesirable social and economic consequences. Economically speaking, when many foreigners, not to mention the operation itself, are spending large amounts of money in an economy where money is scarce, this can cause the inflation rate of the country to increase, diminishing the purchasing power of the people of the country.[34] Socially, too much contrast in wealth between outsiders and nationals can provoke feelings of envy and sometimes can even lead to crime. These negative effects of peacekeeping operations should be taken into account by the UN to be minimized in future initiatives.[35]

FINAL REMARKS

Having contributed to the process of bringing a peace accord into reality, ONUMOZ can be considered a successful UN peacekeeping operation.[36] The ONUMOZ political component, the first of its kind in a UN peacekeeping operation, played an important role as a mediator between the FRELIMO government and RENAMO. It was instrumental in helping these long-standing antagonists reach agreements relating to outstanding issues in the peace process.

Besides monitoring the cease-fire and providing overall security in the country, the military component ensured a thorough demobilization of soldiers before the elections. This component also was mandated to monitor the collection, storage, and destruction of weapons. Many weapons are believed to be stored still in the bush throughout the country. Interestingly, villagers and NGO workers in the field often were aware of the existence and location of some of these weapons. However, since the UN military were not and could not be close to the people, they only occasionally had access to information concerning weapons and ammunition. CIVPOLs actually knew more about where to find weapons and ammunition spread around Mozambique, and they should have been asked.

Having lived and worked with Mozambicans in their communities country-wide, UN Volunteers were the grassroots arm of ONUMOZ. These UN field diplomats not only monitored the elections in Mozambique, but also informally facilitated the coming of post-war democracy in the country. This low-profile volunteer diplomacy—small daily acts that promoted confidence—often remained unnoticed. But they have the advantage of creating an environment for Mozambicans' own self-empowerment.

Although the transition to peace in Mozambique was successfully accomplished by the government and RENAMO with the assistance of the United Nations, the Mozambican people and their leaders actually made the peace come true. Neither massive financial resources nor 10,000 blue helmets would have been able to impose peace where political will and commitment were lacking. In this context, ONUMOZ helped us draw lessons to understand better why some UN peacekeeping operations succeed where others may fail.

Have peace and democracy come to stay in Mozambique? The Mozambican people clearly expressed their choice for peace and democracy: 87.9 per cent of the 6 million or more voters exercised their right to vote for the first time.[37] The duty to spearhead the rebuilding of Mozambique now lies with its leaders. There is, however, still a long way to go towards institutionalizing democracy, which will only be consolidated some years from now at best. Furthermore, an entire country remains to be rebuilt.[38] UN Volunteers serving with national and international development agencies and NGOs still have an important role to play there. Therefore, it is not the end, but the beginning. Let us not forget Mozambique!

NOTES

1. *Report of the Secretary General on the United Nations in Mozambique, 28 January 1994,* UN Doc. S/1994/Add. 1, 2.
2. United Nations Development Programme Internal Document—UNDP/RR/POST/MOZ/REV6 (July 1991), 1–16.
3. An English version of the General Peace Agreement was annexed to the Letter dated 4 October 1992 from the President of the Republic of Mozambique addressed to the Secretary-General, UN Doc. S/24635.
4. Abi-Saab, Georges. "La deuxième génération des opérations de maintien de la paix." *Le trimestre du monde* (4e trimestre 1992): 87–97. Based on two criteria, chronological (extrinsic to peacekeeping operations) and functional (intrinsic to peacekeeping operations), Georges Abi-Saab classifies UN peacekeeping operations into "first generation" and "second generation" peacekeeping operations. "First generation" peacekeeping operations are traditional operations where military troops were deployed to perform traditional tasks such as monitoring and enforcing cease-fires, observing frontier lines, and interposing between belligerent states. "Second generation" peacekeeping operations, on the other hand, are post-Cold War operations designed to address intrastate conflicts whose mandate is not primarily military. Their mandate can include *inter alia* humanitarian, security, administrative, electoral, and police functions as part of a comprehensive peace transition process. See also Ghébali, Victor-Yves. "Le développement des opérations de maintien de la paix de l'ONU depuis la fin de la guerre froide." *Le trimestre du monde* (4e trimestre 1992): 67–85; and Goulding, Marrack. "The evolution of United Nations Peacekeeping." *International Affairs* 69 (1993), no. 3: 451–464.

Voting for Peace

5. For a comprehensive study about the origins and implications of the civil war in Mozambique, see Andersson, Hilary. *Mozambique: a War against the People.* London: Saint Martin's Press, 1992, pp. 1–191; Hanlon, Joseph. *Mozambique: Who Calls the Shots?* Indianapolis: Indiana University Press, 1991, pp. 1–192; and Hanlon, Joseph. *Mozambique: The Revolution under Fire.* London: Humanities Press, 1984, pp. 1–304.

6. The Mozambican government, complying with the UN sanctions against the Rhodesian white settler regime, closed its borders with Rhodesia. In retaliation, Rhodesia attacked border areas in Mozambique where Zimbabwean refugees were concentrated.

7. Andersson, *Mozambique: A War against the People*, pp. 14–15.

8. Andersson, *Mozambique: A War against the People*, p. 15.

9. Andersson, *Mozambique: A War against the People*, p. 60.

10. There is widespread use of black magic and heavy reliance on witch doctors and spirit mediums among the rural people in Mozambique.

11. The Nkomati Accord was considered an unprecedented step because the Mozambican government had been until then supportive of the black movement in South Africa. Furthermore, the signature of this accord was not well regarded by Mozambique's neighbors, who considered it a sell-out to South Africa.

12. See the *Security Council Resolution 797*, UN Doc. S/RES/797 (1992), approving the Report of the Secretary-General on the United Nations Operation in Mozambique, 3 December 1992, UN Doc. S/2489, 1–15.

13. *Security Council Resolutions 879, 916 and 960*, UN Docs. S/RES/879 (1993), S/RES/916 (1994) and S/RES/960 (1994), respectively.

14. For more information on the United Nations Operation in Mozambique, see "Mozambique: Out of the Ruins of War (United Nations mobilizes for peace)." *Africa Recovery*, United Nations Briefing Paper. (May 1993), no. 8: 1–20. See also the *United Nations Volunteers Introductory Briefing Document on the United Nations Operation in Mozambique.* Geneva: UNV, April 1994, pp. 1–38.

15. *Report of the Secretary-General on the United Operations in Mozambique*, 3 December 1992, UN Doc. S/24892, 1–15.

16. Through its five components, ONUMOZ:
    Political: facilitated impartially the implementation of the agreement, in particular by chairing the Supervisory and Monitoring Commission and its subordinate commissions;
    Military: (i) monitored and verified the cease-fire, the separation and concentration of forces, their demobilization, and the collection, storage and destruction of weapons; (ii) monitored and verified the complete withdrawal of foreign forces; (iii) monitored and verified the disbanding of private and irregular armed groups; and (iv) provided security for vital infrastructures, especially in the corridors, as well as for the United Nations and other international organizations active in support of the peace process;
    Humanitarian: coordinated and monitored humanitarian assistance operations, in particular those relating to refugees, internally displaced persons, demobilized military personnel, and the affected local population, and, in this context, chaired the Humanitarian Assistance Committee;
    Police: monitored all police activities in the country, public or private; monitored the rights and liberties of Mozambican citizens; provided technical support to the National Police Affairs Commission established under the General Peace Agreement, as well as assisted the Electoral Division in monitoring all phases of the electoral process; and
    Electoral: provided technical assistance and monitored the entire electoral process.

17. *Final Report of the Secretary-General on the United Nations Operation in Mozambique*, 23 December 1994, UN Doc. S/1994/1449, 1. See H. Valot, this volume.

18. In accordance with the General Peace Agreement, a Mozambican Electoral Law was enacted in December 1993, with a view to establish the legal framework in which the first multiparty elections in Mozambique were to be held. This Electoral Law provided *inter alia* for the establishment at the national, provincial, and district levels of Electoral Commissions and Technical Secretariats for the Administration of the Elections, the

87

organs in charge of the organization of the entire electoral process. In spite of being composed of members proposed by the government, RENAMO, and other political parties, these Commissions and Technical Secretariats were autonomous bodies, independent of all state authorities and political parties.

19. Mozambique is politically divided into provinces, districts, administrative posts and localities. At the national level, the Electoral Division was headed by a director who, besides providing the overall direction to the division, was expected to maintain contacts with the Government of Mozambique, RENAMO, the National Electoral Commission, and the main political parties. At the provincial level, eleven electoral coordinators, one for each province, worked with the provincial electoral authorities and political party leaders.

20. Once deployed, UN Volunteers would attempt to communicate with their provincial coordinators by radios, when the system was operational. Also, UN Volunteers were outstationed at the district level only where suitable living conditions were existent. Otherwise, they remained based at the provincial capitals, and travelled to the districts as required.

21. *Report of the Secretary-General on the United Nations Operation in Mozambique*, 3 December 1992, UN Doc. S/24892, 1–15, and *Security Council Resolution 797*, UN Doc. S/RES/797 (1992). In order to fulfill its mandate, the Electoral Division, through UN professional staff and UN Volunteers: (a) verified the impartiality of the National Electoral Commission and its organs in all aspects and stages of the electoral process; (b) verified that political parties and alliances enjoyed complete freedom of organization, movement, assembly, and expression, without hindrance and intimidation; (c) verified that all political parties and alliances had fair access to state mass media and that there was fairness in the allocation of both the hour and duration of radio and television broadcasts; (d) verified that the electoral rolls were properly drawn up and that qualified voters were not being denied identification and registration cards or the right to vote; (e) reported to the electoral authorities on complaints, irregularities, and interferences reported or observed, and, when necessary, requested the electoral authorities to take action to resolve and rectify them, as well as conducted its own independent investigation of irregularities; (f) observed all activities related to the registration of voters, the organization of the poll, the electoral campaign, the poll itself and the counting, computation and announcement of the results; (g) participated in the electoral education campaign; (h) prepared periodic reports on the evolution of the electoral process, which were submitted to the Secretary-General through his interim Special Representative.

22. For more information on international electoral monitoring, see Beigbeder, Yves. *International Monitoring of Plebiscites, Referenda and National Elections—Self-Determination and Transition to Democracy*. Dordretch: Martinus Nijhoff, 1994, pp. 1–329; *Human Rights and Elections—A Handbook on the Legal, Technical and Human Rights Aspects of Elections*, Professional Training Series no. 2. Geneva: Center for Human Rights, 1994, pp. 1–24; Ebersole, Jon M. "The United Nations' Response to Requests for Assistance in Electoral Matters." *Virginia Journal of International Law* 33 (1992), no. 1: 91–122; and Van Haegendoren, Geert. "International Electoral Monitoring." *Revue belge de droit international* 20 (1987): 86–123.

23. According to the Mozambican Electoral Law, registration was to begin on 1 June 1994 and end on 15 August 1994. The National Electoral Commission, however, decided to extend the registration period so that demobilized soldiers and returnees could have a chance to register as well. This contributed to making the registration period very long and hard for brigade members who were already tired and demotivated.

24. *Report of the Secretary-General on the United Nations Operation in Mozambique*, 2 pril 1993, UN Doc. S/1993/25518, 1–12. For more information about the mine problem, see *Land Mines: Time for Action—International Humanitarian Law*. Geneva: International Committee of the Red Cross, 1994, pp. 1–42; and *Landmines: A Deadly Legacy*. New York: Human Rights Watch, Physicians for Human Rights, 1993, pp. 1–510.

25. Large rectangular piece of cloth Mozambican women wear around their hips as a skirt.
26. Article 25 of the Regulation on International Observation issued by the National Electoral Commission.
27. Protocol III of the General Peace Agreement.
28. *Final Report of the Secretary General on the United Nations Operation in Mozambique*, 23 December 1994, UN Doc. S/1994/1449, 2.
29. The ONUMOZ Electoral Division counted on a total of 1,200 IEOs to observe the voting and the counting throughout Mozambique. These IEOs were briefed in Johannesburg and deployed in the districts shortly before the October elections. Some CIVPOLs, military observers and ONUMOZ staff working in Maputo, as well as NGO workers, also served as IEOs during the elections.
30. *Final Report of the Secretary General on the United Nations Operations in Mozambique*, 23 December 1994, UN Doc. S/1994/1449, 3.
31. *Statement of the Special Representative of the Secretary-General*, 19 November 1994, UN Doc. SG/SM/5488. The members of the Security Council unanimously endorsed the election results in its Resolution 960 (1994) of 21 November 1994.
32. There, one would find not only the Electoral Division, the Technical Unit for Demobilization, UNOHAC, Military Command, and CIVPOL Command offices, but also Administrative, Security, and Finance offices, as well as their respective sub-offices.
33. Internal UNV minute of the comments made by the Special Representative of the Secretary-General in the United Nations Operation in Mozambique to a meeting of UNV personnel held on 30 November 1994 at the UNV headquarters in Geneva.
34. ONUMOZ's approximate annual cost was US$240.8 million. See *United Nations Peacekeeping Information Notes* (New York: United Nations, 1995), 126.
35. That large peacekeeping operations cause social as well as economic consequences in the country where they are established is a fact. Concerning this issue, see Fitzgerald, E.V.K. "The Economic Dimension of Social Development and the Peace Process in Cambodia," and Arnvig, Eva. "Women, Children and Returnees." In: Peter Utting, ed. *Between Hope and Insecurity: The Social Consequences of the Cambodian Peace Process.* Geneva: UNRISD, 1994, pp. 71–94 and pp. 143–182, respectively.
36. Contreras, Joseph. "Lessons from Mozambique—The UN: Peacekeeping missions sometimes work." *Newsweek* (March 13, 1995): 39; and Preston, Julia. "Blue Hat Blues." *Washington Post* (February 19, 1995): C2.
37. *Final Report of the Secretary General on the United Nations Operation in Mozambique*, 23 December 1994, UN Doc. S/1994/1449, 3.
38. UNOHAC played an important role in the coordination of the efforts of UN organizations and agencies, NGOs, as well as of a number of Mozambican entities, to design and implement humanitarian assistance programmes during the period of the ONUMOZ mandate. These programmes slowly shifted from emergence to development. The war being over, emphasis could be placed on the restoration of essential services in rural areas and particularly in areas which were going to receive returning refugees, displaced people and former soldiers. Two thousand wells have been dug or rehabilitated and as many as 700 primary schools and 250 health facilities have been built in rural areas. Much more, however, remains to be done. See the *Final Report of the Secretary General on the United Nations Operation in Mozambique*, 23 December 1994, UN Doc. S/1994/1449, 6.

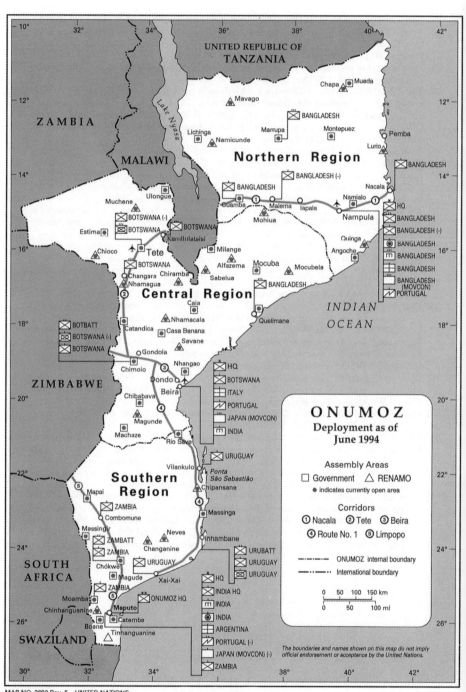

ONUMOZ
Deployment as of
June 1994

Assembly Areas
□ Government   △ RENAMO
● indicates currently open area

Corridors
① Nacala   ② Tete   ③ Beira
④ Route No. 1   ⑤ Limpopo

------- ONUMOZ internal boundary
------- International boundary

0   50   100   150 km
0   50   100 mi

The boundaries and names shown on this map do not imply
official endorsement or acceptance by the United Nations.

MAP NO. 3692 Rev. 5   UNITED NATIONS
JUNE 1994

4

END OF THE WAR MACHINERY: DEMOBILIZATION IN MOZAMBIQUE

Henri Valot

FERNANDO IS 32. Tall, thin, he wears ragged clothes, broken boots. Fernando is strong, easily violent; he often argues, monopolizes his fellow soldiers' attention. He is my first adviser and assistant. With me he has access to the storage room, the object of acute interest among the soldiers, which we visit with the cooks every morning: 150 kilos of corn flour, 100 kilos of rice, beans, salt, sugar, and so on are distributed daily.

When we hear from the airfield nearby the sound of the aircraft marked with the UN letters, he calls to his friends and fellows, boards the truck with them to bring back new farming equipment, food, boxes of civilian clothes to be distributed on the demobilization day, occasional letters to me from Europe and Asia, even military observers on an official visit. Fernando calls me "TUCO," for United Nations Volunteer serving as a Technical Unit Camp Officer. Sometimes he tells me about war, his women,

Henri Valot is a French national born in 1966. A former Protection Officer, he is now pursuing a doctoral degree in political philosophy concerning the question of violence at Paris X University. A UN Volunteer District Electoral Supervisor in Cambodia, he later served as a UN Volunteer Technical Unit Camp Officer with the United Nations Operation in Mozambique from November 1994 to March 1995. He is presently working as a Press Officer at the UN General Assembly.

Mozambican scenes, weapons that misfire too easily, dead bodies left on the road, and his hopes.

Fernando is from Chimoio, in the centre of the country. In 1981, when he was in his late teens, Fernando undertook a rough journey, and arrived in Maputo, the capital and largest city, to look for a job, leaving behind his parents' failure and a land that had become hostile and dry. Although a distant cousin offered him hospitality for some time, Fernando was thrown off-balance in this new environment, so different, so tough. He quickly lost hope, took advantage of the shiniest, easiest things the city had to offer. During this time, which included rationing of goods, his life was made of robbery and bargaining.

Samora Machel,[1] leader of Mozambique at that time, was gathering crowds, making speeches for emancipation. Fascinated by Machel's strength, Fernando could recognize himself in the orator's words when he spoke of unemployment, hooliganism in the city, and the efforts to throw the "non-productive," especially the unemployed internally displaced people, out of the city.

The police arrested Fernando and his friends in the street. He had lost his documents much earlier and could not justify his presence there. He was neither studying nor working. In March 1983, he became a victim of the *Operação Produção*, a forced migration of unemployed young people to communal work groups.[2] At the airport, he understood that he was being sent to Mandimba, in the remote province of Niassa. Surprised and sad, he kept silent in the aircraft taking him to the unknown.

Upon arrival at a communal work site, he settled down with his fellows in a simple but new and comfortable house. Mandimba was not a city. It was not even a village. The inhabitants were suspicious and the party secretary was often inquisitive. Fernando could not even understand their language.[3] Therefore, feeling unable to go on living there, he decided to run away. He walked, often stopping along the road, taking short rests in the houses here and there.

He wanted to return to his native city, Chimoio, but was afraid of being caught again and sent back to a village where life seemed to have stopped, as in Mandimba, which he had fled. One night, a group of very young soldiers, yelling and carrying automatic rifles, surrounded him while he was asleep. They forced him to follow them; they were walking fast and Fernando was exhausted. Threatened at each stop, he could do nothing but follow them in the dark. They walked for a long time. The soldiers wanted to cover his eyes with a blindfold, but Fernando managed to dissuade them from this idea.

The rebel RENAMO (Mozambique National Resistance) soldiers finally arrived at their camp and tied Fernando to a tree with four other prisoners. Some had arrived a few days earlier and were still tied there. Others, he heard, had already died, shot in front of their families. There was a very strict discipline in the RENAMO camp, even though it was often disrupted by collective drinking. After some days, he was released under one condition: that he became the camp commander's slave. He worked as a tent keeper, a cook, and had to comply with all demands. This was the price for his life.

IN THE ASSEMBLY AREA: CHECK-IN

The last day of November 1993 marked the opening of the first areas set aside to assemble and demobilize Mozambique's armed factions. There were 29 camps for government soldiers and 20 camps for RENAMO soldiers throughout the country.[4] Fernando, with a dozen friends, showed up at the doors of our government camp, in Lichinga. At the reception desk was Camp Commander Major Daoud, who had been detached from the Niassa provincial military headquarters to undertake the sensitive and delicate task of demobilization. Major Daoud had been a political commissioner of the Provincial Armed Forces for more than five years, and was a well-known and respected Mozambican in the province.[5] The United Nations Operation in Mozambique (ONUMOZ) was also present in the persons of team leader Major Alaa (Egyptian); his deputy, Captain Farias (Brazilian); and team members Major Volkoff (Russian) and Major Jia (Chinese), who together constituted the UN's military observers in the Lichinga camp. I was among them, the only civilian in the camp, a representative of the Technical Unit for Demobilization, and a United Nations Volunteer.

We had arrived 15 days earlier and had settled in this disaffected camp. It was raining cats and dogs in Lichinga. The Bengali engineers had set up our white tents in the mud. The military observers were installing the communication systems (Radio/INMARSAT).[6] This was my first general view of what was going to be my home, my territory for action. Lichinga camp, located in the neighbourhood of the small capital of the Niassa province in northern Mozambique, had some, if limited, infrastructure. Built in the 1960s as a shelter for the Portuguese Army, it was occupied in 1975 by FRELIMO, the Mozambique Liberation Front, a liberation movement founded in 1961.[7] The camp was damaged, unhealthy, but at least it existed. On the grounds I discovered barracks, warehouses, a generator I hoped I could resuscitate, latrines out of order, and, in the middle of the camp, broken-down trucks, monuments to those killed in the fight for independence, and a basketball court. This should be enough, I thought, to receive the 1,500 soldiers expected in the first stage of the demobilization process in Lichinga.

Fernando is among the very first men to show up at the check-in desk. He carries a rusted AK47, which he will prove to be absolutely out of order under the skeptical eyes of our Chinese major. He hands over this antique piece to the Russian major who unsuccessfully tries to find a reference number to register what had been once a weapon. Through all this, Fernando is attentive. ONUMOZ team leader Major Alaa, deeply moved, takes Fernando in his arms, while Major Volkoff writes on his registers the numbers of the obsolete weapons turned in, and looks through an endless list of names of the soldiers who had volunteered for demobilization. This check-in done, the Technical Unit begins its job. With the assistance of Captain Farias, I take this first group of 50 soldiers to the storage room. Each receives a blanket, a plate, a piece of soap, and there are buckets to be shared among every 10 persons. Fernando offers me his help.

Once they have received these very minimal supplies, I address the soldiers with a short welcome speech. In a slow and clear Portuguese that I had learned years earlier in South America, I introduce my team and the rules of conduct in the assembly area. Suddenly I stop, reading some surprise in the soldiers' eyes. One of them dares to ask me to repeat, and explains, "We could not imagine it to be Portuguese! We expected anything from you but to listen to the language we speak!" Before I continue speaking, I ask if everyone understands Portuguese; ten of them say they had learned it, but do not speak it anymore. However, most of them speak it fluently. In fact, at the time of the independence in 1975, FRELIMO, the liberation movement, had made the political decision to maintain Portuguese as the only official language, so the members of the armed forces had to learn it. Moreover, most of these soldiers had been posted far away from their home provinces or simply displaced all around the country during the war years. Among the 14 local dialects spoken in Mozambique, the only universal means of communication is the Portuguese language.[8]

Once my inaugural speech is finished and understood by most of the soldiers, I take them to the registration desk, where they fill in the assembly forms that will be sent to the Technical Unit's database in Maputo. There, new lists will be established and the government and RENAMO will determine who among these soldiers will be demobilized and who will be integrated into the new armed forces, the Mozambican Defence Forces (FADM).[9]

THE ASSEMBLY AREA

I adopted the Lichinga camp. With Captain Farias, and later with on Fernando, we began work to make it ours. Having arrived on November 15, we had no more than 15 days to build an assembly centre out of the place. The task was overwhelming: we had to clean the barracks, organize the future kitchen, train the registration team, set up a dispensary, draw a circle for a helicopter landing, dig latrines, and set up our own UN camp inside the military camp. We were very eager to see this space dedicated to returning fighters to civilian life.

In our attempt to renovate the camp and improve the living conditions of the assembled military, we benefited from the support of 70 Mozambican soldiers from the provincial military headquarters. They were supposedly in charge of the security of the camp. These soldiers, however, who dreamt of being demobilized but were obliged by the military authority to keep their status, were the ones who stole the food and the few belongings of those who handed over their guns to the military observers. Thus, robbery and strife were permanent residents of the camp.

News of my lively debates on this subject with the military observers reached the camp commander as well as the provincial commander, who called me in. I described to the provincial commander a very basic principle: a group integrated into another group should display the same characteristics. Further, even though weapons had been abolished in this area, the active-duty Mozambican soldiers were carrying guns, disturbing the easy atmosphere of the camp, and threatening security rather than guaranteeing it.

The provincial commander nodded gently, a large smile illuminating his round face, which was marked with the ritual scars of the Makonde ethnic group. He replied that for the moment he did not worry about threats from the soldiers being demobilized. The problem, he said, came instead from the political situation in Mozambique, which was still unstable; the obstacles to implementation of the peace agreement; the United Nations' arrival;[10] and the mistrust between the parties. He touched me when he added, "We, fighters of the Mozambican Independence, have united this country, but have lost another war. I hate seeing my men in disarray, sick and lost, looking forward to demobilization. I cannot accept either that we were not able to solve our problems ourselves, and that we have no other choice now than to rely on United Nations' assistance." Major Alaa, the ONUMOZ team leader, listened to my translation, agreed, and added his support to our observer role, emphasizing our understanding and discretion. Farias, his deputy, winked at me, smiling at my air of dismay.

We returned to the camp in silence. Alaa, the Egyptian team leader, told me that from then on I should be more careful about what I said. I replied that in our camp, the civilian Technical Unit for Demobilization, unlike his, I am not an observer and that, on the contrary, I have to spend every bit of energy to encourage this difficult process of returning fighters to civilian life. I said that I would not make any concessions about the fact that civilian rules of conduct are necessary in this intermediate space of the assembly area.

The invention of civilian rules of conduct starts with decent conditions for rest, health, and food. With help from the 70 soldiers on duty, whom I managed to disarm during the work period, we dug latrines and wells, painted the buildings, cleaned the kitchen, built beds and tables for the dispensary. We painted the camp with the United Nations colours, blue and white. All the equipment was supplied by the regional coordination of the Technical Unit. Its manager, Martin Wanseth, trusted us, and from a SWED-RELIEF[11] budget for the assembly areas, he got the necessary funds. It became like a game: to clean the basketball court, to hang United Nations flags on the buildings for which we are responsible, to set up, ironically, "latrine-commandos" in the sunny mornings, to exchange spades for weapons of the camp "security guards," and, under the terrible eyes of the military, to dig the soil.

TUCOS AND OTHER VOLUNTEERS: FERNANDO

Fernando says he remained too long in the RENAMO camp. There, he saw children learn to kill their brothers, frightened villagers forced to bring food to fighters, the quiet calm after the tempest of an unexpected attack by the government forces, the suffering from infected injuries, the tenderness of a woman, also a prisoner, who became his.

One evening, Fernando was released by the government soldiers. He witnessed a massacre from which his female companion did not escape. He begged the government soldiers to save her, but she was considered property of the "armed bandits" and had to die. He followed the government soldiers, leaving the village in flames behind them. He learned that he was close to Chimoio and expressed the wish to visit his family, who probably believed he had been killed. The soldiers stopped him. He had yet to prove to them that he was not a RENAMO fighter, but a RENAMO prisoner who had been released. They walked for a long time, stopping in villages that were often deserted. When they passed inhabited houses, Fernando noticed the villagers' fright and saw the violent behaviour of the soldiers as they helped themselves to the villagers' limited food.

Eventually they arrived in a camp in the Manica province and Fernando was allowed to rest for a few hours. Then he had to face the endless questions of the camp sergeants. He managed to convince them of his kidnapping by RENAMO, of the violence he endured, and of his ignorance of the logic of war. He was told he would never be allowed to go back home. His compulsory military service was to start on the same day. Mozambique needed new conscripts to counter the aggressions it was facing. Large parts of the country were falling under RENAMO control. The armed movement was burning down community villages, deporting people, destroying roads, bridges, electric lines.[12]

In 1987 Fernando had no choice but to accept his new life as a governmental soldier in the large Manica base. Manica and Sofala, provinces located at the centre of the country, were in the heartland of RENAMO territory. As a result, the pressure there was unrelenting. Fernando, who was under constant watch by the base sergeants, had only logistical duties in the camp. Since he was not given an AK47, he did not take part in the attacks.

In this base, he was neither happy nor unhappy: he just survived. He was regularly victimized by a recurrent malaria. With a colleague, he learned how to make simple guitars. The camp commander did not pay visits to his men. He was too busy trying to get the food rations from Maputo for himself, people would say. There was not enough food, so the fittest soldiers went out of the camp and scouted for more in the villages to survive. The weaker ones suffered from infections, while those who ventured into the fields took the chance of stepping on a mine laid by belligerents.

It was a strange war. Fighting with RENAMO was rare.[13] The civilian population suffered primarily in the sporadic confrontations on the village main squares. Usually, the government soldiers arrived too late, after RENAMO had robbed the village of resources and killed the villagers who tried to oppose them. FRELIMO accused the village chiefs of collaboration with the enemy. Some soldiers, uncontrolled by their officers, took advantage of the people's fear to steal the last chickens or goats of the village.

The Zimbabwean presence on the Beira corridor[14] was intended to support FRELIMO. The protection of convoys was one of the worst military tasks. Gunfire burst out at a turn of the road, the violence of the attacks was terrible, trucks burned. The Zimbabweans fired back but the RENAMO men knew the ground and how to vanish, leaving fire and tears behind them.

DEMOBILIZATION AS A POLITICAL IMPERATIVE

A ghost is haunting southern Africa; it is the incomplete demobilization and the violent resumption of hostilities in Angola in the fall of 1992. There were in Angola, as in Mozambique, 49 demobilization assembly areas. For a period of 17 months beginning in June 1991, soldiers were demobilized and officers were designated to head the new Angolan armed forces. Nevertheless, as soon as the results of the first round of the September 1992 presidential elections were made public, the National Union for the Total Independence of Angola (UNITA) called its generals back and the war resumed that year, worse than before.[15]

These two countries have many similarities. Both are former Portuguese colonies that received independence in 1975, with a single party of socialist obedience after independence (the Popular Liberation Movement of Angola [MPLA] and FRELIMO in Mozambique). Both have rebel movements that were supported by neighbouring South Africa (UNITA in Angola and RENAMO in Mozambique), accompanied by violent confrontations and destruction of the infrastructure and the social networks. In both cases the United Nations observed the demobilization, the disarmament, and the organization of elections.[16]

But there the comparison ends. Angola is a rich country and was strategically essential during the Cold War. No doubt, there are resources in Mozambique, but they remain unexploited. UNITA, autonomous and with powerful means at its disposal, is led by Jonas Savimbi. RENAMO has always been dependent on external support; it became more and more a "coalition of the marginalized,"[17] a disorganized force of the suffering people.

The United Nations cannot, however, forget the bitter Angola experience. Secretary-General Boutros Boutros-Ghali, at the October 1992 signing of the General Peace Agreement of Mozambique,[18] called on the international community to establish an operation in Mozambique with the necessary military, human, and logistical resources.[19] Apart from the verification of the withdrawal of foreign troops from the Mozambican territory (Malawi armed forces protected the Nacala corridor and Zimbabwean forces watched the Beira corridor), ONUMOZ's role during the first stage of the peace process was to supervise the cease-fire and the demobilization of both government and RENAMO troops.

Aldo Ajello, the Special Representative of the Secretary-General, repeatedly emphasized from the time of his arrival in Maputo in 1992 that elections in Mozambique would be possible only after demobilization. The Angolan precedent was still alive in everyone's memory. It happened, however, that the deadlines expressed in the peace agreement could not be reached. The demobilization was supposed to be completed by July 1993 and elections were to be held in October of that year. In May 1993, the first United Nations contingents had just disembarked on the Mozambican territory, even as RENAMO held on to its Maringue base in the centre of the country and left the peace talks. Meanwhile, the first assembly areas opened and military observers and we UN Volunteer camp officers settled in, but with no soldiers to demobilize. Postponement after postponement took place because of the RENAMO demands, because of disagreement over the location of assembly areas in the contested territory, and because of the difficulty that the Ministry of Defence's generals faced in accepting the demobilization of their troops. By September 1993, the process seemed to be permanently interrupted.

This date was also marked by Boutros-Ghali's visit[20] to Mozambique and the elaboration of a new plan for the implementation of the General Peace Agreement. Under this plan, the assembly areas would be opened for soldiers to be demobilized in December 1993, and demobilization would be completed before May 1994 so that elections in the presence of international observers could take place in October 1994.

The parties agreed to the new calendar, then tried to find ways to again postpone the beginning of the demobilization. Special Representative Ajello, a skillful negotiator, led the debates, pushing the two armies to comply with their promises. Both of them watched each other and denounced the other's backward steps and hesitations; mistrust was still present. "National reconciliation," a widely used expression, was no more than words. However, despite the delays, in December 1993 the first soldiers showed up at the doors of the assembly areas. We UN Volunteer camp officers and military observers began to do the demobilizing work.

THE TECHNICAL UNIT FOR DEMOBILIZATION

To support the assembly and demobilization programme in accordance with the General Peace Agreement, the Special Representative of the Secretary-General delegated to the Technical Unit for Demobilization the technical, logistical, and administrative aspects of the demobilization process. This unit was directed by Tom Pardoel, a Dutchman familiar with the Mozambican situation, and Ian During, a Swede representing the SWED-RELIEF organization. They were assisted by specialists in water, nutrition, health, information, and databases who administered the project.[21]

All the technical unit camp officers were UN Volunteers. The first group arrived in May 1993. Forty-nine of them were posted in the various camps in the country, while others served in regional offices. New UN Volunteer specialists would arrive later to replace those on leave. Who were these volunteers who gave one year or more of their lives to work with the demobilization of Mozambican soldiers? Among them were a Togolese cartographer, a Peruvian lawyer, a former French police officer, an Italian social worker. There were so many different profiles it is difficult to draw a common picture. What they all had in common was some kind of interest in the political transition in Mozambique. Among them was the solidarity of evening radio exchanges, occasional visits. Each had a camp made in his own image: Davide built a shower, Afonso sang opera every night to the radio, Gustavo imagined constructing a sun deck by a pond.

For all of them it is an absolutely new experience. Common sense, a certain idea of organization, a curiosity mixed with compassion, and some tact to secure good relationships with the UN military observers and the camp authorities were the essential qualities for a UN Volunteer camp officer. Who among us had earlier experience in the demobilization of military men who had fostered one of the most cruel wars in the last 50 years? None of us. Everything here had to be invented: rules for these soldiers exhausted by military life; a space called the assembly area; and a time to go from military to civilian life.

ABOUT TUCOS AND OTHER UN VOLUNTEERS

The technical unit camp officers were not the only UN Volunteer specialists who participated in the demobilization of Mozambican soldiers. The International Organization for Migration (IOM)[22] also brought to this endeavor an essential contribution, as did the United Nations Office for Humanitarian Assistance Coordination (UNOHAC)[23] volunteers. UN Volunteers serving with IOM transported the former soldiers and their families to the destinations they chose. On the basis of information gathered in the assembly area and of the synthesis made in the Maputo database, these volunteers found local transportation to move the demobilized soldiers to their new homes. Sometimes it meant crossing the whole country. They might have had to travel by truck, aircraft, if not by boat. In any case, IOM relied on local solutions; for example, all buses and trucks available in Mozambique were rented by IOM during July 1994, when more than 20,000 soldiers were transported. IOM ensured security of the roads in order to take former soldiers right to the door of their new homes. Acquaintance with the country, with its old and damaged infrastructure, with its potential, became a natural part of this work. The UN Volunteers serving with IOM also were present on the demobilization day. They arrived in their colourful trucks marked with IOM stickers so they could be easily identified, set up their tables among ours, distributed some equipment for agriculture (tools and seeds), and accompanied the demobilized soldiers to their destinations.

UN Volunteers with UNOHAC, field assistants at the provincial level, monitored the demobilization operation. Their mandate included direction of and assistance to the Reintegration Commission (CORE).[24] While coordinating the distribution of food aid, these UN Volunteers followed with particular attention the movements of demobilized soldiers and their families. Since they were responsible for a training programme, they listened carefully to the needs of the former soldiers. It was only through this close collaboration between the representatives of these different UN agencies and ONUMOZ components that demobilization was possible.

MOBILES AND MOBILITY

Demobilization as a Passage

In the beginning of December 1993, 1,500 government soldiers arrived in the Lichinga camp and the waiting began. The census forms had been sent to Maputo, and we waited with the soldiers for the demobilization dates. We were told that the government had decided to stop the assembly process. In fact, RENAMO had sent only a few men to its 20 assembly areas.

Demobilization as "passage": a soldier's boots in a RENAMO camp during the demobilization process in Muchene, Mozambique. Photo: UN photo 186942/ S. Santimano

For some of the assembled soldiers, the waiting time would last more than six months. As Special Representative Ajello described it, the assembly area was only a transitory place and therefore could not provide the necessary living conditions for a prolonged stay. Moreover, he warned the parties of the ever-present danger to the General Peace Agreement of allowing these men to remain for too long in the transit sites. But the demobilization stopped again. I took advantage of the time left in the camp to question the soldiers. I wanted to understand their past, and what they were feeling during this turning point in their lives.

By "demobilization as passage," I mean the space and time of transition in which the individual is called to remember his origins. Demobilization is the passage from the military status to the civilian one, in which the geographical, social, and relational origins of the individual are examined and questioned. In Mozambique this process had a name, demobilization; a place, the assembly area; a time, six months (rather than the six weeks initially planned). It was, in fact, an empty time during which the soldiers were deprived of their military identity and had to face a future yet to be invented. The assembly area was the place where one began losing one's present identity and began moving on to something else. It was a transitory place, but it was limited on all sides. It was a new space with undetermined characteristics: a military zone that no longer existed, a community of people nobody was really willing to integrate with, and a time of expectation.

Any transition questions an individual's origin or the origins he gives to himself. This is why we asked two simple questions to the soldiers: "Who were you?" (before being a soldier), and "Who will you be?"

There is a multiple character of any origin. An individual's identity is built out of multiple passages, places, and times. During the assembly period, the origins each individual attributed to himself were questioned: his family origin, the beginning of his military commitment, and, above all, the origin to which he referred today in devising a vision of the future. This is when imagination intervenes. Origin is subject to modification through imagination. The individual can, because the present requires it, designate in his memory an original space; he can assign to his individuality a single place of origin and negate all others. The origin is a matter of both imagination and reality; it is subject to re-actualization, if not radical transformation, at every moment of life, as long as it provides ways to manage the present. Therefore it cannot be reduced to a given time or place.[25]

This is the main issue of the demobilization process conducted by the United Nations: it raises the problem of the origin of the Mozambican. Few origins have been more subject to violence during the last three centuries than the identity of the Mozambican society (the colonialism of Portuguese dictator Antonio Salazar, community projects of FRELIMO, the violent response of RENAMO). Which one among the soldier's broken origins will he take as the leading direction, a promise for the future?

Demobilization as Mobility and Displacement

The mobility and displacement aspects of demobilization are understood by the United Nations, which has given IOM the task of transporting the demobilized soldiers to the place of their choice. Demobilization and national reconciliation require some thinking about space: from the sharing of collective space to the necessary reoccupation of private space, as well as the political possibility of circulating freely throughout the country. All of this could be handled just as a question of topography, or at best of logistics, neglecting the social dimension of the demobilization process.

As a matter of fact, mobility is required from the soldiers as soon as the assembly period starts. To wonder about origin or origins and then to physically move requires this mental operation: to imagine oneself somewhere else, different, in a future that remains uncertain for all. In this experiment, the individual is required to transform himself, and that transformation requires him to create a place for the future out of what he conceives first as an origin to recover. The soldier is required to move from the military sphere to the civilian sphere to come. At stake is to find a place, not only physical, but social. These are essential concerns because they reflect not only individual trajectories, but also a collective project for the nation.

Some will say that what Mozambique needs first is to recover its food self-reliance. For that, a return to the land must be organized. But we know that nowadays there is an imperative need for training, that the commercial and social links, destroyed by years of war, must be restored. One should therefore also add that this country needs administrators, technicians, professors, to get out of the dead end it is facing. Therefore, new socioeconomic spaces and places must be created in Mozambique. By carefully reading the registration forms and listening to the hopes of the demobilized, one detects, here and there, the emergence of new social roles.

THE END OF THE WAR MACHINERY

Reintegration

In March 1994, after new and painful delays, the first demobilization took place. The lists eventually arrived from the capital. While we organized ourselves, the soldiers whose names were registered on the list waited silently in the camp. Others, who were not listed, observed, curious and envious. The truck fleet marked with IOM identification arrived early in the morning. Our colleagues set up their tables; the volunteer camp officers organized everything together. Also present were representatives of CORE and of UNOHAC.

The military men who would no longer be soldiers at the end of this day confirmed to the UN Volunteers serving with IOM their itineraries and

Facing the future after years of conflict: portrait of a RENAMO soldier taken at a demobilization ceremony in Maringue, Mozambique. Photo: UN photo 186968/ G. Neuenburg

destinations. Then they received from the camp officer their demobilization cards and the checkbook that would entitle them to the reintegration subsidies, civilian clothes, a few kilos of food, a bucket, instruments for agriculture, and the equivalent of three months' pay. The demobilized men gathered in a corner of the camp and exchanged their worn military combat dress for colourful trousers and shirts. Belts, used boots, and military caps would never be used again, trousers and shirts would no longer hide the scars of these years of hunger and violence, all of these slowly piled up in a corner of the yard. Other demobilized soldiers sat on the ground counting the money given to them. Many of them had not been paid by the government for a long time. As for RENAMO, it avoided giving financial compensation and paid its warriors in kind.

When the first IOM truck left the assembly area, a scream was heard in the camp, a cry of happiness and release. Fernando was sitting next to me; I could see that he was skeptical. Not all of them would be demobilized. The need for conscripts for the new army (FADM) was the flip side of demobilization. By December 1994, out of the 30,000 men it had expected, the FADM was composed of merely 11,000 men. The newly elected government is now responsible for recruitment to create an army for the needs of Mozambique.

The financial subsidies received by the demobilized soldiers on the day of their return to civilian life were an important part of the social reintegration plan. According to the Reintegration Support Scheme (RSS),[26] six months' pay was disbursed by the government to each man, followed by an 18-month allowance from a fund administered by the United Nations Development Programme (UNDP). The demobilized men received their first checkbook, which allowed them to retrieve money from an established bank in the country. The pay, it goes without saying, was not high: 75,000 Meticais (US$15) a month for a simple soldier. If this sum means nothing in a large city, it has significant value in the countryside, where money is scarce.

The CORE has set up offices in the provincial capitals. With the support of the UN Volunteers working with the International Labour Organisation (ILO),[27] CORE offers training and technical learning schemes for demobilized men who wish to acquire a skill. It encourages the creation of micro-enterprises. The Information and Reference Service (IRS),[28] established by IOM, provides administrative assistance to demobilized men who are experiencing difficulties in obtaining what is owed to them. The IRS also has some knowledge of the local employment opportunities, and it progressively builds a professional job-search network to which the demobilized soldiers have access. When ONUMOZ left Mozambique, UNDP and IOM projects became the essential elements of the reintegration process.

Among the 91,691 assembled government and RENAMO soldiers, 78,078 soldiers were demobilized and transported to the locations of their choice within Mozambique, not including an almost equal number of their dependents, while the remainder joined the new army.[29] The demobilized soldiers now benefit from the reintegration programmes.

Violence and Disarmament

Between December 1993 and September 1994, the Cease-fire Commission had counted some 700 "incidents" related to the demobilization of soldiers. Some were dramatic. In Quelimane, the provincial capital of Zambezia, the military, fed up with waiting, attacked shopkeepers in the city. In Angoche, Nampula province, the fighting between police and assembled soldiers ended in casualties and deaths.

These rebellions had many causes, including the waiting time in the assembly areas, the refusal to integrate the FADM, the fear of the future, the disobedience to a disintegrating military authority, and the lack of the promised new benefits of demobilization such as food and agricultural instruments. Some of the incidents took place inside the assembly areas, where civilians in charge of demobilization were taken as hostages, and road blocks were set up outside camps.

In June 1994, a new incident on the Beira-Chimoio road was disclosed to us, and it was both worrying and reassuring. Two hundred demobilized military men stopped cars, took passengers as hostages, and demanded the demobilization of their fellow soldiers in the camps. This group was composed of former military men from RENAMO and FRELIMO. For the first time, the enemy brothers went on strike together, for the same claim. This was a proof that, even with difficulty and pain, reconciliation had made progress. It was no longer an empty promise; soldiers gave it reality, and, by their actions, taught it to their superiors.[30]

The Cease-fire Commission, responsible for the demobilization and disarmament of troops, collected in the assembly areas the weapons of the belligerents. Apart from automatic weapons and mortars, more than 1 million rounds of ammunition and land mines were collected. After being transported to the regional storage rooms, these weapons were selectively handed over to the new Mozambican armed forces.

It is well known that the weapons handed over were only the tip of the iceberg, and that they were usually not working. Some sources even say that about 1 million weapons still circulate in Mozambique. The country is full of weapons to which the United Nations has no access. The former belligerents cooperated reluctantly, and gave the military observers false or incomplete data. The government bases are easier to identify, but RENAMO denies knowledge of where the weapons are hidden.

The country is large; it appears to be impossible to screen it for weapons. Apart from the military arms there are also thousands of weapons kept by civilians. As with the mine clearance in roads and fields in Mozambique,[31] disarmament cannot be completed within the time frame of ONUMOZ's mandate.

The hidden armaments, held by the ex-belligerents or by the civilian population, are a threat to the country. The demobilized soldiers often had no life experience other than wartime survival; they lived day after day with a weapon in hand. After a difficult sociological and psychological period, they joined a civilian society that was just re-emerging from its ashes; it still does not know how to give the former soldiers the place they think they deserve. The ex-fighters have lived outside the law for years. Today, they must comply with the rules of this state that is being reconstituted and respect the customs of a society that is gaining strength again. A social group that was once an actor in and responsible for the fighting must dissolve itself and accept the decimation of its force.

Two threats accompany this process of national reconciliation: the inaction of the demobilized men as they search for their origins, and the armaments inherited from the years of war. Special Representative Ajello uses pacifying language and tries to calm the media[32] and the political and religious leaders who are predicting the worst. Ajello regularly repeats that weapons as such cannot be the cause of violence, only its instruments. Asked to explain the difficulties of the Cease-fire Commission over uncollected weapons, he states that this is an endless task and admits that the United Nations alone could not complete it. He emphasizes that his role is to work with the parties on political solutions that would prevent or invalidate the use of these weapons.

The parties, however, see their responsibilities as being reduced. Demobilized military men are re-organizing far from their traditional leadership. Armed bands appear on the roads of Mozambique. The most pessimistic of national and international observers fear the worst.

The Cease-fire Commission, led by Colonel Pier Segala, has carried on its endless task. In September 1994, it began the post-demobilization verification. Thousands of additional arms were discovered as civilians told the military observers about arms storage places that the combatants never mentioned. It has even been necessary to disarm the militia and the paramilitary groups that have played an important role during the war. In December 1994, Colonel Segala produced his final report: a total of 189,827 weapons and large amounts of ammunition were collected during the entire disarmament process in Mozambique.[33]

DEMOBILIZATION AS A CIVILIAN PROCESS

The former military men were brought back to civilian life at the end of the long assembly process. They had to take off their boots and exchange their combat dress for civilian trousers to be released from military obligations. According to the General Peace Agreement, the demobilization was a military act under the control of the armed forces.

However, the commanding officers of the camp have been confronted from the very beginning of the assembly process by a very violent opposition by the future demobilized soldiers. Once integrated and registered, these soldiers wanted to be absolutely free from the military rule. Hence, military rule was openly ignored in the assembly area by the soldiers as well as by the military in charge of the security. The commander soon felt threatened by this group, which he did not know how to control anymore. The assembled soldiers started to settle in their own way the differences they had with the military hierarchy.

The assembly period generated unexpected forces and out-of-control behaviours. The refusal to obey the military rule was aggravated by the ignorance of the soldiers concerning civilian rules of conduct. Food distribution was inevitably an occasion for fighting. Robbery was common among assembled military men, and the strong, bad-quality alcoholic beverages made for disaster in the camp social life.

From these observations, which constitute the demobilization experience of one UN Volunteer in Mozambique, I have drawn the following conclusions:

Demobilization is a passage, in which the identity and origin of the individual is questioned, and it is therefore a very significant sociopsychological transformation of a vulnerable group.

The assembled soldiers refuse to obey the military rule. The assembly area must, therefore, have its own rules.

Demobilization has numerous social meanings and consequences for the individual as well as for the state.

Contrary to the principle that demobilization is a military act, it appears much more as a civilian process. The reintegration projects start in the assembly area itself once the military men have abandoned their arms. The reintegration opportunities and the required mental exercise of displacement and mobility should be recognized from the start of the assembly period. Moreover, the temporary gathering of the soldiers allows a better knowledge of their needs and wishes. The assembly area can become this convivial place where the military men can play, work, exchange ideas with civilians, or simply rest. The technical unit was aware of that when it set up information, recreation, and cultural programmes in assembly areas. However, the Technical Unit's priority remained logistical and administrative work; few resources were given to reintegration.

Closing Impressions

Isolated in the north of Mozambique, Lichinga is paradoxically one the cultural capitals of the country. There, with the support of Keith Warren, a British gentleman in love with this African land, a cultural association, the *Casa Velha*, publishes a local newspaper, organizes concerts and dance shows, and promotes health education in the most remote villages. This association also is a school for the youngsters of the province, who have the opportunity to learn how to undertake projects and how to transmit knowledge.

The youth of the *Casa Velha* cared about demobilization and insisted on participating in the assembly area activities, thereby opening opportunities for the soldiers. A programme was set up: young people were responsible for the TV set and the video movies offered to the soldiers. Others were in charge of managing the daily camp radio and had the opportunity to interview soldiers. We also played soccer together.

Then came the day, so long expected, of the soccer match between assembly area soldiers and civilian sportsmen of Lichinga. More than 1,000 demobilized soldiers were standing on the edges of the soccer ground, and they screamed their support for their fellows. The referee was an employee of the bank. He bravely faced huge pressure from the military group. The civilian team, which had dominated from the beginning of the match, eventually opened the score. The soldiers were vexed, but carried on with even more energy. They wanted to win the game. A second goal in favor of the civilian Lichinga team transformed the atmosphere; the public screamed that there had been treachery. They claimed that the referee had been bought. He was violently attacked by the players of the assembly area. He managed to flee, his cheek bleeding, his shirt torn.

Before long, we wanted to play again, but nobody in Lichinga volunteered to referee. The city players were tired, so we played a game between us, volunteers and the demobilized.

End of the War Machinery

Fernando

Much later, in July and August 1994, I was escorting journalists to Manhiça, one of the new Mozambican Defence Force bases,[34] located north of Maputo. We were attending a shooting exercise when I heard a familiar voice calling me. Turning back, I saw Fernando lying in the grass, holding his gun. He stood up and came to embrace me. Wearing the regular combat dress of the new army, relaxed, he looked like a different person. But after the numerous discussions we had had on his future, his repeated desire to take a break from the military, I could not understand why he had decided to join the army again. He explained that his name never appeared on the demobilization list, and therefore he had learned too late that he had been selected for the FADM. Among his fellow soldiers, some had been demobilized, and some had refused to be registered for the new army, insisting on being demobilized. As far as he was concerned, he got scared by civilian life. He had been touched by the trust placed in him by the camp commander and decided to postpone his return to civilian life. He was going to help make the new army of Mozambique. The lack of volunteers for the new army was troubling him. It seemed to him Mozambique needed a strong, united army.

NOTES

1. Samora Machel governed Mozambique from 1975 to 1986. He died in a plane crash over South Africa in 1986. The causes of this accident are still questioned. Samora Machel replaced, in 1969, Eduardo Mondlane, founder and leader of FRELIMO, who died from a parcel bomb in Dar-es-Salaam, Tanzania, at the FRELIMO base. For more information on the struggle for independence, see Mondlane, Eduardo. *Mozambique: de la colonisation portugaise à la libération nationale.* Paris: L'Harmattan, 1979, pp. 1–257; and Isaacman, Allen and Barbara Isaacman. *Mozambique: From Colonialism to Revolution 1900–1982.* Boulder: Westview Press, 1983, pp. 1–235.
2. In 1983 to 1984, the Mozambican government decided that the young unemployed offenders living in the main towns of the country (Maputo, Beira, Nampula) were also to become part of the *operação produção* or "production operation." The objective of this operation, which gathered people from different parts of the country into community villages, was to increase production by concentrating the work force.
3. The inhabitants of Mandimba, located in Niassa province in the northeast of Mozambique, speak the dialects Macua and Jawa. Fernando, coming from the center of the country, speaks Sena and Ndau.
4. *Report of the Secretary-General on the United Nations Operation in Mozambique* 28 January 1994, UN Doc. S/1994/89, 2.
5. During the war of independence, FRELIMO had an armed wing, the Forças Populares de Libertação de Moçambique (FPLM), which contributed to the withdrawal of the colonialist forces. In 1974, the FPLM successfully controlled the north of Mozambique.

This armed wing turned into the Forças Armadas de Moçambique (FAM) when Mozambique became independent on 25 June 1975.

6. Apart from the regional radio network, countrywide communication was possible through Inmarsat (a satellite fax system).

7. Founded in 1961 by Eduardo Mondlane, the independence front Frente de Libertação de Moçambique (FRELIMO) defined itself from the beginning as a non-racist, nationalist, and non-aligned movement. It fought in a hard geo-political environment, and its first political decision, at the time of the independence, was to respect the United Nations resolutions establishing political and economic sanctions against the apartheid system of South Africa and Rhodesia. This decision revealed to be a costly one for Mozambique when it had to turn to foreign support. As a result, FRELIMO adopted a Marxist-Leninist orientation in 1977, establishing links with socialist countries, mainly East Germany.

8. Mia Couto, a young Mozambican novelist widely published in Europe, writes in this Mozambican Portuguese, spoken by the soldiers. Through this vivid language, filled with the African nonchalance, he tells the stories and expresses the hopes of the Mozambican society. See Couto, Mia. *Terra Sonâmbula, Cada homen é uma raça, Cronicando, Vozes anoitecidas*. Lisbon: Ed. Caminho. *Vozes anoitecidas* was translated by David Brookshaw as *Voices Made Night*. Oxford: Heinemann, 1990, pp. 1–115; and *Terra Sonâmbula* was translated into French by Maryvonne Lapouge Pettorelli as *Terre somnambule*. Paris: Albin Michel, 1994, pp. 1–250.

9. The General Peace Agreement of Mozambique provided for the constitution of the new Mozambican Defence Forces (FADM), composed of 30,000 troops, 15,000 from the government and 15,000 from RENAMO. However, 98 per cent of the assembled soldiers in government and RENAMO assembly areas refused to integrate into the new armed forces. As a result, the parties to the agreement tended to add names of a certain number of soldiers against their will to the FADM lists. At the end of June 1994, while incidents were multiplying in the camps, Aldo Ajello, the Special Representative of the Secretary-General, referring to the agreement, which foresaw the registering of assembled soldiers for the FADM on a volunteer basis, managed to convince both government and RENAMO to respect the will of their men. He also asked them to consider a reduction of the planned number of troops. As a result, the commanding officers of the assembly areas were asked to consult the remaining soldiers on their preferences and to respect their will.

10. In brief, the United Nations was requested to monitor the cease-fire between the parties, FRELIMO and RENAMO, to coordinate the humanitarian assistance, and to observe the elections.

11. SWED-RELIEF is the governmental Swedish cooperation body that has contributed to the emergency and development assistance in Mozambique. The Scandinavian countries, through their government offices and NGOs, have always supported Mozambique in its battle against apartheid in its neighbouring countries. After the signing of the General Peace Agreement, SWED-RELIEF was engaged particularly in the demobilization process, providing each assembly area with US$5,000 for basic rehabilitation.

12. For further information on the civil war in Mozambique, see Hanlon, Joseph. *Mozambique: Who calls the shots?* Indianapolis: Indiana University Press, 1991, pp. 1–192.

13. Geffray, Christian. *La cause des armes au Mozambique: anthropologie d'une guerre civile*. Paris: Karthala, 1990, pp. 6–7.

14. About the Beira Corridor, see Van Dis, Adriaan. *En Afrique: récit*. Arles: Actes sud H. Nyssen, 1993, pp. 1–153.

15. On November 20, 1994, UNITA and the Government of Angola signed the Lusaka Protocol, promising a new era of hope for peace following the most recent two years of conflict. Nonetheless, at the time of writing, implementation of the Lusaka Protocol remains precarious, and scattered fighting continues in certain regions of the country.

16. Gasseau, Jacques. "L'espace lusophone dans l'Afrique australe d'aujourd'hui." *Le trimestre du monde* (2e trimestre 1993): 137–152.

17. See the series of articles written by the French researcher, Michel Cahen, published in *Savana*, a Mozambican newspaper, in November 1994. See also Cahen, Michel. *Mozambique: La révolution implosée: Etudes sur douze ans d'indépendence 1975–1987*. Paris: L'Harmattan, 1987, pp. 1–170. Cahen studied the civil war and then accompanied Afonso Dhlakama, the RENAMO leader, during his electoral campaign throughout the country in 1994. Like Geffray, *La cause des armes au Mozambique*, pp. 1–248, Cahen does not reduce RENAMO to its initial rightist support, but tries to understand the unavoidable position it occupied during the peace negotiations. Controlling large areas of the country, RENAMO, even if it did not have any clear political programme, was supported by some groups of the Mozambican society that refused the FRELIMO authority. Geffray also describes the progression of RENAMO in Nampula province in the early 1980s and the rising support it gathered among groups excluded by the new regime (traditional tribal chiefs, young unemployed, people adversely affected by the villagization programme).

18. The General Peace Agreement of Mozambique (GPA) was signed in Rome on 4 October 1992 after years of negotiations mediated by the Italian government and the Santo Egidio religious community. It includes seven protocols concerning the cease-fire, humanitarian assistance, transition to a multiparty system, and elections. For more detailed information, see *General Peace Agreement of Mozambique*, bilingual edition English/Portuguese. Amsterdam: African-European Institute (AWEPAA), 1993, pp. 1–96.

19. *Report of the Secretary-General on the United Nations Operation in Mozambique*, 3 December 1992, UN Doc. S/24892, 1–16.

20. *Report of the Secretary-General on the United Nations Operation in Mozambique*, 1 November 1993, UN Doc. S/26666, 2.

21. The budget of the Technical Unit was a composite one. It was constituted soon after the signing of the General Peace Agreement, with the support of donor countries. SWED-RELIEF provided logistical support and funded regional coordinators. The Swiss Cooperation contributed to management costs. The European Union provided the non-food items used in the assembly areas. The World Food Programme (WFP) was in charge of the food in the camps; the World Health Organization (WHO) was responsible for basic health care; the United Nations Children's Fund (UNICEF) took care of sanitation; and the International Organization for Migration (IOM) provided transportation for the demobilized soldiers and their families.

22. IOM contributed to the peace process by transporting not only demobilized soldiers and their families but also other vulnerable groups, such as the internally displaced and refugees. Well-informed about the local transport facilities and the road situation, this organization exceeded its tasks by providing administrative and social support to the reintegration of these groups.

23. UNOHAC, following the 'Declaration by the Government of the Republic of Mozambique and RENAMO on the guiding principles for humanitarian assistance' that was signed in Rome on 16 July 1992, coordinated the humanitarian assistance programmes. This office carried out extensive information gathering throughout the country on various topics, such as population density, road accessibility, health, education, water sources, and agricultural production, and it created a database absolutely necessary to any emerging development programme. See UNOHAC Internal Document, *UNOHAC Map Series Humanitarian Assistance Programme in Mozambique*. February 1994.

24. CORE, one of the Peace Commissions, was among the main political instruments for the implementation of the General Peace Agreement. The other Peace Commissions were the Supervision and Control Commission, led by Aldo Ajello, Special Representative of the Secretary-General; the Cease-fire Commission; and the Joint Commission for the formation of the Mozambican Defence Force. Represented in the Peace Commissions

were FRELIMO, RENAMO, ONUMOZ and delegates of the International Community. See *General Peace Agreement of Mozambique*, Annexes III and IV.

25. Concerning "passage" and "origin," see Sibony, Daniel. *Entre-deux: l'origine en partage.* Paris: Seuil, 1991, pp. 1–402.

26. The RSS, funded by a UNDP-controlled trust fund, was implemented through a local bank, the *Banco Popular de Desenvolvimento*, and was well represented at the district level.

27. Some of the former TUCOs were at the time of this writing working under the auspices of the ILO. They were carrying out a training programme on basic techniques and occupational activities for the demobilized soldiers.

28. UN Volunteers were also working at the time of writing in IRS provincial offices. This means that some UN Volunteer specialists had the opportunity to work with both demobilization and reintegration of soldiers in Mozambique.

29. *Final Report of the Secretary-General on the United Nations Operation in Mozambique.* 23 December 1994, UN Doc. S/1994/1449, 3.

30. The General Peace Agreement had to impose itself in an atmosphere of deep mistrust between the signatories. But following the elections, a new culture of peace, coming from the soul of the society, could potentially control the leaders and build the national reconciliation.

31. "Demining is our failure," Aldo Ajello repeatedly said. Mozambique counts more than 2 million mines that have caused at least 10,000 deaths and 80,000 injuries, among the civilian population, according to Handicap International. After an unexplained delay, ONUMOZ finally carried out a demining program on the main roads of the country. For more information on disarmament and demining, see *Final Report of the Secretary-General on the United Nations Operation in Mozambique.* 23 December 1994, UN Doc. S/1994/1449, 1–9.

32. For instance, the first issue of *Mozambique Inview*, the independent Mozambican newsletter, on 8 June 1994 was entitled 'Armed Separatists Re-emerge in Mozambique.'

33. *Final Report of the Secretary-General on the United Nations Operation in Mozambique.* 23 December 1994, UN Doc. S/1994/1449, 4.

34. In Manhiça camp, infantry battalions of the new army were being trained by Mozambican instructors under the supervision of British advisers. The formation of the FADM was not under ONUMOZ's mandate. The United Kingdom, Portugal, and France were assisting the Mozambican government in training infantry battalions, special forces battalions, units of logistic specialists, and a company of sappers. Additional support to the training of the new army was also provided by Zimbabwe and Italy. See *Final Report of the Secretary-General on the United Nations Operation in Mozambique.* 23 December 1994, UN Doc. S/1994/1449, 4.

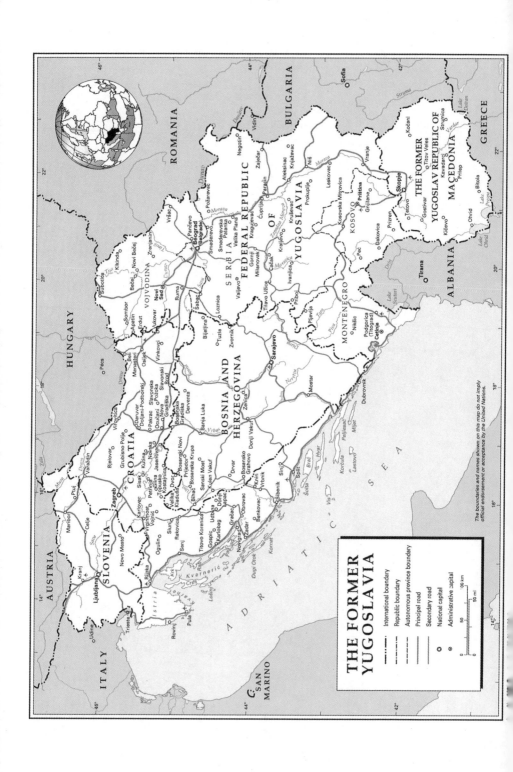

THE FORMER
YUGOSLAVIA

	International boundary
	Republic boundary
	Autonomous province boundary
	Principal road
	Secondary road
○	National capital
◎	Administrative capital

The boundaries and names shown on this map do not imply official endorsement or acceptance by the United Nations.

5

CAUGHT IN THE CROSSFIRE: DILEMMAS OF HUMAN RIGHTS PROTECTION IN FORMER YUGOSLAVIA

Benny Ben Otim

SOME LESSONS CANNOT be learned in a classroom. I have seen the results of conflict in my own country—poverty, hunger, and death—all the tragedies one encounters in a disaster. Born and raised in northern Uganda bordering Sudan, I was exposed early in life to the suffering of refugees. While living in Uganda, little did I know that one day I would arrive at Gatwick airport in the United Kingdom as an asylum seeker and refugee myself. Neither could I have imagined that some 10 years later I would land at the Zagreb airport, this time as one of 18 United Nations Volunteers deployed in the former Yugoslavia to assist and protect refugees and people in flight within their own country.

In this chapter I present my experience as a UN Volunteers Protection Officer serving with the United Nations High Commissioner for Refugees (UNHCR). The refugee problem is primarily a human rights problem because violations of human rights are directly responsible for the movement of people across international borders.[1] Thus "[s]afeguarding human rights is necessary to prevent conditions that force people to be-

Benny Ben Otim is a Ugandan national born in 1952. A lawyer graduated from the University of Florida, he was a UN Volunteer Protection Officer with the United Nations High Commissioner for Refugees in Banja Luka, Bosnia-Herzegovina, from November 1992 to April 1993. He is currently a staff member of UNHCR working in Zagreb.

come refugees, and is a key element in protecting them,"[2] according to the UNHCR.

I also discuss the dilemmas of human rights[3] protection in the former Yugoslavia. I confess that I have mixed emotions about this crisis, one of the most complex of the post-Cold War period, marked by mass rape, "ethnic cleansing,"[4] and the deliberate targeting of civilians and international personnel. From a purely objective perspective, as well as my own as a person desiring to see the cause of human rights advanced, I can be constructively critical of the role of the United Nations and of the other international players in this context. As someone who is now involved in protection work, I appreciate the dilemmas this situation poses as I experience the practical difficulties myself.

THE SLIDE INTO WAR

As the winds of democracy blew across Yugoslavia in the 1990 elections, they brought with them the demise of this country as a federal state.[5] In 1991, the Socialist Federal Republic of Yugoslavia, with a population of approximately 22 million divided into 24 ethnic groups, including the three major groups of Serbs, Croats, and Slovenes, ceased to exist.[6] Out of its ashes, five states emerged: the Federal Republic of Yugoslavia (Serbia and Montenegro), the Republic of Bosnia-Herzegovina, the Republic of Macedonia,[7] the Republic of Croatia, and the Republic of Slovenia.

The confrontation resulting from the emergence of two of the states,[8] Croatia[9] and Bosnia-Herzegovina,[10] has not ended. Further, two internationally unrecognized entities within the former Yugoslavia, the so-called Republic of Serb Krajina (RSK) in Croatia under the control of the Knin authorities,[11] and the Serbian Republic of Bosnia and Herzegovina, which would regroup the Bosnian Serb autonomous regions currently under the control of the Pale authorities,[12] are still involved in a violent struggle to emerge as distinct states.

At the heart of the conflict in Croatia is the presence in certain areas of large Serb populations that are seeking autonomy and eventual unification with Serbia. The presence of a Serb majority in these regions dates back to the beginning of the nineteenth century.[13] It is the presence of Serbs in 20 per cent of Croatia, in areas Croats consider their own, that has led to recurring problems in the region, in 1941[14] and again 50 years later.[15]

The situation in Bosnia-Herzegovina, where I was stationed, with its mixed population of Serbs, Muslims, and Croats, is even more complex and problematic. Unlike in Croatia or Serbia, no single group constitutes a significant majority of the population. The 4.3 million inhabitants are 43.7 per cent Muslim,[16] 31.4 per cent Serb, and 17.3 per cent Croat.[17] Throughout this crisis, the position of the Bosnian Muslims, who are fighting on several fronts[18] during an arms embargo declared by the United Nations,[19] has been difficult. With the support of Serbs from Serbia and Montenegro and in spite of international condemnation, the Bosnian Serbs were able to occupy 70 per cent of Bosnia-Herzegovina.

The breakup of Yugoslavia has been marked by armed conflict characterized by appallingly brutal and wanton violations of human rights and humanitarian law.[20] The human impact has been catastrophic, leaving millions throughout the former Yugoslavia, mainly in Bosnia-Herzegovina and Croatia, in need of food, medicine, and shelter.[21]

The UN has been substantially involved in providing humanitarian assistance in former Yugoslavia since the start of the crisis. In November 1991, in direct response to the deteriorating situation, UN Secretary-General Boutros Boutros-Ghali authorized UNHCR to act as the lead agency[22] for humanitarian assistance, not only to refugees who have crossed international borders, but also to internally displaced persons (IDPs), as well as civilian populations affected by the crisis.[23]

THE UN'S RESPONSE

In June 1991, when serious hostilities broke out in Croatia and Slovenia after both republics declared themselves independent, the initial attempt to find a political solution to the crisis came from the European Community (EC).[24] Because of ambiguous and conflicting signals from the EC itself, as well as from individual EC members,[25] the EC's attempt to settle the conflict was unsuccessful. This failure led to the direct involvement of the UN.

The United Nations Protection Force (UNPROFOR)[26] was established in February 1992 under the Vance Plan[27] for an initial period of 12 months.[28] In August 1992, an International Conference on the Former Yugoslavia was convened, combining the efforts of the UN, the EC, and other international organizations.[29]

Since the establishment of UNPROFOR, the military and civilian police (CIVPOL) components have worked alongside UNHCR in protection work, particularly in the UN Protected Areas (UNPAs) in Croatia[30] inhabited by Croatian Serbs. In Bosnia-Herzegovina, UNPROFOR also supported protection efforts by UNHCR.[31] Additionally, personnel from the UN Centre for Human Rights (UNCHR) have also been monitoring human rights violations since 1994.[32]

However, throughout the war, massive and systematic violations of human rights and grave violations of humanitarian law did not provoke a sufficiently firm or serious response from the international community to stop the violations.[33] In 1993, Cable News Network broadcasted reports of heavy casualties suffered by the civilian population because of the Bosnian Serb blockade of UN humanitarian efforts in eastern Bosnia-Herzegovina (Srebrenica, Gorazde, and Zepa). Because of the continuing failure of the international community to stop the carnage, the Security Council declared Srebrenica a "safe area" to be kept free of armed attacks under the enforcement action of Chapter VII of the UN Charter. The safe area was expanded later to cover five other areas, including Sarajevo.[34]

In each of the six safe areas, UNPROFOR was to monitor security conditions and provide protection to the civilian population. The Bosnian Serbs gave little credence to the concept of safe areas and continued to blockade and shell these areas at will. Rather than imposing an end to the Bosnian Serb blockade of Srebrenica and Gorazde, the UN opted for expensive air drops of food and other relief supplies to the population of the areas. Since the safe areas could never be considered completely safe, the concept lost its meaning.[35]

In an effort to put teeth into a host of UN Security Council resolutions[36] that demanded unimpeded delivery of humanitarian assistance and respect of civilians in safe areas, the UN authorized in March 1993 limited North Atlantic Treaty Organization (NATO) air strikes to prevent the strangulation of Sarajevo and to protect the safe areas.[37] UNPROFOR itself was authorized by the Security Council to deter attacks against the safe areas.[38] However, periodic NATO air strikes and UNPROFOR's reactions on the ground were ineffective, and violations of humanitarian law continued unabated.

To address specific allegations of human rights violations, a special session of the UN Commission on Human Rights was convened in August 1992 in Geneva, Switzerland, to discuss the human rights situation in the former Yugoslavia, and a special rapporteur was appointed.[39] In his first report, he wrote that "[h]uman rights violations are being perpetrated by all parties to the conflicts. There are also victims on all sides. However, the situation of the Muslim population is particularly tragic: they feel that they are threatened with extermination."[40] Human rights field offices were established in the territories of Croatia, Macedonia, and

Bosnia-Herzegovina to monitor the regional human rights situation,[41] while the Federal Republic of Yugoslavia declined to give consent.

In October 1992, in response to the continued violations, the Security Council established an impartial Commission of Experts[42] to investigate grave breaches of the 1949 Geneva Conventions.[43] The commission visited the former Yugoslavia in April 1993 to carry out on-site investigations.

As a result of various reports, the UN Security Council then established in 1993 an International Tribunal composed of eleven judges and a prosecutor to sit at The Hague. The tribunal is charged with prosecuting those responsible for serious violations of international humanitarian law in the former Yugoslavia since 1991.[44]

By 1993 more than 3.6 million refugees, internally displaced persons, and war victims needed protection throughout the former Yugoslavia. War-torn Bosnia-Herzegovina alone accounted for more than 2 million people in need of both protection and humanitarian assistance.[45] Delivering assistance and providing protection to this immense number of people not only presented a logistical nightmare for UNHCR, but it also required a large number of experienced personnel.

VOLUNTEERING WITH UNHCR

As the lead agency, UNHCR was presented with the challenge of providing personnel at short notice. To cope with the increasing needs, it was inevitable that UNHCR would have to either recruit new staff or turn to other organizations for assistance. United Nations Volunteers was among the organizations called upon by UNHCR. In 1992, UNV started fielding volunteers within UNHCR teams.

Our UNV group was made up of lawyers, social workers, logistics officers, and radio operators, as well as a programme officer.[46] When I arrived at UNHCR in November 1992, the entire Protection Unit for Bosnia-Herzegovina in UNHCR Zagreb headquarters consisted of only one person. I was sent to the Banja Luka field office in Bosnia-Herzegovina as the first protection officer in one of the most troubled areas, its very name synonymous with ethnic cleansing. There, most local staff had only a rudimentary command of English and few had ever heard of UNHCR.

In Banja Luka

From the day of my arrival in Banja Luka, I realized what would be the three defining realities of my job: deliberate policies to remove minorities, no international consensus on solutions, and regular denial of access by combatants to people in need.

The Bosnian Serbs were dead set to get rid of minorities by whatever means, violent if need be, until all Muslims and/or Croats were driven from territories under Bosnian Serb control. To that end they carried out the deliberate policy of ethnic cleansing. Where a minority was slow in moving out, the house would be blown up with dynamite. Other ingenious methods to move minorities included use of apartheid-type regulations limiting living space, and dismissal from employment of parents whose children did not respond to draft calls.

For those who did not live through the situation in Bosnia-Herzegovina, the effects of cleansing upon first sight were shocking. In his report back to UNV, the chief of UNV's Humanitarian Relief Unit (HRU) described what he saw on a field trip we took together in 1993. "Bosanska Gradiska is a pretty town, with tree-lined streets and squares, cafés, bistros, and all the allure of a prosperous cosmopolitan western European town. However, the mosque was now a heap of rubble, and the Muslim population all but eliminated."[47]

From Bosanska Gradiska we went to Omarska, a Muslim village whose population was victimized by ethnic cleansing. "On the way, we passed a large fertilizer factory, alleged by some locals to be the site where many bodies from massacres are disposed. Some had complained to UNHCR about the bad smell now emanating from the plant. Omarska and its environs are a scene of utter destruction: entire rows of houses rendered uninhabitable, windows and roofs blown away, and gutted by fire. Contents plundered. And on the roof of each one, a large circle with an "X" inside, painted in black, to identify it as a house to be eliminated."[48] The families living in these houses were among the more than 50,000 Muslims and Croats who had been forced out of this area. This was the repeated reality we faced on the ground in the former Yugoslavia.

Furthermore, no international outcry or pleas by international organizations such as UNHCR would stop this. Instead, organizations operating in the field could expect to meet strong resistance and planned obstacles, such as severely restricted movement, until the cleansing was a foregone conclusion.

It also quickly became apparent that the flurry of publicity on diplomatic activities hid sad truths: that the governments represented in the Contact Group,[49] in the Security Council, and in the UN made statements on human rights issues that were not heeded, and that there was no agreed-upon strategy or consensus on how to solve the crisis unleashed by the breakup of Yugoslavia. This lack of a coherent political strategy raised several troubling questions for organizations and personnel operating on the ground, in the forefront of the crisis.

While UNHCR consistently asserted its neutrality, demanding that it should be allowed to carry out its humanitarian work unhindered by the fighting parties, most of the antagonists, particularly the Bosnian Serbs, regularly blurred the political and humanitarian lines. The practical results of this blurring activity meant that issues faced on the ground, no matter how small, became political issues. UNHCR has been denied access by the Bosnian Serbs to areas where threatened populations are located, even when authorization had been given earlier.

I visited Vrbanja, a Muslim village about five kilometres from Banja Luka, with the chief of UNV's Humanitarian Relief Unit after a woman told us about the situation there. We drove through the village but were unable to reach her house. Instead, we were intercepted by Bosnian Serb irregulars in unmarked cars who waved us back. The "cleansing" was probably ongoing but we could not get to the other side of the village, despite our official local authorization to do so.[50]

Dilemmas

A major human rights dilemma for UNHCR in the former Yugoslavia was whether to carry out large-scale evacuations of vulnerable people, which would literally mean that UNHCR—the refugee protector—could be seen as helping to create refugees. The alternative was to attempt to provide protection and security to threatened minorities where they lived, a totally unrealistic option in a situation of ethnic cleansing. This dilemma produced a paralysing fear on the part of UNHCR staff and field workers such as UN Volunteers assisting UNHCR that by becoming directly involved in transfers UNHCR would be accused of promoting ethnic cleansing.

This accounts for UNHCR's original choice to limit its activities to monitoring, rather than to become directly involved in evacuations. For myself and some other UN Volunteers, monitoring ethnic cleansing and dutifully reporting the violations to our superiors was simply not enough. We could not help being moved by what we saw, the widespread and recurrent incidents of killing, rape, and maiming of civilians. In early 1993, the UNHCR field office in Banja Luka learned of an elderly woman who had been raped in front of her family as a warning that they had two days to move out, or else the entire family would be killed.

Dilemmas of human rights protection: a woman on return to her devastated house in the former Yugoslavia. Photo: UNHCR/A. Hollmann

By coincidence the officer-in-charge and I, both UN Volunteers, were on duty at the time, which made the decision an easier one. We resolved together to do something more than just monitoring the situation. So after using our good offices with the Bosnian Serb authorities, we obtained exit papers, loaded the elderly woman and her family into a UNHCR vehicle, and, with a lot of negotiations along the way, we successfully moved the family to Croatia. We waited with trepidation for a possible rebuke from senior UNHCR officials. When our report did not provoke the reaction that we feared, we became bolder and carried out more such transfers, and soon other UNHCR colleagues joined the bandwagon.

In the words of Sadako Ogata, United Nations High Commissioner for Refugees, the critical issue posed by this crisis is: "How long and how far can a humanitarian institution go on in assisting and, to some extent, saving the victims, without damaging its image, credibility and principles and the self-respect of its staff in the face of manipulation, blackmail, abuse, humiliation and murder?"[51]

Reflection on this question must begin with a humanitarian organization's decision to become involved in the crisis. Once it became involved in the former Yugoslavia, UNHCR, a humanitarian and non-political UN body, could not dictate its position independently of the UN. The decision to assist in this kind of conflict is not an easy one for a UN body, especially if UN military muscle is lacking and the major international players are unable to agree on solutions. Additionally, UN agencies are indirectly associated with UN military forces. The International Committee of the Red Cross (ICRC), regularly involved in conflicts, shuns any close identification with the UN military apparatus in the former Yugoslavia, thereby religiously guarding its impartial stance. The crisis in the former Yugoslavia has reaffirmed the view that collective prevention of both aggression and violations of international humanitarian law depend on the concomitant will of the international community to decide on a course of action and enforce its decisions, which may, in turn, require military action. Since the UN has no independent force of its own, how will it ever succeed in a raging conflict? Should we throw up our hands and give up the little that the UN can achieve in alleviating the suffering of the people? To me the answer is a resounding "no." We must persevere, but the UN must also heed the criticism that is leveled against it and redouble its efforts to become an effective instrument in complex emergencies, including addressing both humanitarian needs and the roots of the crisis. As Jan Eliasson, the former Under-Secretary-General for Humanitarian Affairs, observed: "Relief without going to the root causes of the problem is like ... putting up an umbrella in a hurricane.... We have to remind the parties in the conflict ... that there has to be a process of dealing with the root causes and getting solutions to the basic political problems."[52]

UNHCR was charged in former Yugoslavia with providing humanitarian assistance and protecting refugees and displaced persons. In Banja Luka itself, in my view, the Bosnian Serbs were diametrically opposed to this protection and were determined to carry out ethnic cleansing at all costs and to disrupt humanitarian aid. They were equally determined to test international will and to manipulate the international community by both denying access to threatened populations and by the indiscriminate use of military force against civilian targets.

Neither of these activities provoked a firm response by the UN beyond the creation of more resolutions. The frustration caused by watching people suffer and die exacted a high toll on the morale and health of UNHCR staff. Invariably, this led to depression, burnout, and high turnover of staff, who, sometimes after only short periods, would leave the area for other UNHCR operations.

In the future, there may be more Yugoslav-type crises. In response to the dilemma of becoming involved in "live war" situations, UNHCR has appointed an adviser to the high commissioner on operations in war theatres and has incorporated other policy innovations, such as those covering evacuations of vulnerable persons, as a last resort.

According to this new policy, "[e]vacuation is a last resort, in that it acquiesces in the very displacement that preventive efforts aim to avoid. But in some circumstances it is the only way to save lives. There is a very fine line between refusing to facilitate ethnic cleansing and failing to prevent needless deaths. During the war in Bosnia-Herzegovina, humanitarian agencies have been forced to confront this dilemma on a number of occasions. In Srebrenica the line was clearly on the point of being crossed, and UNHCR and UNPROFOR decided to continue evacuating the most vulnerable members of the town's population."[53]

UNV Contribution to UNHCR

The presence of UN Volunteer specialists at the early stages of the operation when UNHCR was stretched thin on the ground proved to be crucial for several reasons. Our arrival helped jump-start the UNHCR operation, and our assistance contributed to the expansion of the operation. Though UN Volunteers often had little or no previous UNHCR experience, they brought with them maturity and flexibility in addition to their own specialized experience in their respective fields, all of which proved valuable in dealing with the challenges posed in the field.

Protection work in the former Yugoslavia was often done by the seat of the pants, determined as it was by the fluctuating daily circumstances confronting minorities. The range of protection activities to moderate the wanton killings of minorities included mediation with the "central" government, local municipalities, militia, and often individual soldiers at the roadblocks, who were law unto themselves. UN Volunteer specialists were involved in all of this work.

We also monitored and reported human rights violations, provided protection to "extremely vulnerable individuals," i.e. the elderly, sick, unaccompanied minors, and those under direct threat of violence, and provided the UN presence in threatening situations. Sometimes when we received advance notice of planned attacks on particular families or villages, the UNHCR and UNV staff would position themselves between the attackers and the minorities, often intermingling physically with those threatened until the threat passed or until the people concerned could leave the area safely. This approach was consistent with the concept of showing "presence" and was not discouraged by UNHCR. To my knowledge, no UN Volunteers were injured in these activities.

The maturity brought by the UN Volunteers I encountered serving with UNHCR was particularly crucial in dealing with the Bosnian Serbs. It is common knowledge among all humanitarian workers in the region that encounters between international humanitarian staff and the Bosnian Serbs often have been characterized by unpleasantness and friction. The Bosnian Serbs often would agree to requests by international humanitarian organizations only when they were confronted with great firmness. This intransigence was made worse by the noticeable habit of talking for hours on end. Understandably, field staff got tired of this and regularly attempted to short-circuit these diatribes.

However, listening could often mean the difference between success or failure. While it required the pragmatic approach of sitting, sometimes for hours, and hearing arguments regarding the righteousness of claims, this strategy paid off for me in my day-to-day work. By listening, I was able to build some degree of trust or friendship that could lead to later opportunities to call on these same individuals for access to areas, even those in the process of being "cleansed." Our role as international observers could be a moderating influence in these situations.

Efforts to understand people and their culture were vital to our work. Developing working relationships with the community leaders could even lead to dramatic results. For example, in February 1993, 120 Muslim survivors of ethnic cleansing in a Sanski Most village, some still bleeding from wounds, escaped to Banja Luka and took refuge in a local mosque. The Banja Luka Serb authorities would not allow them to travel farther unless they produced exit permission from Sanski Most Serb authorities. Attempts by the UNHCR field office and senior officers from Zagreb to get papers from Sanski Most had proved futile. Meanwhile, nightly grenade attacks were being launched against the mosque. At the request of UNHCR supervisors, I travelled to Sanski Most, visited the mayor, and drank a few "rakija" with him before making a personal appeal for permission to transport the people from the area. After this meeting, the mayor authorized his assistant to travel the next day to UNHCR Banja Luka to deliver the documents.

Perhaps the most telling contribution of UN Volunteers in the former Yugoslavia was our occasional ability to influence the direction of UNHCR policy decisions. Oftentimes decisions regarding day-to-day field responsibilities were shouldered by UN Volunteers due to the rapidly changing circumstances. Under these conditions, UNHCR headquarters in Geneva and the Zagreb office could offer only general guidance. Because specific policy guidelines were being developed and refined after the fact, field staff members were often left to use their own best judgment when confronted with unforeseen situations.

SOME LESSONS

The marriage between UN Volunteer specialists and UNHCR staff was not always a smooth one at first. Working in a cooperative spirit sometimes means using gentle persuasion to influence others. In the end this kind of consensus-building approach does pay off and volunteers should be prepared to go the extra mile to build good relations where they are serving.

In protection matters, an identifiable and distinct volunteer role may be difficult to sustain. In the former Yugoslavia, UN Volunteers were not easily identifiable as UN Volunteers, except to those knowledgeable about the UNHCR system. We were structurally incorporated into UNHCR's operations and were considered UNHCR staff. As a matter of policy, UNHCR desired the complete integration of UN Volunteers into the UNHCR operational structure. Inevitably, this meant the distinct character of the volunteer contribution was not always recognized. Nevertheless, I believe UN Volunteers have made, and continue to make, meaningful contributions as volunteers within UNHCR's operation to alleviate the suffering of some of the victims of this conflict.

For humanitarian organizations such as UNHCR, participating in these types of emergencies has highlighted the need for strong and clear policies encompassing ground rules for dealing with parties that flagrantly abuse international norms. Other measures that may help include: greater use of the media to articulate the organization's concern in order to drum up public support as early as possible; effective mechanisms for building institutional memory from day-to-day field experience; an organized and concerted effort to apply lessons learned; and training to blend in support professionals (such as those from UNV) to avoid friction between traditional and other staff and to produce solid field reports for policymakers.

CONCLUSION

"We the peoples of the United Nations, determined ... to reaffirm faith in fundamental human rights, in the dignity and worth of the human person...."[54] These words of the preamble to the Charter of the United

Nations evoke in many people today, instead of joy, a nagging uncertainty. In light of the ongoing war in the former Yugoslavia, the reaffirmation of the Charter preamble rings hollow. The war has shaken faith in the UN's ability to deal firmly with gross violations of humanitarian law and human rights.

My experiences while growing up influenced me and led to my service as a UN Volunteer and to the work I am continuing to do with United Nations High Commissioner for Refugees. It is difficult though rewarding work, and is absolutely necessary. A strategy I use to handle pressure in the field is to keep a specific objective in mind rather than a grand vision. There is an immense personal satisfaction in each good act done to assist a refugee.

At a global level, the problems in the former Yugoslavia have demonstrated the urgent need for finding mechanisms for peaceful and orderly processes of change in the post-Cold War era, as well as the need to revise the UN's response to the new conflicts around the world. The large number of UN resolutions regarding former Yugoslavia may reflect a universal wish for peace and pacific solutions to this dispute, but this wish does not necessarily translate into reality unless there is the international will to back up these noble sentiments.

Despite the best intentions and dedication of all UN personnel in the field, so long as the UN itself does not articulate a clear distinction between its human rights and humanitarian role on the one hand, and its role in finding political solutions to conflicts on the other hand, it will come in for criticism. In the former Yugoslavia, humanitarian assistance has taken place in the absence of any political and military solution, thereby fueling the conflict. As a consequence, the parties do and may continue to use the blockade of humanitarian assistance as a weapon of war.

Compounding this fact is the division in the Security Council,[55] and the result has been uneasy diplomatic accommodation between those who advocate strong action and those who argue for cautious approaches to promote a political solution. While the Security Council acts at the political level, others are directly involved in the mechanics of human rights and humanitarian work, which by its very nature requires neutrality and distance from political considerations. Herein lies the dilemma for the UN.

NOTES

1. UNHCR, *The State of the World's Refugees—The Challenge of Protection*. New York: Penguin, 1993, p. 7.

2. UNHCR, *The State of the World's Refugees*, p. 8.
3. Refugees differ from other people in need of humanitarian aid because they also need international protection. Refugees cannot look to their governments and state institutions to protect their rights and physical security. In this context, according to UNHCR, "[t]he essential elements of international protection ... are admission to safety, exemption from forcible return, non-discrimination and assistance for survival.... Protection must include physical security of refugees. There are two dimensions of physical protection. One is personal security from physical attack whether from armed forces, death squads, or lone assassins. Physical protection also means keeping people alive through humanitarian assistance. Food, water, sanitation and medical care are fundamental to survival." UNHCR, *The State of the World's Refugees*, p. 5.
4. The term "ethnic cleansing" is used to describe methods employed to force the flight of minority populations from their homes and territory, including the use of terror tactics to coerce such populations to flee.
5. Yugoslavia itself was a product of World War I. In 1918, with the end of the war, the Kingdom of Serbs, Croats, and Slovenes was formed under the Serbian Prince Regent Aleksandar. The name of the country was changed by the king in 1929 to the Kingdom of Yugoslavia, "Land of the South (Yugo) Slavs," to signify state and national unity. In 1943 to 1944, the communists, who had fought as partisans alongside the Allies in World War II, took power after defeating the Nazi occupiers of Yugoslavia. Until his death in 1980, their leader, Josip Tito, was the undisputed head of a Soviet-type, federated Yugoslavia. Despite the semblance of stability under Tito's leadership and the attempts by the communists to hold Yugoslavia together, nationalism and the desire for independence among the various groups did not die. Rather, they remained dormant, buried very near the surface during the Cold War. For a concise description of the history of Yugoslavia, see *Eastern Europe and the Commonwealth of Independent States 1994*. London: Europa, 1994, pp. 87–94 and pp. 721–726.
6. The former Yugoslavia also is home to three major religions, Muslims, Orthodox Christians, and Roman Catholic Christians. For a detailed discussion of interethnic issues in former Yugoslavia, see Draganich, Alex N. *Serbs and Croats: The struggle in Yugoslavia*. New York: Harcourt Brace & Co., 1992; Laftan, R.G.D. *The Serbs, The Guardian of the Gate*. New York: Dorset Press, 1989; Ramet, Sabrina P. *Nationalism and Federalism in Yugoslavia 1962–1991*. Bloomington: Indiana University Press, 1992, pp. 1–346.
7. Pending settlement of the disagreement with Greece over the name of this new state, Macedonia is provisionally referred to within the United Nations as "the former Yugoslav Republic of Macedonia." See *Resolution 817*, 7 April 1993, UN Doc. S/RES/817/1993.
8. The declaration of independence of Slovenia also led to an outbreak of fighting between the Yugoslav People's Army (JNA) and Slovenian military forces. The violence arising from the birth of Slovenia as a state did not, however, acquire the same proportions as in Croatia and Bosnia-Herzegovina.
9. The elections in Croatia were followed by a Croatian declaration of independence in 1991, which, in turn, was answered with a military uprising by the Serbs in Croatia.
10. In Bosnia-Herzegovina, the 1990 election results conformed to the nationality and religious affiliation of the parties, with each national group—Serbs, Croats, and Muslims—voting for their respective parties. The Muslim party won the election by a slim majority, reflecting the demographics of the area. In a move that mirrored those of Croatian leaders, the Muslim political leaders declared Bosnia-Herzegovina an independent state in 1992. The Bosnian Serb response was to take up arms and fight for a separate state within Bosnia-Herzegovina.
11. The "Knin authorities," named after the capital of the region, Knin, control three Serbian Autonomous Regions, the Krajina, Slavonia, Baranja, and Western Srem.
12. The Serbian Autonomous Regions are Bosanska Krajina, Eastern and Old Herzegovina, Romanija, Northern Bosnia. The Pale authorities are named after Pale, on the out-

skirts of Sarajevo. As of the writing of this chapter, the worst fighting in months began in Sarajevo between Bosnian Serbs and Bosnian Muslims. The fighting, described by some UN officials as the most serious since 1993, sent civilians in Sarajevo scurrying for basement shelters for the first time since the start of a four-month cease-fire signed in December 1994 (UN Doc. S/1995/8) and ending 1 May 1995, the longest cease-fire since the beginning of the war. See *International Herald Tribune* (17 May 1994): 1.

13. In the beginning of the nineteenth century, the Austro-Hungarians established a military frontier ("Vojna Krajina" in Serbo-Croatian language) on their southern flank and persuaded Serbs fleeing from the Turkish invasion force to populate the area.

14. In April 1941, an independent State of Croatia emerged with the support of the Germans and Italians. As a result, a civil war waged by Tito's resistance forces broke out. By 1944, the Croatian state had collapsed and was restored to Yugoslavia.

15. At the time of writing this chapter, the war in Croatia had also resumed after the four-month cease-fire. See "Croatian Troops Move to Retake Serbian Enclave," *International Herald Tribune* (2 May 1995): 1; and Cohen, Roger. "Serbs Shell Zagreb With Cluster Bombs, Casualties Put at 126," *International Herald Tribune* (3 May 1995): 1.

16. The reason for the large concentration of Muslims in Bosnia-Herzegovina compared to the other regions in the former Yugoslavia can be traced to the period when the Ottoman Empire occupied the Balkans. While the Ottomans forcibly converted Serb Orthodox Christians and Slovene/Croat Roman Catholic Christians to Islam throughout the region, the greatest number of conversions made in Bosnia-Herzegovina was among the Bosnian Bogomils, a religion independent from the Catholic or Orthodox faiths. See generally Encyclopedia Brittanica, Micropedia, Volume II, p. 115 "Bogomils," and Stoyanovitch, M.D. *The Great Powers and the Balkans 1875–78.* Cambridge: Cambridge University Press, 1938.

17. See population statistics in *Eastern Europe and the Commonwealth of Independent States 1994*, pp. 182–195.

18. In the beginning of the conflict with the Bosnian Serbs, the Bosnian Muslims were aided by both the Bosnian Croats and the new state of Croatia. However, this alliance did not last. The Bosnian Muslims and their former allies, the Bosnian Croats and Croatian forces from the state of Croatia, turned their weapons against each other in May 1993 further aggravating the situation in Central Bosnia-Herzegovina. It was not until early 1994 that, under pressure from the United States, Croatians and Bosnians struck an uneasy alliance in the form of a confederation. As a result of peace talks held in Washington D.C. in late February 1994, Bosnian Croats and Bosnian Muslims signed two documents, the Framework Agreement Establishing a Federation in the Areas of the Republic of Bosnia and Herzegovina with a majority Bosniac and Croat Population, and the Outline of a Preliminary Agreement for the Confederation between the Republic of Croatia and the Federation. Subsequently, on 10 May 1994 an agreement for establishing a Bosniac-Croat Confederation was reached; UNPROFOR was closely involved in the implementation of all its military aspects.

19. The Security Council, by means of Resolution 713 adopted on 25 September 1991, decided "... under Chapter VII of the UN Charter, that all States shall, for the purposes of establishing peace and stability in Yugoslavia, immediately implement a general and complete embargo on all deliveries of weapons and military equipment to Yugoslavia ... ," UN Doc. S/RES/713/1991.

20. International humanitarian law historically has been conceived to provide protection for the victims of international armed conflicts. Human rights law, on the other hand, has been concerned with the protection of human rights in situations of peace. These systems of protection have developed and functioned under different institutional "umbrellas"; humanitarian law under the International Committee of the Red Cross (ICRC) and human rights law under the United Nations and various specialized and regional agencies. Applicable in times of war (humanitarian law) and of peace (human rights), both laws are converging. Human rights are increasingly focusing on the protec-

tion of individuals in situations of international and internal armed conflicts, and international humanitarian law is becoming more and more concerned with the regulation of intrastate behaviour in violent situations. See particularly Meron, Theodor. "Human Rights and Humanitarian Law: Growing Convergence." In: *Human Rights in Internal Strife: Their International Protection*. Cambridge: Grotius, 1987, pp. 1–172.

21. *UNHCR Information Notes on Former Yugoslavia No. 11/93*. Geneva: UNHCR, 1993; and *UNHCR Briefing Kit*. Geneva: UNHCR, January 1995.

22. As lead agency, UNHCR has been coordinating the efforts of UN agencies operating in the territory, such as UNHCR itself, the United Nations' Children Fund (UNICEF), the World Health Organization (WHO), the World Food Programme (WFP), as well as many NGOs. The International Commission of the Red Cross also has been operating in former Yugoslavia. After its creation in 1992, the UN Department of Humanitarian Affairs has been assisting UNHCR in its task.

23. According to UNHCR, "[i]nitially, UNHCR's mandate was limited to people outside their country of origin.... In recent years, moreover, the General Assembly and the Secretary-General have increasingly frequently called on UNHCR to protect or assist particular groups of internally displaced people who have not crossed an international border but are in a refugee-like situation inside their country of origin." UNHCR, *The State of the World's Refugees*, p. 170.

24. *The United Nations and the Situation in the Former Yugoslavia*. New York: UN Department of Public Information, 15 March 1994, p. 1.

25. While the EC offered its "good offices" to find a peaceful settlement, the EC itself and some individual members, notably Germany, recognized the independence of Slovenia and Croatia.

26. *Resolution 743*, 21 February 1992, UN Doc. S/RES/743/1992 approving the *Further Report of the Secretary-General Pursuant to Security Council Resolution 721 (1991)*, 15 February 1992, UN Doc. S/23592 established UNPROFOR for an initial period of 12 months with the following mandate: to ensure that United Nations Protected Areas (UNPAs) were demilitarized through the withdrawal or disbandment of all armed forces in them, and that all residents in UNPAs were protected from fear of armed attack. In order to carry out its mandate, UNPROFOR was authorized to control access to UNPAs, and with a view to ensure non-discrimination and protection of human rights, to monitor the functioning of the local police. Later, by means of *Resolution 762*, 30 June 1992, UN Doc. S/RES/762/1992, UNPROFOR's mandate was enlarged to comprise the undertaking of monitoring functions in the "pink zones"—certain areas of Croatia controlled by the Yugoslav People's Army and largely populated by Serbs, but outside the agreed UNPAs' boundaries.

27. The Vance Plan, which included a cease-fire in Croatia, the establishment of the United Nations Protected Areas, and the deployment of UNPROFOR, was brokered by Cyrus Vance, the UN special envoy for former Yugoslavia.

28. On 31 March 1995, approving the report of the Secretary-General of 22 March 1995, UN Doc. S/1995/222 and Corr. 1, the Security Council decided to split UNPROFOR's operations in Croatia, Bosnia-Herzegovina, and Macedonia into three different peacekeeping operations: the United Nations Confidence Restoration Operation in Croatia (UNCRO) by means of Resolution 981, UN Doc. S/981/1995; the United Nations Protection Force in Bosnia-Herzegovina (UNPROFOR) by means of Resolution 982, UN Doc. S/982/1995; and the United Nations Preventive Deployment Force (UNPREDEP) by means of Resolution 983, UN Doc. S/983/1995. Their respective mandates were described in the above-mentioned report of the Secretary-General and extended until 30 November 1995.

29. Also taking part in the International Conference on the Former Yugoslavia were the Conference on Security and Cooperation in Europe (CSCE) and the Organization of the Islamic Conference (OIC). Conceived to remain operational until a final settlement of the conflict has been reached, the International Conference on Former Yugoslavia

is managed by the Steering Committee and has six working groups, an Arbitration Commission, and a Secretariat. The Steering Committee was co-chaired by Cyrus Vance, representative of the Secretary-General of the United Nations, and Lord Owen, representative of the presidency of the European Community. (At the time of the writing of this chapter, Cyrus Vance had left the Steering Committee and Thorvald Stoltenberg had taken his place.) As a result of the conference, the Vance/Owen Peace Plan for Bosnia-Herzegovina was initially agreed to by the parties in the conflict in October 1992, but was subsequently rejected by the Bosnian Serb Assembly. Under the plan, Bosnia-Herzegovina would have become a decentralized state divided into 10 largely autonomous provinces, three for each major ethnic group—Muslims, Serbs, and Croats. Sarajevo province would have remained a mixed community. Later, other plans (HMS Invincible package, the European Union Action Plan) were proposed under the framework of the International Conference, but the parties to the conflict were unable to reach any agreement; at the time of writing hostilities were ongoing in the former Yugoslavia.

30. UNPAs in Croatia are areas in which Croatian Serbs constitute the majority or the substantial minority of the population and where tensions have led to conflict. Three areas declared UNPAs by the Security Council were eastern Slavonia, western Slavonia, and Krajina.

31. *Resolution 776*, 14 September 1992, UN Doc. S/RES/776/1992, approving the *Report of the Secretary-General on the Situation in Bosnia and Herzegovina*, 10 September 1992, UN Doc. S/24540, authorized UNPROFOR's operation in Bosnia-Herzegovina under the mandate to support the UNHCR efforts to deliver humanitarian relief throughout the Bosnian territory, and in particular to provide protection at UNHCR's request, where and when UNHCR considered such protection necessary.

32. In 1993, several monitors were deployed in Zagreb, Croatia, in a field operation established by the Centre for Human Rights. For a description of the scope and character of this field operation, see the sixth *Report on the Situation of Human Rights in the Territory of Former Yugoslavia* submitted by the special rapporteur of the Commission on Human Rights, 19 May 1993, UN Doc. E/CN.4/1994/4, 1–9.

33. For a vivid description of the situation, see UNHCR. "A Week in Bosnia-Herzegovina in the Year 1992—Excerpts from UNHCR Situation Reports: 19–25 June 1993." In: UNHCR. *The State of the World's Refugees*, 82.

34. *Resolution 819*, 16 April 1993, UN Doc. S/RES/819/1993, declares Srebrenica and its surroundings a "safe area." *Resolution 824*, 6 May 1993, UN Doc. S/RES/824/1993, expanded the "safe areas" to include the capital of Bosnia-Herzegovina, Sarajevo, and such other threatened areas, in particular the towns of Tuzla, Zepa, Gorazde, and Bihac.

35. Attempting to refine the concept of safe zone, the Secretary-General, in his Report of 9 May 1994 to the Security Council, considered the safe area concept as a temporary mechanism by which some vulnerable populations could be protected pending a comprehensive negotiated political settlement for the conflict. Furthermore, safe areas are declared as such so people can be protected. The declaration of safe areas is not intended to defend territory and UNPROFOR is not to be considered as part of the conflict.

36. Resolutions 713 (1991), 721 (1991), 724 (1991), 727 (1992), 740 (1992), 743 (1992), 749 (1992), 752 (1992), 757 (1992), 758 (1992), 760 (1992), 762 (1992), 764 (1992), 769 (1992), 770 (1992), 771 (1992), 787 (1992).

37. In order to ensure compliance with the "no-fly zone" established in the air space of Bosnia-Herzegovina (Resolution 781, 9 October 1992, UN Doc. S/RES/781/1992), the Security Council, by means of Resolution 816, 31 March 1993, UN Doc. S/RES/816/1993, authorized, under Chapter VII of the UN Charter, NATO (member states, acting nationally or through regional arrangements) to take the necessary military measures (air strikes). France, the Netherlands, Turkey, the United Kingdom, and the United States offered to take part in the operation.

Caught in the Crossfire

38. UNPROFOR's mandate concerning Bosnia-Herzegovina was further extended by Resolution 836, 4 June 1993, UN Doc. S/RES/836/1993, also under Chapter VII of the UN Charter, "... to enable it, in the safe areas referred to in Resolution 824 (1993), to deter attacks against the safe areas, to monitor the cease-fire, to promote the withdrawal of military or paramilitary units other than those of the Government of the Republic of Bosnia and Herzegovina and to occupy some key points on the ground, in addition to participating in the delivery of humanitarian relief to the population as provided for in Resolution 776 (1992) of 14 September 1992." UNPROFOR was also authorized, "... acting in self-defence, to take the necessary measures, through the use of force, in reply to bombardments against the safe areas by any of the parties or to armed incursion into them or in the event of any deliberate obstruction to the freedom of movement of UNPROFOR or of protected humanitarian convoys."

39. The special rapporteur was appointed to investigate allegations of human rights violations, to make recommendations for ending such violations, and to gather information on possible human rights violations which may constitute war crimes. See *Resolution 1992/S-1/1* adopted by the UN Commission on Human Rights, Geneva, Switzerland.

40. *Report on the Situation of Human Rights in the Territory of the Former Yugoslavia* submitted by Tadeusz Mazowiecki, special rapporteur of the Commission on Human Rights, 28 August 1992, UN Doc. E/CN.4/1992/S-1/9, 1–18.

41. See follow-up to recommendation of a special rapporteur, Commission on Human Rights, *Resolutions 1992/S-2/1* and *1993/7*.

42. *Resolution 780*, 6 October 1992, UN Doc. S/RES/780/1992. In this resolution, as well as in *Resolution 764*, 13 July 1992, UN Doc. S/RES/764/1992, and further in *Resolution 808*, 25 February 1993, UN Doc.S/RES/808/1993, the Security Council affirms that all parties are bound to comply with the obligations in international humanitarian law and in particular the Geneva Conventions of 12 August 1949.

43. Convention for the Amelioration of the Condition of the Wounded and Sick in Armed Forces in the Field (Geneva Convention I), 12 August 1949, 6 UST 3114, TIAS no. 3362, 75 United Nations Treaty Series (UNTS) 31; Convention for the Amelioration of the Condition of the Wounded, Sick, and Shipwrecked Members of the Armed Forces at Sea (Geneva Convention II), 12 August 1949, 6 UST 3217, TIAS no. 3363, 75 UNTS 85; Convention Relative to the Treatment of Prisoners of War (Geneva Convention III), 12 August 1949, 6 UST 3516, TIAS no. 3365 UNTS 287.

44. The Security Council adopted Resolution 808, 25 February 1992, UN Doc. S/RES/808/1992, establishing the ad hoc International Tribunal, based on the recommendation of the Commission of Experts (see the report of the Commission of Experts, UN Doc. S/25274) and on several reports of violations of international humanitarian law (see the report of the European Community investigative mission into the· treatment of Muslim women in the former Yugoslavia, UN Doc. S/25240—annex I of Resolution 808, 22 February 1993, UN Doc. S/RES/808/1993; the report of the committee of jurists submitted by France, UN Doc. S/RES/25266; the report of the commission of jurists submitted by Italy, UN Doc. S/25300; and the report transmitted by the permanent representative of Sweden on behalf of the chairman-in-office of the Conference on Security and Cooperation in Europe (CSCE), UN Doc. S/25307). Recently the tribunal agreed to take over genocide accusations against Bosnian Serb leaders for possible prosecution. Prosecutors expect to indict the Bosnian Serbian president, Radovan Karadzic; his military commander; and his former secret police chief by the end of the year. See *International Herald Tribune* (17 May 1995): 1 and 9.

45. See UNHCR, *The State of the World's Refugees*, p. 79.

46. The UN Volunteers team was comprised of three lawyers (protection officers), four social workers, four logistics officers, six radio operators, and one UNV programme officer, who was to provide all the necessary support for all the UN Volunteers.

47. O'Donnell, Frank. *UNV/HRU Report on Mission to Croatia and Bosnia-Herzegovina*, 30 April 1993. O'Donnell was then the chief of UNV's Humanitarian Relief Unit.

48. O'Donnell, *UNV/HRU Mission Report to Croatia.*
49. The Contact Group, composed of the foreign ministers of France, Germany, the Russian Federation, the United Kingdom, the United States, the European Union Commissioner for Foreign Affairs and the two co-chairmen of the Steering Committee, was established in April 1994 and also has been devoted to finding a peaceful solution to the former Yugoslav conflict. See *United Nations Peace-Keeping—Information Notes.* New York: United Nations, 1995, p. 93.
50. This incident was reported in O'Donnell, *UNV/HRU Mission Report to Croatia.*
51. Excerpts from the opening address of Sadako Ogata, United Nations High Commissioner for Refugees, at the Conflict and Humanitarian Action Conference held on 22–23 October 1993 at Woodrow Wilson School of Public and International Affairs, Princeton University, USA.
52. *UN information document—Notes for Speakers, Human Rights.* New York: UN, 1993, p. 36.
53. UNHCR, *The State of the World's Refugees*, p. 91.
54. Preamble to the Charter of the United Nations signed on 26 June 1945 (San Francisco, USA). See Goodrich, Leland, Eduard Hambuo, and Anne Patricia Simons. *Charter of the United Nations—Commentary and Documents.* New York and London: Columbia University Press, 1969, pp. 1–732.
55. At the time of writing, the Security Council, responding to European concerns, has been holding closed-door sessions to review the UN's role in the former Yugoslavia. UN Secretary-General Boutros Boutros-Ghali outlined four alternatives facing the organization: a broadened mandate; maintenance of the 22,000 peacekeeping troops currently stationed in the region; total withdrawing all troops; or reduction of troop levels.

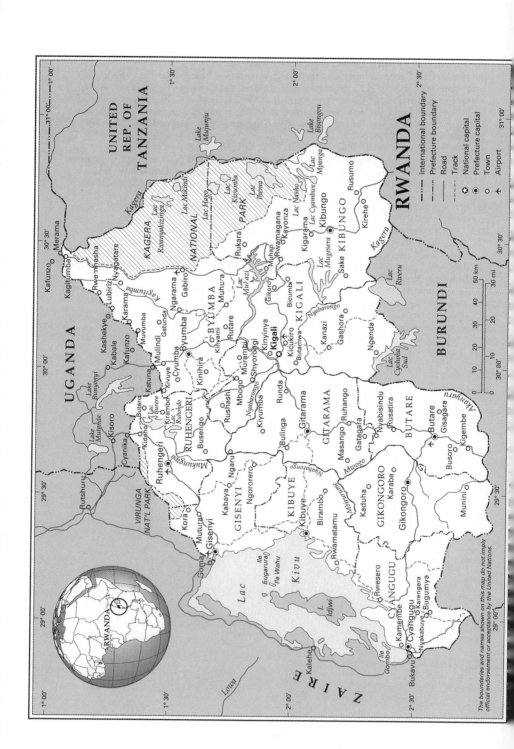

6

BACK FROM RWANDA: CONFRONTING THE AFTERMATH OF GENOCIDE

Stephen P. Kinloch

RWANDA IS A paradigm of the kind of situation the United Nations should be prepared to face in the future. It dramatically highlights the need for the UN organization to be able to act extremely quickly to protect human rights and provide emergency humanitarian assistance to threatened civilians. According to UN Secretary-General Boutros Boutros-Ghali: "The delay in reaction by the international community to the genocide in Rwanda has demonstrated graphically its extreme inadequacy to respond urgently with prompt and decisive action to humanitarian crisis entwined with armed conflict."[1]

From the point of view of a UN Volunteer who served in Rwanda as a Field Officer with the UN High Commissioner for Refugees (UNHCR), this contribution sets out lessons that can be drawn from the Rwandan tragedy. The crisis situation faced by the United Nations in Rwanda, the precedent created by the French-led Turquoise Operation, and, most of

Stephen P. Kinloch is a French and British national born in 1964. A doctoral candidate at the Graduate Institute of International Studies in Geneva, he is currently writing a dissertation on the idea of a UN permanent international military volunteer force. A UN Volunteer Field Officer with the United Nations High Commissioner for Refugees in Rwanda from August to October 1994, he also volunteered for UN peacekeeping operations in Cambodia, former Yugoslavia, and Somalia.

all, the personal experience of seeing the suffering of Rwandans constitute a basis for wider reflection on the future of the UN organization's intervention capability.

FROM GENESIS TO APOCALYPSE

For a foreigner freshly disembarked from a French/German Transall aircraft onto the tarmac of Kigali airport on 1 August 1994, nothing could be more striking than the contrast between the surrounding tranquil beauty and quietness of the hilly capital, and the dreadful pictures of Rwanda in the mind of the rest of the world. Only the strange and mournful atmosphere of a ghost city, reinforced by the scars of the recent fighting and looting on public buildings, private houses, and vehicles on the street, indicated to me that a disaster beyond imagination had occurred in the "Land of the Thousand Hills."

Rwanda is such a delightful country that, according to local legends, God spends his days busy in the world, but goes back to Rwanda to sleep every night. Known as the country of the "everlasting spring," it has been a relatively prosperous African state, benefiting from a high-altitude climate and fertile land. The importance to the economy of the major crops, tea, coffee, and bananas, is reflected in the fact that 90 per cent of the population lives on "rugos," small family farms. Every available piece of land is carefully cultivated.[2]

Before going to Rwanda I did not know much about the history of the country. Later, while in Rwanda, I happened to come across a schoolbook in what remained of a public library looted during the crisis. According to the book, the country, first inhabited by Batwas Pigmies, was agriculturally developed by Hutu farmers of Bantu origin and later dominated by Tutsis, who had emigrated from the mid-Nile region. Whether or not these accounts are factual, they have been used largely to legitimize colonial policies based on ethnic discrimination as a means to establish foreign domination over the country. Ethnic cleavages and competition for power have remained ever since they began to be manipulated by colonial powers, and have fostered increased tensions.[3]

The cyclic ethnic violence recently experienced by Rwanda started in 1959 when widespread massacres provoked the departure and exile of about 150,000 Tutsis to Uganda and Congo. The slaughter was described at the time as the most horrible and systematic massacre since the extermination of the Jews by the Nazis.[4] After the legislative elections and the referendum on monarchy in September 1961, the Hutu-led military coup of Gregoire Kayibanda and consecutive ethnic clashes were followed by a coup in 1974, led by Hutu General Juvenal Habyarimana, who then became President of Rwanda.

On April 6, 1994, a plane carrying the presidents of Rwanda and Burundi was shot down. This fatal crash was the starting point of a wave of violence and systematic massacres of Tutsis and politically moderate Hutus in Kigali[5] and other parts of the country with the active participation of the *interahamwe* militia.[6] These events prompted the seizure of power by the rebel Rwandan Patriotic Front (RPF) at the beginning of July 1994.

The consequences of the tragedy were appalling: more than 500,000 Rwandans perished between April and July 1994 in one of the most dreadful genocides in recent history. This would be equivalent to 2 million to 4 million deaths in France, 4 million to 8 million in Bangladesh, 5 million to 10 million in Brazil, or 9 million to 18 million in the United States.[7] An estimated 2.5 million refugees fled to neighbouring countries—Burundi, Tanzania, and Zaire—in a massive population exodus of biblical dimensions. Millions were affected by food shortages inside Rwanda. More than half a million internally displaced persons moved to the "safe humanitarian zone" (Turquoise Zone) in the southwest of Rwanda. One can only wonder how a country such as Rwanda could become the theatre of such an apocalyptic tragedy.

WHEN THE INTERNATIONAL COMMUNITY FAILS TO APPEAR

One recent political cartoon worth more than a thousand academic speeches pictured a UN military officer pointing, during a briefing, to four different cases of UN involvement. In these cases, the UN appeared, did something, and failed (Somalia); did something and appeared to fail (Cambodia); appeared to do something and appeared to fail (Bosnia). Finally, in Rwanda, the UN simply failed to appear.[8]

In Rwanda, the United Nations not only did not fulfill its mission, but, in my view, it withdrew when it was most needed. Finally, it was not able to intervene when it was urgently requested to do so. Despite the massive effort of the international community to alleviate the suffering of the Rwandan people, no humanitarian crisis has so clearly pinpointed the limitations of the United Nations system's capacity to prevent disaster, or to respond in time to a disaster on such a scale. The UN Secretary-General acknowledged, "We all must recognize that, in this respect, we have failed in our response to the agony of Rwanda, and thus have acquiesced in the continued loss of human lives."[9] The story of recent UN involvement, with the United Nations Observer Mission Uganda-Rwanda (UNOMUR),[10] United Nations Assistance Mission in Rwanda (UNAMIR I and UNAMIR II), and eventually the Turquoise Operation, can therefore be described as a series of lost opportunities. Its cost was extremely high in terms of a failed relief effort, and, much worse, in terms of human life.

Where is the UN?

The events following the death of the President of Rwanda on 6 April 1994, took everyone by surprise, since earlier ongoing negotiations had given some reasons for hope.[11] The Arusha peace talks had been successfully concluded in August 1993 with the signing of a comprehensive peace agreement in Rwanda that called for, among other measures, repatriation of refugees, demobilization and reintegration of the armed forces, and a democratically elected Rwandan government. To this end, the first United Nations Assistance Mission in Rwanda (UNAMIR I) was created in October 1993.

However, UNAMIR I, which was to be composed of 2,519 troops from 23 countries, completely failed. Not only was it never able to interpose itself between the government's Rwandan Army Forces (RAF) and the rebel Rwandan Patriotic Front, but it could not prevent or respond to the genocide[12] since its original mandate did not allow it take action when the carnage started.[13] On 5 April 1994, the Security Council expressed its concern at the delays in the implementation of the peace accords and over the deterioration of the security situation in the country.[14] The Security Council decided to extend the mandate of UNAMIR I up to the end of July 1994. But after 10 UNAMIR Belgian soldiers were killed, Belgium withdrew its battalion while several UN local personnel were massacred. In early April 1994, the evacuation of humanitarian personnel was recommended.

The Security Council was given the choice among: massively reinforcing the weakened UNAMIR I and giving it powers under Chapter VII[15] of the Charter to avert combat and massacres; reducing UNAMIR I to 270 troops, rendering the relief effort impossible; and withdrawing completely. The Security Council did not hesitate to decide, on 21 April, for the second alternative,[16] reducing UNAMIR in size and making it impotent. However, given the scale of the massacres and of the refugee flows, the UN Security Council soon had to revise its position and launch a new operation.

UN or not UN

The second United Nations Assistance Mission in Rwanda (UNAMIR II) was formally created in mid-May 1994. A force of 5,500 troops was authorized by the Security Council to protect refugees and facilitate the delivery of humanitarian aid.[17] However, a week after the Security Council's action, only Ghana had formally committed troops for Rwanda. By June, three countries—Ghana, Senegal, and Ethiopia—had made firm commitments to supply 2,200 troops. However, none of the governments possessing the necessary troops had offered to provide fully trained and equipped military units.[18] As a result, the deployment of UNAMIR II was postponed, causing what the Secretary-General described as "deplorable delays."[19]

The UN was left with only one option: to allow France, which had taken the initiative to lead the multinational Turquoise Operation three months after the start of the massacres, to create a "safe humanitarian zone" in south-western Rwanda to prevent a further exodus of Rwandans to Zaire and Burundi. Authorized in June under Chapter VII of the Charter, the multinational Turquoise Operation force was composed of a total of 2,500 troops; the French soldiers were assisted by military units of seven other countries. The operation was intended to assure security and protection of displaced persons and civilians in Rwanda until the full deployment of UNAMIR II.[20] UNAMIR troops were eventually deployed gradually in the Turquoise Zone after the French departure of 22 August 1994.[21]

With 2,500 troops and 5,000 tons of equipment, Turquoise Operation, although late and limited in time, yielded significant results in addition to the protection it gave to displaced persons in the south-western Turquoise Zone.[22] In Goma, hundreds of aircraft delivered more than 10,000 tons of humanitarian relief supplies. In Cyangugu and Goma, major medical assistance was provided. Also, tens of thousands of bodies were buried. The French troops, asked by the UN to remain in Rwanda as long as UNAMIR II remained undeployed, left a month later.[23]

The Turquoise Operation was extremely controversial and heavily criticized, given France's past involvement in Rwanda, in particular its well-known support to the Hutu-led former government.[24] However, humanitarian aid workers such as Béatrice d'Ervau and Laure Marine from Action Internationale Contre la Faim generally acknowledged that "even if France was not the most appropriate country to intervene in Rwanda because of its past, it was the only one to have expressed the desire to do so and be prepared to lend assistance."[25] Although it was controversial, the French-led Turquoise Operation demonstrated what could be accomplished on short notice with a limited but highly professional and motivated humanitarian force.

IN THE EYE OF THE STORM

The Rwandan crisis constituted a tremendous challenge for all organizations in the field. During a single year, the international community had to respond to all phases of the continuum from crisis to rehabilitation. However, because of the security situation and the lack of military protection, most of the staff of UN and non-governmental organizations (NGOs) had been evacuated from Rwanda shortly after 6 April 1994,[26] including 16 United Nations Volunteers.[27] The UN Volunteers were temporarily moved to Nairobi before being redeployed with other UN agencies that established bases in strategic locations in countries bordering Rwanda to cope with the flow of refugees.[28] Nineteen additional UN Volunteers were urgently recruited in May 1994 to work with the United Nations High Commissioner for Refugees in Burundi, Zaire, and Tanzania; with the United Nations Children's Fund (UNICEF) at the border with Uganda and Rwanda; with the World Food Programme (WFP) and the United Nations Educational, Scientific and Cultural Organization (UNESCO) in Tanzania; and with the United Nations Rwanda Emergency Office (UNREO) in Kenya.[29] After the crisis, the first UN Volunteers to arrive in Rwanda landed in Kigali on 1 August 1994 and were assigned to work with UNHCR as field officers.

In the Field with UNHCR

Fax transmission of 29 July 1994. UNHCR. Emergency Preparedness and Response Section: "PLEASE NOTE THAT THE FOLLOWING UNVS WILL BE ARRIVING NAIROBI EITHER ON THE 31ST OF JULY OR 1ST AUGUST 1994. WE ARE UNABLE TO CONFIRM EXACT ETA[30] TO NAIROBI AS ALL UNVS ARE TRAVELLING FROM SOMALIA AND THERE IS AN INCIDENT OF FIGHTING NEAR THE EMBASSY THAT MAY DELAY THEIR ARRIVAL. THEY WILL HAVE TO TRAVEL ON SHORT NOTICE ON ANY AVAILABLE FLIGHT AS SOON AS THEY ARE ABLE TO DO SO." Five UN Volunteers who were willing to participate in the emergency operation, including me, were being transferred on a one-day notice from Mogadishu to Kigali. Although deployed within a fortnight, we, along with many relief workers and organizations, arrived too late. Three months after the massacres, hundreds of thousands of Rwandans had already died in Rwanda and in refugee camps outside the country. The worst had happened.

One can hardly imagine the responsibilities our mission involved, particularly in view of the consequences for the returnees that we transported or assisted. As in many other UN operations, the main difficulty for UN Volunteers operating in the field often was the lack of coordination inside the relief agency itself. In an emergency, the relief system should be even more organized than in normal conditions. In the field, however, this principle is often reversed, and emergency is unfortunately sometimes used as an excuse for inadequate management. Yet, the stressful working conditions of the relief workers were incredibly easy compared to the suffering of the Rwandans themselves, who walked with extreme dignity for miles and miles in a mass exodus to Tanzania, Burundi, or Zaire, out of fear of an atrocious death at home.

In early August, UNHCR did not have a single truck at its disposal in Rwanda. My first mission, therefore, was to drive to Tanzania to bring back a few trucks being used by an NGO operating in the Ngara camps at the border. Once I had passed through the suburbs of Kigali, I started to see people walking on the road, sometimes going north, but most of them fleeing south. Hundreds of people were on the move on foot or bicycle, clutching bags of flour, buckets, sleeping mats. There were children running behind their mothers, old women, exhausted men. The remains of individual tragedies were visible along the road: here flour spread on the ground; there an armchair or a bed too heavy to be carried farther; empty huts hurriedly built and just as quickly abandoned by people running from death. We could feel the tremendous suffering of these people. I was overwhelmed by a terrible feeling of powerlessness standing right in the face of disaster. At the same time, I felt ferocious rage and anger that such a situation had been allowed to happen, that so little had been done to prevent it.

The "Safe Haven"

Once we had gotten the trucks, my main mission consisted in setting up an office in the "safe humanitarian zone" (Turquoise Zone) in the southwest, where more than 350,000 Rwandans were living in camps in dreadful conditions. With very limited means, we were to start a process of voluntary "repatriation," i.e., an organized system of transporting people to their places of origin. It was believed that this would have its own psychological impact on those remaining in the camps by helping restore confidence.[31]

On the move again: internally displaced Rwandans boarding UNHCR trucks to depart from Gikongoro, in the Turquoise Zone, Rwanda, August 1994. Photo: UNV/Stephen P. Kinloch

Before the withdrawal of the French forces from the "safe haven" of the Turquoise Zone, the international community feared that thousands of Hutus might cross the border to take refuge in Zaire from fear of retaliation on the part of the Rwandan Patriotic Front.[32] Relief organizations feared catastrophic scenarios in which the refugee movement could even be larger than the one in Goma, where almost 1 million people had fled. Moreover, the September planting season was coming; since land was scarce in Rwanda, any peasant who had vacated his land for the planting season stood the chance of having it cultivated by others and possibly lost, which would lead to permanent conflict. On the one hand, UNHCR did not feel it was appropriate to openly encourage refugees to go back home because of the uncertainty over their future safety in Rwanda. On the other hand, UNHCR wanted to prevent more border crossings, to avoid creating another situation like that in Goma. The Rwandan army had agreed not to occupy the south-west as long as the situation remained unstable. A policy of re-establishing confidence in the south-west was therefore adopted, and it was decided to facilitate the return of those who spontaneously requested it.[33]

Such an enterprise was extremely delicate, given the uncertainty over safety in the rest of the country. Nobody knew the fate of those returning home. Horrible rumours were being spread in the camps by those who had undertaken the journey home and had come back. People who had taken refuge in the "safe humanitarian zone" did not feel secure anymore when the Turquoise Operation ceased. In fact, the UN troops soon demonstrated by their passive attitude that they would not protect civilians as the French had, and that it would not be long before the RPA soldiers (Rwandan Patriotic Army, formerly the Rwandan Patriotic Front) would enter the zone. When the new government's soldiers were eventually allowed by UNAMIR to do so, harassment and searches of civilians soon started in the camps.[34] Why then remain there? Some of those who had not yet fled to the borders dared to leave the Turquoise Zone.

We started transportation on 23 August on the basis of lists established by UN military observers. It was the day after the French troops' departure. With the precious assistance of the local staff, hard-working Tanzanian drivers, and a few trucks in rather bad condition, we managed to transport about 250 people a day to Kigali and other destinations along the way. This was, in fact, the very beginning of what would be later called the "Homeward Operation."[35] The nature and the scale of operations changed when the goal changed to transporting as many people as possible out of the camps before the imminent rainy season. With the Homeward Operation, the displaced persons were going to be transported from Gikongoro and Cyangugu, using all the transportation available, including that of UNAMIR, International Organization for Migration (IOM), and UNHCR.

The Kizi check point lay between the former Turquoise Zone and the rest of the country controlled by the government. There the returnees were searched and registered. Sometimes the search would take place under the rain, the heavy rain of Rwanda. The passengers in the trucks would have to spend the night on the spot if the search had not been carried out before dawn or if there had been an accident along the difficult road from Cyangugu, delaying the arrival of the convoy. The RPA officer was absolutely inflexible and would not authorize UNHCR to build a shelter. Therefore we would often come at night and supply these poor people, who had already undertaken a long and hazardous journey, with plastic sheeting, blankets, biscuits, and water.

*The human dimension of the tragedy: an old Rwandan man in Cyanika refugee
camp, south-west of Rwanda, 1995. Photo: UNV/Vanya Kewley*

The Last Checkpoint

One day, I was at the Kizi checkpoint at about 11 a.m. A long line of
trucks stood waiting. The returnees carried only a few personal belongings with them, sometimes packed in the basket called *agaseke* in which,
according to the Rwandan custom, the groom's family traditionally
puts presents for the bride at the time of the wedding. They were asked
to step out of the trucks and were searched extremely meticulously,
women, babies, and old people.

I talked with the Rwandan Patriotic Army officer at the registration
point for my report on whether returnees had been arrested, and, if
so, on what charges and where they would be taken. A person could be
arrested on the charge of "participation to the genocide" if two witnesses
were found to accuse the person. There was nobody to defend those
accused, except for the UNHCR field officer, who could only ensure that
the returnees were given the chance to explain themselves.

On my way back to the convoy, as I passed the long line of returnees
waiting to be registered by their new authorities, I noticed two British
soldiers talking to each other on the road. Coming closer, I heard one

asking in a very normal voice: "Where is everybody going? And ... what about the body?" "Which body?" I asked. "Over there!" they replied. I looked in the direction he was pointing and I saw a truck that had been deserted by its passengers. A corpse was, in fact, lying in the truck among a few bags and personal belongings. The soldiers, apparently scared by the risk of contamination, had not dared remove it, even though it was wrapped in a straw mat. The convoy would have to start off quickly to reach Kigali before dawn. "I'll take care of it," I said. "It" was an old lady who had suffered from dysentery and who had been too weak to stand the journey. I took her body in my car to a field nearby. It was my first burial.

In the afternoon of the same day, while I was still at Kizi checkpoint, I was summoned by a member of the local staff. A child had died in one of the convoys. I was taken to a woman carrying a baby on her back, according to the African custom. But the child's head was completely covered, giving a strange and sinister look to what would have normally been a charming and lively image. The woman seemed to be almost ashamed, lost. This had been her only child; he also had had dysentery, and had not survived the journey.

With the local staff member, I took the woman, still carrying her child, to the field nearby. We wrapped the small package in a mat. We dug close to the place were the old woman had been buried that morning. The woman did not cry or express anything. Her pain was unspeakable. She looked as if she could not understand what was happening. Several small children from the neighbourhood silently gathered around the freshly dug hole. Maybe they could also not understand what was going on, why this small human being, like them, was being wrapped in a mat, put in a hole, and covered with red soil. It was the most simple and striking ceremony I had ever experienced.

I accompanied the woman, who had remained silent, back to the convoy, and she boarded a truck, as if nothing had happened. I checked that all the trucks had left with their passengers in the direction of the transit centre. Then I took the UNHCR car and went back to Gikongoro, in the Turquoise Zone. Outside, nothing seemed changed. But everything looked unreal around me. The freshly cultivated field looked like a series of immense cemeteries, and the small, regular hills made with care by the peasants, as graves everywhere.

LOOKING AHEAD

Months later, I was in Geneva, buying roses for someone I loved. Beautiful, fresh, lively roses. The seller wrapped them into a white paper as he would usually do, but he also covered the opening at the top. What so disturbed me all of a sudden? I did not know, but I could not stand the sight of it. The image of the child at Kizi checkpoint, which had been buried deep in my mind, suddenly surfaced. I understood my reaction and removed the paper, so that the heads of the flowers could be seen.

How could one ever forget? What is unforgettable is the suffering of individual Rwandans, so often left out by the media, as it emphasizes pictures of mass graves, the expression "genocide," the somehow reassuring collectivization of death. Seeing the suffering of individual people gives the tragedy another dimension, a dimension that is not possible to neglect, ignore, or forget. At stake is the credibility of the United Nations, and also of its ideals. Solutions should be found to prevent such tragedies from happening again.[36]

UN Military Response

As disastrous as it may be, the tragedy of Rwanda could, paradoxically, offer some positive results if its lessons are learned and applied. One of the lessons of the international community's failure in Rwanda is that in certain circumstances humanitarian assistance cannot be provided without the protection of or the close cooperation with the military. A force must be able to go into operation very quickly on the ground. "A military intervention was needed at the very beginning and this just did not happen," said the secretary-general of *Médecins Sans Frontières* (Doctors Without Borders), who added: "A small contingent of soldiers, perhaps 2,000 or so, could have stopped the killings by protecting people in the churches and hospitals and securing a few areas in the country."[37] After Rwanda, the old idea of aid without protection or United Nations intervention is "scandalous if not absurd."[38]

The Turquoise Operation has demonstrated that, contrary to recent arguments,[39] there are instances where a relatively small, professional, well-trained, motivated, and readily available force can make a difference, at least in terms of saving lives. The UN's dependence on member states to contribute forces, often with insufficient training, language skills, or commitment, has resulted in deplorable consequences. According to the Secretary-General, "Our readiness and capacity for action has demonstrated to be inadequate at best, deplorable at worst, owing to the absence of collective political will."[40]

In Rwanda, as the Secretary-General has pointed out, the UN faced a situation different from those encountered in traditional peacekeeping operations during the Cold War: "We used to be involved in a classic war or international war. Suddenly we have something new, which is the failed state. No more government. Yugoslavia, Somalia, Rwanda: No more government."[41]

The difficulties encountered by the Secretary-General in securing the necessary troops highlighted as never before the limits of the UN's intervention capability. Under current procedures, two to three months can elapse between the Security Council authorization of a mission and its becoming operational in the field.[42] However, the main limitation the UN faces regarding intervention in crises has been the reluctance of member states to become involved where their direct interests are not at stake. Moreover, the UN has proven to be totally dependent not only on the political will of member states but on what Winston Churchill called "the ebb and flow of national politics." It is particularly significant that U.S. President Bill Clinton's new directive on peacekeeping,[43] by putting strict conditions on the participation of U.S. troops in international operations, played an important role in preventing the United States and in dissuading other countries from getting involved early in the Rwandan crisis.[44]

Even when the necessary troops were available, the UN suffered from a lack of credibility. One of the main factors of success in a military operation is the motivation of the troops and their willingness to take risks. Because of the strong domestic pressures exerted by public opinion and media at home, member states often are reluctant to suffer casualties in crisis operations. As a matter of fact, in Rwanda, as in Yugoslavia, the United Nations chose to make its priority the security of the UN force itself, not the security of the civilians it should have been protecting.[45] Peacekeepers are drawn from national contingents. "United Nations commanders and their staff have no say in the source of contingents and have to work with what they get," according to Lt. Gen. John Sanderson, the force commander of the UN operation in Cambodia.[46]

Using specially trained armed forces made up of individuals who volunteer for the job rather than national military contingents could be a way to overcome the problem. Creation of such a UN military volunteer force was eloquently described by Sir Brian Urquhart.[47] According to the former UN under-secretary-general for special political affairs, there is a need for a "... highly trained international volunteer force, willing if necessary to fight hard to break the cycle of violence at an early stage in low level but dangerous conflicts, especially ones involving irregular militias and groups."[48] Boutros-Ghali himself commented: "I am not against a foreign legion, but the problem is that we must obtain the agreement of the member states."[49]

In order to gain the acceptance of the member states, such a rapid deployment force should have its functions clearly defined in advance, and should be allowed to intervene only in specific cases where a limited emergency military operation is needed to protect human rights or provide humanitarian assistance in collapsed states or at the request of a state. A relatively small force could be used preventively to deter an aggressor, provided that a commitment to back up the force if necessary was clearly expressed by member states before the intervention. Given the current cost of UN military operations and the current financial situation of the world organization, innovative solutions should be found to create and maintain such a force, thereby avoiding the uncertainties of national contributions.[50]

Volunteerism and Humanitarian Relief

United Nations Volunteers was able to field experienced and motivated relief workers on very short notice as soon as the main UN agencies started operating again in Rwanda.[51] Had it been requested, it could have done so earlier. Presently UNV is still largely dependent on other UN agencies to deploy UN Volunteer specialists.[52] The question remains open whether, instead of waiting until an agency requests UN Volunteers to implement its own emergency programmes, UNV could respond earlier by quickly fielding UN Volunteers under UN auspices in the needed areas.[53] Another idea to increase UNV's readiness would be to keep a reserve UNV "brigade." The brigade, operating on standby at all times, could be tapped and pressed into action immediately.

The diversity of skills of UN Volunteer specialists makes them well-prepared to cope with the various necessities on the civilian side of operations of a crisis. In Rwanda, a few UN Volunteers who served as UNHCR field officers were nurses who used their expertise in emergency medical operations in addition to their tasks in logistics and protection. Some UN Volunteers, experienced in military matters, were able to effectively interact with the military side of the operation and with local authorities. The legal background of other UN Volunteers gave them the knowledge to deal efficiently with protection matters. Intensive joint training and rehearsals with UN military personnel before the mission are more essential than ever to prepare the volunteers to react and coordinate relief efforts as efficiently as possible in emergencies.

Because of their close contacts with the local population, their interest in community participation, and their experience in development projects, UN Volunteers can be natural bridges between crisis and development.[54] In Rwanda, one of the most shocking aspects of the humanitarian operation was the lack of links between the emergency operation, which included food, water, shelter, and transportation assistance, and the mid- or long-term development and reconstruction. It was particularly striking, to mention one example, to see the tea factories, most of which had been looted, remain unattended while tea crops were rotting in the fields. This was a disaster in itself because of the importance of tea in the Rwandan economy and because the manpower to rehabilitate the factory was readily available.[55]

The potential negative effects of the influx of basic emergency humanitarian assistance from the outside—such as increased dependence, the absence of a long-term development perspective, and lack of community-based initiatives—could be partly alleviated by deploying UN Volunteers to encourage community-based activities and to facilitate the recruitment and training of local volunteers. New approaches to humanitarian relief can be adopted on the basis of cooperation rather than assistance by strengthening local capacity.[56] Given the necessary resources, the UN Volunteers Programme can, with its long experience in development, be a supplier of very specific kinds of humanitarian assistance built on both specialized emergency response skills and skills for development.

Based on my own experience, I know that the UN Volunteers who transferred from Somalia to Rwanda did so not only because the transfer was requested, but because they did not feel useful or busy enough in the Mogadishu headquarters of the United Nations Operation in Somalia (UNOSOM). Whatever our original personal motivations for becoming a volunteer, we did not come to Rwanda for financial gain or for promotion within a bureaucracy, but to put all our energy in a mission we considered valuable. Volunteers can help improve the image of the UN, which is too often perceived as a stiff bureaucracy perpetuating the interests of a few civil servants pursuing career strategies. Saving as many lives as possible and easing people's pain is what UN Volunteers and so many other relief workers from different NGOs and UN agencies try to bear in mind every day in the field.

CONCLUSION

"Abandoning the Rwandan people to their fate would set a dangerous precedent, indicating that the international community tolerates indiscriminate warfare, killing and intolerance of minority groups," warned the president of the International Red Cross Committee in early May

1994.[57] What has happened could happen again. The Rwanda tragedy has ancient and well-known roots, which meant that current events were to some extent predictable. Once it became clear that intervention was required in order to save lives, could not the international community have acted more quickly?

If such crises are, in fact, new situations, should not the UN have new means at its disposal? Rwanda shows what should be avoided. But it also shows, in spite of the ambivalent character of the Turquoise Operation, what is possible. Since humanitarian assistance is in many instances impossible without military protection, the UN organization needs to increase its military preparedness and rapid deployment capacity. New solutions, such as the creation of a UN permanent military force, have to be found in order to overcome the reluctance of member states to get involved in conflicts where their direct interests are not at stake.

The considerable responsibilities given to UN Volunteers in the field and at country headquarters have already shown volunteers' contributions in Rwanda[58] and other peacekeeping and emergency operations to be impressive and significant. Volunteers have proved to be an appropriate instrument in humanitarian emergency operations. In view of the cost of UN operations—more than US$3.5 billion in 1993—the UN can truly benefit from the presence of volunteers in the field and at headquarters. Volunteers are a tremendous source of energy, motivation, and dedication, animated by the United Nations' own ideals.

Above all, what will never be forgotten by those of us who have been in Rwanda at the time of the crisis is the human dimension of the tragedy. One could easily identify with the victims, whether modest farmers or highly educated persons. The local staff, refugees, or displaced persons themselves sometimes held university degrees of higher level than the international personnel they were working with. People like you and me who had lost all their belongings, if not relatives, were gathered in camps, transported in trucks, and sometimes died during the journey.

For those who participated in the emergency relief effort "... the tragedy of Rwanda is almost impossible to comprehend unless you have been there, seen it, heard it, and smelt it. It is a tragedy not of some impersonal collective nouns—a nation, a million people, an ethnic group—but of individuals, mothers, fathers, little children."[59] In a country where hundreds of thousands of people died in horrible conditions, the death of a single child was still a disaster of immeasurable dimensions.

Few other experiences can more poignantly demonstrate that such situations should be avoided at all costs. This intimate knowledge of the tragedy can produce the necessary motivation and determination to look for solutions to prevent it from happening again. The Rwanda crisis could go a long way in teaching us how to answer the hard questions, and thus it could have far-reaching consequences, if its lessons are properly learned. Shall we let it be a lesson?

NOTES

1. *Report of the UN Secretary-General on the Situation in Rwanda*, 31 May 1994, UN Doc. S/1994/640.
2. At the heart of the Great Lakes region between central and eastern Africa, Rwanda is bordered by Uganda on the north, Tanzania on the east, Zaire on the west, and Burundi on the south. The population of 7.4 million is divided into three ethnic groups: Batutsis (14 per cent), Bahutus (85 per cent) and Batwas (1 per cent), who share the same customs and the Kinyarwanda language. French is also an official language. Rwanda is a relatively small territory of 26,340 square kilometres, the size of Brittany, but it has the highest population density in Africa, with 284.7 inhabitants per square kilometre as of 1991. See "Le Rwanda: Quand la Folie meurtrière Déclenche un Génocide." *DHA News* (May–August 1994): 15–17.
3. Although some Hutus had progressively been integrated into the ruling class under the Tutsi-dominated feudal system, the ethnic division was strengthened under the German protectorate, following Count Von Goetzen's exploration in 1896, and under the Belgian protectorate established after World War I. Plaut, Martin. "Rwanda—Looking Beyond the Slaughter." *The World Today* 50 (August–September 1994), no. 8–9: 149–153.
4. Goose, Stephen D. and Frank Smyth. "Arming Genocide in Rwanda." *Foreign Affairs* 73 (September–October 1994), no. 5: 88.
5. If the ethnic roots of the recent outbreak of violence and massacres cannot be ignored, neither should they be regarded as the sole and unique cause of the tragedy. The interests, interferences, and influence of foreign states after independence in 1962, and the internal politics and foreign policies of Rwanda, have among other factors played an important role in the drama. Neither were the recent massacres committed by only one ethnic group against another: "... thousands of Hutus have also been victims, massacred by those same death squads out of suspicion that they sympathized with the rebels or simply because they were not card-carrying members of Mr. Habyarimana's party, the National Republican Movement for Democracy and Development." Richburg, Keith B. "Rwanda Blood Lust: Not Just Tribal." *The International Herald Tribune* (16 May 1994): 7.
6. Name given to the special militia created by the president of Rwanda, Juvenal Habyarimana, following his coup.
7. *Report of the Secretary General on the Situation in Rwanda*, 31 May 1994, UN Doc. S/1994/640.
8. Political cartoon by MOIR, in the *Sydney Morning Herald*, 25 July 1994.
9. *Report of the UN Secretary-General on the Situation in Rwanda*, 31 May 1994, UN Doc. S/1994/640.
10. The resumption of hostilities between the armed forces of the government and the Rwandan Patriotic Front in the northern part of the country in early February 1993 prompted the Security Council to authorize, by its Resolution 846 of 22 June 1993, the establishment of the United Nations Observer Mission Uganda-Rwanda (UNOMUR) on the Uganda side of the common border, for an initial period of six months. See *The United Nations and the Situation in Rwanda*, Reference Paper. New York, United Nations, Department of Public Information, August 1994, p. 1.

11. See *The United Nations and the Situation in Rwanda*.
12. Dubrulle, Carole and Yves Kameli. "L'ONU en Panne d'Imagination." *Le Monde* (26 May 1994): 5.
13. *Report of the UN Secretary-General on the Situation in Rwanda*, 31 May 1994, UN Doc S/1994/640.
14. Resolution 909, 5 April 1994, UN Doc. S/RES/909/1994.
15. Enforcement actions are authorized under Chapter VII of the Charter of the United Nations. "Chapter VI 1/2" is an expression used to describe the peacekeeping practice elaborated at the time of the Cold War.
16. Resolution 912, 21 April 1994, UN Doc. S/RES/912/1994.
17. Resolution 918, May 17, 1994, UN Doc. S/RES/918/1994.
18. UN Press Release, SC/5973, 3 January 1995. See "A Dose of Honesty—Boutros-Ghali Admits Failure as UN Efforts to Broker Peace Come to Nought." *The Weekly Review* (3 June 1994): 34–35.
19. See "For the last two months I have tried to obtain from the different Member States their participation in the United Nations Force and I have not been able to obtain them." In: *Remarks of the Secretary-General outside the Security Council after the Formal Meeting on Rwanda—22 June at 1:45 P.M.*, Geneva, U.N. Information Service, 22 June 1994. See also *Report of the Secretary-General on the Situation in Rwanda*, UN Doc. S/1994/924, August 3, 1994, 5.
20. Troops from the following countries were participating in the operation: Senegal (243), Mauritania (10), Chad (132), Egypt (7), Congo (40), Guinea-Bissau (35), Nigeria (43). See "L'Intervention Française au Rwanda." *Raids* (October 1994), no. 101: 6–32.
21. See *Progress Report of the Secretary General on the United Nations Assistance Mission in Rwanda*. 6 October 1994 and 8 November 1994 (S/1994/1133 and S/1994/1344).
22. For the first time the French army established a command system to coordinate humanitarian aid, civilian affairs, and military operations by creating a Planification Cell and a Humanitarian and Civilian Affairs Cell.
23. Five hundred Ghanian UN soldiers were eventually positioned in the southwest of Gikongoro. These troops later were to be complemented after the French departure of 22 August 1994 by troops from Ghana (822), the United Kingdom (499), Canada (394), Ethiopia (271), as well as Malawi, Zambia, Zimbabwe and a logistical/medical Australian contingent.
24. The impartiality and neutrality of the force was questioned, in view of France's support to the former Hutu-led government and its alleged role in training the militia held responsible for the massacres. See Wonyu, Emmanuel. "Rwanda, ce que l'Histoire Retiendra." *Afrique 2000* (August 1994), no. 18: 27–30. Also Dowden, Richard. "French Press on with Rwanda Mission." *The Independent* (21 June 1994).
25. d'Ervau, Béatrice and Laure Marine. "The UN, Ineffectual and Inert." *Crosslines Global Report* 2 (July–October 1994), no. 4–5: 34.
26. It should be noted, however, that International Committee of the Red Cross (ICRC) and several *Médecins Sans Frontières* (MSF) volunteers remained in Kigali and in other cities of Rwanda during the entire emergency period. A small UN interagency team was dispatched to Kigali in mid-April to work in close cooperation with the United Nations peacekeeping forces to support field cooperation capacity and to conduct a quick-needs evaluation. See *Strengthening of the Coordination of Humanitarian and Disaster Relief Assistance of the United Nations, Including Special Economic Assistance: International Decade for Natural Disaster Reduction*, General Assembly, 49th Session, Economic and Social Council, Substantive Session of 1994, UN Doc. A/49/177 & E/1994/80, 21 June 1994. However, the UN Department for Humanitarian Affairs (DHA) office and the recently created United Nations Rwanda Emergency Office (UNREO) were not re-opened in Kigali before the end of July 1994. See "Operational Coordination of Humanitarian Assistance in Rwanda." *DHA News* (May–August 1994): 28–29.

27. The emergency humanitarian involvement of the United Nations Volunteer (UNV) programme started as early as July 1993, after almost 10 years of continuous UNV presence and activity in the country. By 6 April 16 UN Volunteers were operating in Rwanda with UNHCR logisticians, UNICEF nutritionists, and WHO epidemiologists. A programme of 50 UN Volunteers working for the reintegration of demobilized soldiers and the facilitation of community participation in post-war projects had been prepared in the context of the Round-Table for Humanitarian Assistance and Reconstruction organized by the United Nations Development Programme (UNDP) scheduled for February 1994. The conference did not meet, mainly due to the reluctance of the contributing countries to support the effort. *UNV Activities and UN Agency Operations within the Context of the Rwanda Crisis (as of 1 September 1994)*. Geneva: United Nations Volunteers, September 1994, p. 8.

28. A July appeal for US$434.8 million to cover emergency and rehabilitation needs was launched by the Secretary-General, and by early September, US$137 million had been pledged, in addition to US$200 million in food, medicine, and logistical aid. UNHCR, WFP, UNICEF, other agencies, and numerous NGOs had already started to shift resources in coordination with DHA, the main objective being to provide the flood of refugees with basic food and non-food humanitarian aid. At the end of July 1994, the UNV programme was confronted with a sudden and exponential demand for UN Volunteer specialists. The 22 July Consolidated Appeal for the Persons Affected by the Crisis in Rwanda, included a UNV appeal for $894,000 for the deployment of 43 UN Volunteers. By 1 September, 8 UN Volunteers were already in the field and 122 UN Volunteers were to be posted in different UN agencies operating in Rwanda or neighbouring countries, such as DHA, WFP, UNHCR, UNESCO, UNICEF, IOM, UNHCR, UNDP/OPS, or ICAO, pending availability of financing.

29. Twenty in Zaire and Tanzania with UNHCR, 1 at the border with Uganda and Rwanda with UNICEF, 3 in Tanzania with WFP and UNESCO, and 1 in Kenya with UNREO.

30. "ETA" stands for estimated time of arrival.

31. Other duties included the monitoring of the humanitarian situation in the camps, human rights monitoring at the border between the Turquoise Zone and the rest of the country, and logistics for the supply of basic humanitarian aid such as blankets, plastic sheeting, food, etc.

32. The Rwandan Patriotic Front (RPF) became the Rwandan Patriotic Army (RPA).

33. *Interim Report of the Secretary General on the United Nations Assistance Mission in Rwanda*. UN Doc. S/1994/1113, 6 October 1994.

34. The UNAMIR mandate to "... contribute to the security and protection of displaced persons, refugees and civilians at risk in Rwanda including through the establishment and maintenance, where feasible, of secure humanitarian areas ..." was reaffirmed in November 1994. Cf. Draft Resolution S/1994/1360, Press Release SC/5956, 30 November 1994. However, after the departure of the French troops from the Turquoise Zone, several incidents made it clear that the local civilian population was no longer protected, in spite of the UN military presence. Under the pressure of the new government, and contrary to promises made earlier by UNAMIR to the population, I witnessed the arrival of Rwandan Patriotic Army soldiers who had been allowed to enter the "safe haven," first without weapons. This was to have tragic consequences, as was demonstrated by the massacre of 23 April 1995, in which thousands of Hutu refugees were killed in Kibeho camp. See "2,000 Hutu Refugees are killed in Rwandan Massacre, UN Says." *The International Herald Tribune* (24 April 1995): 1 and 9. See also "High Commissioner Condemns Brutality in Rwanda." *UNHCR Update on Rwanda* (24 April 1995).

35. Later, The Rwandan government, together with UNAMIR, UNHCR, IOM, and UNREO, devised a plan called "Operation Retour" (Homeward Operation) to transport internally displaced persons from camps in Gikongoro to their homes in the prefectures of Butare, Gitarama, Kigali, and Kibungo.

36. See Minear, Larry. "Human Values Are at Stake in Rwanda." *The Christian Science Monitor* (28 October 1994): 19.
37. "Doctors Cannot Stop Genocide." *Crosslines Global Report* 2 (July–October 1994), no. 4–5: 15.
38. See Heuze, Marie. "No Aid Without Protection: An International Responsibility." *Crosslines Global Report* 2 (July–October 1994), no. 4–5: 28.
39. See Hillen, John F. III. "Policing the New World Order: The Operational Utility of a Permanent U.N. Army." *Strategic Review* 22 (Spring 1994), no. 2: 54–62.
40. *Report of the Secretary-General on the Situation in Rwanda.* UN Doc. S/1994/640, 31 May 1994.
41. "Boutros-Ghali Speaks Out." *Time* (1 August 1994): 19.
42. Boutros-Ghali, Boutros. "Empowering the United Nations." *Foreign Affairs* 71 (Winter 1992/1993), no. 4: 92.
43. Presidential Decision Directive 25, following the United States' setbacks in Somalia and Haiti.
44. Sciolino, Elaine. "The Peacekeeping Front: Clinton is Pulling Back." *The International Herald Tribune* (7–8 May 1994): 3. See also Pringle, Peter. "America Hampers Dispatch of Extra UN Troops for Rwanda." *The Independent* (18 May 1994); and Dowden, Richard. "Don't Blame the UN for an American Mess." *The Independent* (18 May 1994).
45. "Soldiers exist to fight and, if necessary to die. That is the contract a soldier undertakes. The democracies, not to speak of the United Nations, no longer seem to take this very seriously." Pfaff, William. "The Death of an Ideal Darkens Europe." *The International Herald Tribune* (1 December 1994).
46. Lt. General John Sanderson, *International Humanitarian Law and the Role of Military Establishments*, Speech to Australian Red Cross Regional Conference. Canberra: Australian Defense Studies Centre, 12–14 December 1994, p. 17.
47. "Time has come when governments should consider establishing a separate and distinctive United Nations Humanitarian Security Police." In: Childers, Erskine and Brian Urquhart. *Renewing the United Nations System.* Uppsala: Dag Hammarskjöld Foundation, 1994, p. 118. See also Urquhart, Brian. "For a UN Volunteer Force." *The New York Review of Books* 40 (15 July 1994) no. 11: 3–4.
48. *Ibid.*, p. 3.
49. *Transcript of Press Conference by the Secretary-General Boutros Boutros-Ghali Held at Headquarters on 5 January 1995*, UN Press Release SG/SM/5518, 5 January 1995, p. 5.
50. "I believe that it is desirable in the long term that the United Nations develop such a capacity, but it would be folly to attempt to do so at the present time when the Organization is resource-starved and hard pressed to handle the less demanding peace-keeping responsibilities entrusted to it." *Supplement to the Agenda for Peace: Position Paper of the Secretary-General on the Occasion of the Fiftieth Anniversary of the United Nations.* UN Doc. A/50/60, S/1995/1, 3 January 1995, 18. "Just as the UN cannot discharge its responsibility if it is held hostage—as in Rwanda—to the hesitations of the member-countries to provide forces even for fully authorized peacekeeping operations, so a UN Volunteer Force needed for rapid deployment would be hamstrung if it were subject to the uncertainties of national contributions, including the perennial problem of arrears." *Our Global Neighborhood. The Report of the Commission on Global Governance.* New York: Oxford University Press, 1995, p. 111.
51. The acceleration of the deployment of UN Volunteers in the field is a challenge for UNV: the usual procedure of recruitment takes a minimum of three to six weeks. To work more effectively in crisis, UNV established in 1991 a Humanitarian Relief Unit (HRU) for emergency interventions. Additionally, for Rwanda, an in-house Task Force was specifically set up and extra-budgetary funds were used to accelerate and facilitate the recruitment process.
52. In general, UNV provides volunteer specialists to agencies such as UNHCR and WFP to meet emergencies, such as the one that erupted in Rwanda in July 1994.

53. *Between Crisis and Development: Volunteer Roles and UNV Contribution—Response from Somalia,* 4th UNV Special Consultation 20–21 October 1994. Geneva: United Nations Volunteers, September 1994, pp. 4–5.

54. "What emerges from case reviews, both from the comments of those supervising UN Volunteers, and from the UN Volunteers themselves, is their clear desire to associate closely with the problems of the local population, and from an integrated socio-economic perspective." *Between Crisis and Development, Volunteers Roles and UNVs' Contributions,* Discussion Paper for UNV's Special Consultation in Geneva, 20–21 October 1994. Geneva: United Nations Volunteers, September 1994.

55. See "Rwanda Crisis Blow for Africa's Development." *Africa Recovery* 8 (April–September 1994), no. 1–2: 4–6.

56. A UNV Project (RAF/95/V01) "Support to NGOs and Community-based organizations in the Great Lakes Region of Africa for Capacity Building in Humanitarian Assistance and Peace-Building Initiatives" is currently being implemented in cooperation with "Africa Synergies" and a Consortium of 24 national NGOs in Burundi, Kenya, Rwanda, Rwanda, Tanzania, Uganda, and Zaire.

57. Sommaruga, Cornelio. "For Urgent Action to Stop the Massacres in Rwanda." *International Herald Tribune* (5 May 1994).

58. To support the Centre for Human Rights initiative in the field of human rights in Rwanda, a project executed by UNV and financed through a cost-sharing arrangement between USAID and UNDP for a total amount of US$1,027,000 was approved by UNDP, the Centre for Human Rights, and the Government of Rwanda in December 1994. This project covers the deployment of five human rights field officers recruited directly by the Centre for Human Rights and 26 UN Volunteer specialists, including 20 human rights specialists, 1 backstopping officer, 3 car mechanics, 1 radio technician, and 1 generator specialist.

59. Walker, Peter. "A Taste of Things to Come." *Crosslines Global Report* 2 (July–October 1994), no. 4–5: 23.

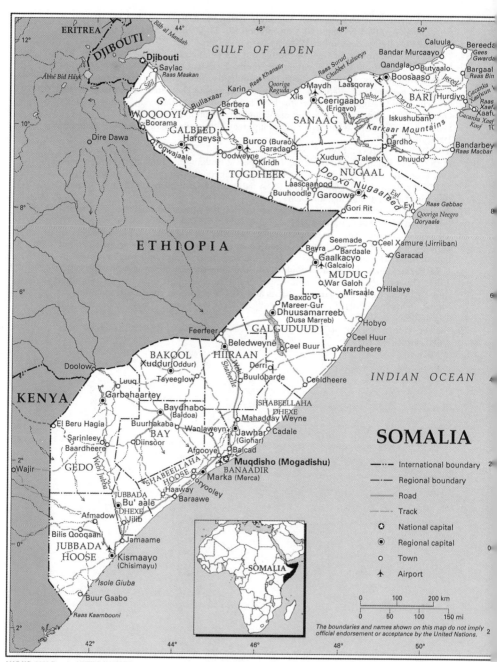

SOMALIA

- ----- International boundary
- ----- Regional boundary
- ———— Road
- ———— Track
- ⊛ National capital
- ◉ Regional capital
- ○ Town
- ✈ Airport

0		100		200 km
0	50	100	150 mi

The boundaries and names shown on this map do not imply official endorsement or acceptance by the United Nations.

MAP NO. 3690 Rev. 3   UNITED NATIONS
MARCH 1994

7

BEHIND THE COMPOUND WALL: VOLUNTEERISM UNDER CHALLENGE IN SOMALIA

Anthony C. Nweke

IN SEPTEMBER 1994, I was driven for the first time, along with some United Nations officials, from Mogadishu International Airport to the former U.S. embassy compound in Somalia, headquarters of UNOSOM (United Nations Operation in Somalia). We travelled in two buses escorted by a convoy of armoured personnel carriers and military jeeps. Six soldiers armed with automatic weapons sat in each bus. After 20 minutes on a dusty and bumpy road, avoiding the city, we reached a compound that was fenced and fortified. Those living and working inside had no contact with Somalis except for people recruited locally to work for UNOSOM as cleaners, security officers, translators, and drivers. Because of the security measures, access to the compound was difficult for Somalis who were not employed by UNOSOM. I learned that the heavily fortified headquarters building was not immune to stray bullets or mortar rounds, which sometimes hit the compound when fighting among clans broke out. Our protection against this was flak jackets and helmets. Regular evacuation exercises to shelters were designed to prepare for an orderly exit

Anthony C. Nweke is a Nigerian national born in 1968. He served as a UNV Policy Research Analyst in the Office of the Special Representative of the Secretary-General in the United Nations Operation in Somalia from September 1994 to March 1995. He holds an M.S. degree in Political Science from the University of Lagos.

should the factions become hostile to the UN. Out there, beyond the compound wall, was Somalia.

SOMALIA

The Somali society defies the over-simplified and widespread pre-conceptions that describe it as chronically unable to organize itself according to Western concepts. A well-known specialist on Somalia, Professor I.M. Lewis, asserted that the interriver region of southern Somalia, where most victims of the 1992 humanitarian tragedy were located, "... has the most stable traditional pattern of local government." He therefore believed that "restoring the power of the local elders through involving them in food distribution and encouraging the re-establishment of a locally accountable police force ... should not be too difficult."[1]

On the other hand, the Somalis are extremely individualistic. Somali society is fundamentally egalitarian; decisionmaking processes are democratic "almost to the point of anarchy."[2] Somalis are proud and sensitive to any action, especially by foreigners, that appears to sully their pride and to demean their integrity. They love listening to news about events in the world, especially as it relates to them. It is natural for them to circulate information among the various segments of their society and to organize themselves against anything they consider obnoxious to their culture.

The nomadic character of most of the population has deeply influenced the Somalis and is reflected in their traditional clan behaviour. These ancestral traditions are sometimes very difficult for an outsider to understand. For instance, stealing referred to as "camel raiding" in the past, is a normal practice among the clans. It is considered a virtue to organize a successful camel raid. As a consequence, in modern times most fighting in the country has been due to the looting and counter-looting of vehicles by the clans. The clans resolve such disputes through the meeting of clan elders in a tribal assembly called *shir*.[3] In the shir, peaceful means of settling clan disputes and proper punishments are discussed. One sight common in north Mogadishu is the crude public amputation of those found guilty of stealing by the Sharia court.

The shir arrangement also acts as a check on another source of violence among the Somalis: payment of *diya*.[4] An underlying assumption in Somali society is that when a person commits a homicide, the guilt does not remain solely with the individual. Guilt is transmitted to all members of his or her kin, who become guilty in the eyes of the aggrieved party by reason of their blood connection to the killer. To pacify an aggrieved party, the diya-paying unit gives monetary compensation collectively to the kin of the murder victim. This demonstrates the importance attached to the clan by the Somalis. The population is divided into clans and sub-clans, which traditionally act as a kind of trade union that fights for the interests of members.

Scientific socialism[5] did not spell the end of the loyalty to the clan.[6] Rather, the socialist government led by Siad Barre transformed these loyalties into a political strategy, and made family ties even more important. Thus, "clan balancing became a standard operational procedure for any clan"[7] wishing to control political power in Somalia. Under Barre, corruption and nepotism were rife, and the country's economic, administrative, and political systems were filled according to clan affiliations. Clan rivalries thus became even more pronounced.

FROM INTERVENTION TO ISOLATION

A 1978 revolt against the Barre regime and continuing civil war culminated in 1991 in Barre's overthrow. When Siad Barre left Mogadishu in January,[8] about 12 political factions were struggling to take control of the country, with each faction representing a major clan. The lack of a strong and well-organized democratic opposition, the lust for power by the individual clans, and the destruction of the Somali centralized state[9] led to continued civil war. Eventually, Gen. Mohamed Farah Aidid and Interim President Ali Mahdi emerged as principal rivals. At the same time the collapse of state institutions, especially the police and judiciary, spawned paralysis of governance, breakdown of law and order, general banditry, and chaos.

In the spring of 1992, at the height of the Somali civil war, the UN Security Council passed Resolution 751 establishing the United Nations Operation in Somalia (UNOSOM I),[10] emphasizing provision of humanitarian assistance. UNOSOM I did not assume any direct responsibility for ending the fighting or resolving the political impasse.[11] Later events demonstrated that humanitarian relief could not be effectively delivered in the presence of armed conflict,[12] and this led the UN to review the basic premise underlying its efforts in Somalia.

At the end of the year, a Unified Task Force (UNITAF) was deployed under Chapter VII of the UN Charter,[13] with the principal goal of establishing a secure environment, which included disarming Somali clans, to deliver urgently needed humanitarian assistance. With 37,000 troops, and at a cost estimated at US$1 billion, UNITAF did significantly improve the humanitarian situation in Somalia. However, UNITAF did not, in fact, seek to disarm the factions,[14] and the situation in Mogadishu worsened.

When the Security Council adopted Resolution 814 in March 1993, expanding the size and mandate of UNOSOM (now referred to as UNOSOM II) to compel the Somali militia to disarm,[15] the Somali political factions saw this move as a direct challenge to their military power. This eventually proved to be counterproductive to UNOSOM II's efforts to achieve a political settlement between the two main factions, the Somali National Alliance (SNA) and the Somali Salvation Alliance (SSA).[16] In June, 25 UN Pakistani soldiers were killed, another 54 were wounded, and 10 were taken hostage in an ambush by Somalis.

Another resolution,[17] adopted after the ambush, was interpreted by UNOSOM II as requiring the capture of Gen. Aidid. This led to a massive show of force by UNOSOM against the USC (United Somali Congress)/SNA. By ordering the arrest of Gen. Aidid and declaring war against his faction, UNOSOM II lost its neutrality and was no longer seen as an impartial arbiter between factions.

The entire UN operation in Somalia became premised on the assumption that its task must extend beyond military and humanitarian roles (UNOSOM I) to include the promotion of national reconciliation and re-establishment of effective government (UNITAF; UNOSOM II).[18] This multipronged approach was congruous with the new dimensions of "second generation" peacekeeping operations in other recent UN missions (e.g. UNTAC in Cambodia; ONUMOZ in Mozambique).[19] The problem presented by warring Somali clans and the drift into peace enforcement eventually jeopardized the safety of UN personnel in Somalia.

In spite of some widely recognized successes in providing humanitarian assistance, Somalia, for the UN, was an experiment in peacemaking and peace enforcement[20] in a failed state without structures. At the very least there had been an underestimation of the difficulty, resulting in increased problems. In Somalia, as one observer commented, the UN perceived itself as having "the potential of being the world's police and humanitarian rescue services ... of a world community."[21] Not long after the UNOSOM II operation took off in May 1993, its apparent inability to prioritize tasks caused several members of the Security Council to doubt about the likely success of the UN operation.[22]

IN THE COMPOUND

By April 1994, most UNOSOM II international civilian personnel in Mogadishu were living at one of two official compounds,[23] separated from the Somalis and the country. The deployment of the first group of UN Volunteers to UNOSOM in Somalia, April 1994,[24] coincided with this confinement to compound life in Mogadishu. Three-quarters of the 120 UN Volunteers serving in Somalia between April 1994 and March 1995 were concentrated at UNOSOM headquarters. For six months, I was to experience this unusual life while I served as a UN Volunteer Policy Research Analyst with the office of the Information and Operations Center (SIOC) under the Special Representative of the Secretary-General (SRSG). The confinement at the compound was a unique situation. It molded the experience of the UN Volunteers in Somalia in a way that was distinct from the experience of UN Volunteers in UN missions elsewhere.

The UNOSOM Way of Life

Within the U.S. embassy's main compound, life was not as boring as one would expect. The artificial circumstances of living inside the compound could be relieved by the amenities provided to the international personnel. There was a gymnasium where people went for exercise after working hours. Most international staff members were assigned to air-conditioned self-contained rooms at some recently prefabricated houses referred to as the "500-man camp." These 500-man camp barracks were much more comfortable than the fortified "Norcoy" containers that served as accommodations at the beginning of the operation, but their thin walls were anything but bulletproof. Rations of water boilers, bottled water, soap, and other useful items were given to us.

Civilian and military personnel converged three times a day at the mess hall with tickets for meals. The battalions of the various countries represented in the mission maintained post exchange stations where a relatively wide variety of items, from electronic gadgets down to toiletries, could be purchased.

Inside the compound we heard about events in the various parts of the country through reports from UNOSOM zone and subzone offices.[25] The *Soomaaliya Maanta*, the UNOSOM daily newspaper, and the UNOSOM weekly news bulletins were our main sources of information. Social life was limited, but all the more important for that fact. Interaction with people from different parts of the world was very enlightening. In one interesting discussion I had at the mess hall one night with two fellow

UN Volunteers, an Irishman and a Nigerian, our Irish colleague asked about the federal arrangement in Nigeria. My Nigerian colleague and I explained this to him, agreeing on some points between ourselves and arguing over others. For his part, the Irishman explained to us the grievances of the Irish Republican Army.

The sedentary life at the compound also provided ample opportunity to learn, especially in the areas of electronics and office equipment. Most of the UN Volunteers were from third world countries.[26] Most said that working with UNOSOM II had exposed them to many innovations that they had not encountered before.[27] I personally benefited from such exposure. Coming from Nigeria, where computers are not commonplace, I used my time to familiarize myself with the equipment.

Meanwhile, battles raged outside the compound. Frequently awakened by the sound of heavy gunfire, we knew fighting was going on among the clans. Movement in and out of the compound was under very tight security. There were air and land shuttles during daytime hours to other safe locations like the airport. Occasionally, shuttle operations were obstructed by Somalis staging demonstrations.[28] Heavy fighting also regularly hindered the air shuttle services. During these times, high frequency radio announcements informed us that a particular route had been closed or that shuttle services were suspended.

The marked disparity between the living standard in the compound and the world outside was a source of envy and disaffection among Somalis. Hence, Somalis, especially those laid off from UNOSOM II employment, used all sorts of means to extort money from UNOSOM authorities. These methods ranged from claiming overtime allowances and accumulated fringe benefits to stealing UN vehicles and office equipment or attacking convoys of UNOSOM vehicles. Somali elders sometimes demanded compensation for the deaths and injuries resulting from confrontations between UNOSOM troops and gangs of bandits. Somalis accused UNOSOM authorities of spending the bulk of the money on the faction leaders and neglecting the people. News filtered in that Gen. Aidid was planning to overrun the compound and was promising his militia that once UNOSOM II was driven out of Somalia it would enjoy the amenities at UNOSOM headquarters.

Against this background, there was a real fear that careless staff might be abducted by the militia, to be held for ransom to UNOSOM authorities. Some international staff also were suspicious of the Somali employees of UNOSOM II, who they believed were providing faction and community leaders with information about UNOSOM II activities within the compound.

Behind the compound wall: a UNOSOM soldier surveying the city of Mogadishu. Photo: UN photo 159854/M. Grant

The Special Representative's Information and Operations Centre

UN Volunteers whose work contributed directly to the national reconciliation process in Somalia were generally clustered in three UNOSOM groups: Division for Political Affairs (DPA), Policy, Planning and Information Division (PPI), and, to some extent, SIOC. UN Volunteers assigned to PPI were charged with updating a review of the historical development of the Somali political factions. They also analyzed sociopolitical developments in Somalia and developed strategies for the reconciliation of the political factions, which were then submitted to UNOSOM authorities. One UN Volunteer was transferred out of the compound to a zone office as a political affairs officer. There, he participated in various talks held by the zone director with the faction leaders. He also monitored and analyzed zone political developments, prepared daily situation reports, and facilitated informal contacts between rival political factions.

The Special Representative's Information and Operations Centre and the Policy, Planning and Information Division both started reporting directly to the Special Representative of the Secretary-General in September 1994. The two sections, which should have been reinforcing each other, instead functioned independently. PPI was the think tank of the SRSG for long-, medium-, and short-term planning of all aspects of UNOSOM's operations. PPI was also set up to advise the SRSG on various Security Council mandates relating to the mission, to provide ideas for the work of UNOSOM, and to assess UNOSOM policies at various intervals.

SIOC, on the other hand, was the civilian information wing of UNOSOM; it provided the SRSG with data on the security situation in Somalia. We collected and synthesized political, humanitarian, military, and security information, and reported to the Under Secretary-General for Peacekeeping Operations in New York. SIOC also arranged the itinerary for the daily movement of the SRSG and acted as a liaison between the director for zone operations and the zone offices.

I went to SIOC to synthesize and analyze incoming information to determine the trends of events and to make recommendations on UNOSOM II policies.[29] The office wanted to go beyond reception of information from the zone offices to actual site visits to ascertain and confirm reports. This had been carried out through regular reconnaissance operations in Mogadishu, sometimes including the regions where the zone offices were located. Since the people doing the assessment were ex-military officers, analysis of the situation in the zones had been dominated previously by security concerns.

Limits of Policy Analysis in a Closed Environment

In the course of my work, I unfortunately had only one opportunity to visit a zone office. Direct contact with the Somali people was generally limited to Somalis attached to SIOC and the force commander. I was occasionally able to interview some local staff members when I had a special report to prepare. One result of this limited access to the Somali people was that we often relied on second-hand information. Sometimes other UN Volunteers visited zone offices to assess the progress of the political reconciliation efforts. They ended up being briefed by the UNO-SOM officers stationed there. Thus, the sum of what they learned had already been reported by those zone offices. The effect was that we had few opportunities to develop new information in order to contribute meaningfully towards nation-building in Somalia.

Given these limitations, UN Volunteers did their best to contribute to informing policy by using whatever information they could gather and analyze. Early on in my assignment, I assessed the prospect of national reconciliation and the Somali National Alliance's acceptance in Somalia.[30] In the first report, I wrote that it was an illusion for UNOSOM to hope that the Somali factions would convene a national reconciliation conference, because of certain pressing issues that had not been resolved, especially the basis for representation. I suggested that to prevent a resurgence of a civil war, UNOSOM channel all its energies towards diffusing mounting tensions over the control of the country's major infrastructures, particularly the airports and seaports. Whether or not the paper directly contributed to this evolution, UNOSOM did start efforts to encourage the Mogadishu-based factions to form joint committees to oversee the airport and seaport.

The second assessment had to do with major criticisms against UNO-SOM's policies. I suggested that the statements and actions of UNOSOM at that time tended to vindicate the criticisms. I recommended that instead of the UNOSOM authorities' watching to see what would come out of the Somali National Alliance-sponsored national reconciliation conference, the SRSG should intensify consultations to try to bridge the gap between the two main faction leaders, Gen. Farah Aidid and Ali Mahdi Mohammed, the Somali National Alliance and Somali Salvation Alliance chairmen. I also suggested that consultations could be broadened to include other segments of the Somali civil society. Within the period the paper was submitted, the SRSG stated that he understood that his statements may have alluded to support of the SNA and said that he would continue his efforts towards bringing the faction leaders together.

VOLUNTEERISM UNDER CHALLENGE

The very peculiar UNOSOM environment was an experimental cage or laboratory where the conditions for effective volunteerism can be reviewed.[31] Volunteers served in various other sectors, including humanitarian relief assistance, national reconciliation, rehabilitation and reconstruction of Somali society, and administrative and technical support. One would logically think that this important involvement by UN Volunteers in fields of activity so crucial to the operations in Somalia would have boosted the motivation of the volunteers. Security risks, which were real, could have acted as a catalyst or adversely affected their motivation, but in fact the volunteer spirit of the UN Volunteers was not adversely affected by security considerations. However, the Somalia experience taught that by quartering UN Volunteers and regular UN staff together in a single location for an extended period of time, and in a mission which had lost its objective, the voluntary spirit can be adversely affected.

UNV Fields of Activity

Leaving their compound life and escorted by heavily armed security forces, UN Volunteers serving in the humanitarian area were able to fulfill their specific responsibilities by assisting the Division for the Coordination of Humanitarian Affairs (DCHA); they worked mainly in resettlement, immunization, rejuvenation, and coordination of humanitarian efforts.[32] A UN Volunteer worked at the community level assisting with basic social and economic needs. Another UNV humanitarian officer was involved in arranging medical care for Somalis of all ages, including immunizing children and organizing visits to the communities by international non-governmental organizations concerned with health care delivery. Access routes for health facilities were surveyed to ensure that medical supplies were available to Somalis, especially in Mogadishu.[33]

UNV resettlement officers played a significant role in organizing the resettlement of internally displaced persons and assisted in restoring socioeconomic life to their communities. Those who served with UNOSOM's rejuvenation programme participated in designing a Small Scale Projects Programme aimed at encouraging the active participation of Somalis in planning and implementing economic activities in their communities. These UN Volunteers worked closely with community-based organizations in identifying, designing, and implementing projects to encourage Somali self-reliance.

A woman and her child in Somalia: above all, volunteers are motivated to work with people. *Photo: UN photo 154595/David Heiden*

More than a dozen UN Volunteers assigned to the Justice Division worked in various capacities as in corrections, juvenile justice, crime prevention, human rights, and support to justice programmes at the zone offices.[34] UN Volunteer correction officers regularly visited the prisons in Somalia and advised on the welfare of prisoners. They also gave advice on such other issues as salaries for prison officers and provision of firearms and identity cards; they prepared the draft of a manual for training custodial corps. A UNV juvenile officer assisted in monitoring the treatment of juvenile offenders and participated in recruiting teachers for UNOSOM's street children project in North Mogadishu. The rising tide of crime was addressed by a UN Volunteer crime prevention officer, who played an active role in establishing technical training programmes to provide young people with the skills to make a living without resorting to crime. This work included frequent visits to the Mogadishu Central Prison to discuss prison conditions and identify areas in which UNOSOM could facilitate improvements.

UN Volunteer human rights officers were involved in resolving complaints of human rights violations reported to the Justice Division. They also facilitated implementation of proposals for establishing human rights clinics throughout Somalia by the Human Rights Unit of the Justice Division. Two UN Volunteers with the Justice Division were later sent to the zone offices. There they facilitated the rehabilitation of the criminal justice systems in their assigned regions and assisted in procuring administrative kits to aid the programmes of the division in the zones, and the Somali judicial and custodial corps.[35]

All UN Volunteers in the substantive divisions left the mission before the final UNOSOM II mandate expired in March 1995. This had partly to do with the suspension of most humanitarian, reconstruction, and development activities in Mogadishu.

Can Volunteers Operate in Any Conditions?

The paradox of UNOSOM II was that a mission aimed at freeing Somalis from war and hunger was itself imprisoned on a small piece of U.S. land with very limited access to the world outside. While access to that world existed, it was exercised with the constant risk of ambush and death for those who ventured outside the compound. The mission itself had to some extent lost its goals and hope in solving the problems of the Somalis.

Most of the UN Volunteers were deployed to administrative and technical support units, where their responsibilities did not make use of the professionalism for which UN Volunteers are known.[36] Functions such as operating telephones and VHF radios and sending facsimile messages, done by some UN Volunteers, could be perceived as not requiring extensive specialized training. Such responsibilities did, in fact, require technical and professional skills, and were crucial to the operations. However, it was difficult at first sight to assess the direct impact of those positions on the overall operations, and UN Volunteers occupying them were granted little recognition for their contribution.

The UN Volunteers playing support roles were many miles away from their usual role described in the UNV/Programme and Administrative Support Unit (PASU) report as "working at the local level and building the human resource capacities of the grassroots based groups."[37] Even UN Volunteers assigned to the substantive divisions were unable to fully assess their contribution to UNOSOM II policies. Although UN Volunteers at the Division for Policy Planning and Information sometimes brain-stormed on UNOSOM II's mandate issues and recommended to UNOSOM authorities possible strategies for realizing objectives, they were unable to determine their influence on policy.

UN Volunteers deployed to zone offices had a similar experience. They did not often have the opportunity to interact at the grassroots either. By providing administrative and logistics support to the offices, they, however ironically, exposed their lives to direct threats. For example, a volunteer deployed to a zone office was threatened twice at gunpoint because the Somalis believed he was withholding their payments for the goods they supplied during the Lower Juba Reconciliation Conference held in Kismayo.[38]

The uncertainty of the future of UNOSOM II was another important factor that affected all staff, including UN Volunteers, and that contributed to the special psychological atmosphere in the compound.[39] More important, UN Volunteers ultimately felt caught in a conflict between the demands of their voluntary calling and the needs of the organizational structure in which they worked. In contrast to regular UN employees, who had the satisfaction of substantial financial benefits from the job, to work with people and interact with them over time was one of the main motivations of volunteer specialists, but this did not take place. Deprived from their most immediate and visible satisfaction, volunteers could feel, and be perceived by others, as being under-utilized. This abnormal situation caused some UN Volunteers to question the validity of their volunteering.

Rethinking UNV Involvement

The United Nations Volunteers Programme has been devoted traditionally to development through community-based approaches. United Nations Volunteers also strives to play "its full role in making the talent and commitment of volunteer specialists available to the UN system as a whole—in humanitarian relief work, democratization and protection of human rights."[40] Unfortunately, not all of the living and working arrangements in Somalia were conducive to these goals. Thus, it was common to see those UN Volunteers living in the confined compound world, lacking the vital contact with the people of Somalia, and diverting their energies into UNOSOM staff work.

"The image of the UNV Programme in the field depends on the functions that it supports and the level of professionalism at which the UNVs could operate."[41] The placement of UN Volunteers within the various units in UNOSOM II was skewed in favour of the administrative and technical support roles, which were not related directly to the traditional goals of the United Nations Volunteer Programme.[42] At the workshop organized by UNV/PASU, most UN Volunteers said they believed they performed well in relation to their job descriptions, but they understood that it was difficult to relate their achievements to the goals of the UN in Somalia.

Since the regional peace conferences were convened in the regions where the zone offices were located, the UN Volunteers at the zone offices could have been used to monitor the progress and impacts of the peace conferences on the overall national reconciliation efforts of UNOSOM II. They could have done this through discussions with either the local UNOSOM employees or by visiting informally with communities. Somalis are not averse to visitors who appreciate their traditions, and this work may not have been as difficult as it might have seemed at first glance.

UN Volunteers also could have assisted in reactivating and making more relevant the UNOSOM II accredited regional and district councils,[43] which had not been functioning effectively. It was unfortunate that only one UN Volunteer served with the Division of Political Affairs, which was responsible for the work of the councils. In zone offices, especially in regions such as Baidoa, where relative peace prevailed and some governmental institutions functioned, UN Volunteers could have monitored and reported on the work of these councils.[44]

Could the United Nations Volunteer Programme have entered into joint or collaborative projects with UNOSOM II in areas that were directly related to the stated aims and objectives of the programme? The advantage of this approach is that it would have enabled United Nations Volunteers to take part early in the planning and implementation stages of the UNOSOM projects in which UN Volunteers would be involved. Some specific projects in which United Nations Volunteers could have joined advantageously were outlined in the UN Secretary-General's March 1993 report to the Security Council, where he noted the major challenges for the international community in Somalia.[45]

Rethinking of options by the United Nations Volunteer Programme started in December 1993, when the deputy executive coordinator of UNV at that time stated that a United Nations Volunteers Programme for Somalia would be launched with 100 professionals involved in grassroots work for rehabilitation and development.[46] Further efforts in this direction continued with the signing in November 1994 of an agreement for a joint project supported by the UN Development Programme (UNDP) and United Nations Volunteers. Under the agreement, UNDP and UNV planned to intensify agricultural production in Juba Valley, Lower Juba Region. The objectives of the $500,000 project included "the establishment of an agricultural services system, rehabilitation of small-scale agricultural infrastructure, and the introduction on a pilot basis, of a credit system for small farmers."[47] Apart from UNDP, the Food and Agriculture Organization (FAO), some district councils in Somalia, and local NGOs were to actively participate in implementing the project.

CONCLUSION

UNOSOM II's display of military force as one of the main instruments for establishing peace and stabilizing the situation in Somalia and the compromise of its neutrality through peace enforcement efforts led to further deterioration of the security situation. It was under this anarchic setting that UN Volunteers came to Somalia to lend support to UNOSOM II goals and objectives. The consequent concentration of the majority of UN Volunteers within UNOSOM headquarters in Mogadishu limited their range of activities. This led to a peculiar experience in Somalia compared to the experiences of UN Volunteers serving in other UN missions.

For many UN Volunteers, the lack of contact with Somalis often confined their roles to support of regular UN staff. The administrative and technical support positions held by some UN Volunteers and the ancillary roles played by others did not leave room for all UN Volunteers to evaluate their contributions to UNOSOM II. Their efforts, while productive, were only a small gesture against the immensity of Somali suffering and privation. On the other hand, the UNOSOM II environment put undue pressure on the United Nations Volunteers Programme. The UNV management was not in a position to define specifically its own goals within the Memorandum of Understanding for participation in the mission.[48]

UN Volunteers are defined by the programme as "men and women who are genuinely interested in helping others and in dedicating some years to doing so in another country and culture—with all the job satisfaction which that offers, but also the difficulties it can entail."[49] It would have been preferable if grassroots outreach efforts could have been identified and then carried out by volunteers. Given the context, the deployment of UN Volunteers in Somalia sometimes could be seen only as a cost-saving device.

Volunteerism is a two-way process: while UN Volunteers contribute by their efforts to operations, they need to know that their work makes a real difference and that their role in making that difference is recognized. At the same time, they learn more about themselves and the community in which they work. When volunteers are cut off from the results of their efforts and from the country in which they are serving, the basic elements of volunteerism—motivation, commitment, dedication—can be altered.

The quartering of the UN Volunteers with UN regular staff members in Somalia changed some volunteers' perceptions of volunteering, and it ultimately damaged their motivation and sense of value as volunteers. Volunteerism requires reciprocity and exchange to be a vital force. At the very least those volunteering their skills and abilities need to know they are respected for who they are as much as what they bring. As Paul J. Ilsley asks in his book *Enhancing the Volunteer Experience*: "What's the point of being a volunteer if you're not treated as an equal?"[50]

NOTES

1. Lewis, I.M. "Priorities in Somali Actions." *Guardian Weekly* (13 December 1992): 2.
2. Lewis, I.M. *A Modern History of Somalia: Nation and State in the Horn of Africa.* London: Longman Group Limited, 1980, p. 10.
3. The clan elders who usually "act as deputies ... are not elected representatives, but chosen on the basis of age and influence inside the clan...." See Bongartz, Maria. *The Civil War in Somalia: Its genesis and dynamics—Current African Issues 11.* Uppsala, Sweden: The Scandinavian Institute of African Studies, 1991, p. 10.

4. According to I.M. Lewis, a "'diya-paying' group consists of close kin united by specific contractual alliance whose terms stipulate that they should pay and receive blood compensation in concert." See his *A Modern History of Somalia*. Boulder: Westview Press, 1988, p. 11.

5. Somalia became independent in 1960 with the unification of the former British Somaliland in the north and the Italian trusteeship territory in the south. In 1969 during a bloodless coup, Siad Barre's military government formed a Supreme Revolutionary Council (SRC) whose members were drawn from the army and police. The SRC announced that it had acted to preserve democracy and justice, and to eliminate corruption and clanism. It also introduced scientific socialism "as an alternative to tribalism, claiming that it fit(ted) naturally with the tradition of sharing material possessions." The leadership stated that there was no contradiction between scientific socialism and Islamic religion and stressed the need for popular participation in governance through local councils, worker management committees, and self-help development projects.

6. Ngugi, C. Muiru. "Somalia: Good riddance to aliens or to saviours?" *Daily Nation* (Nairobi) (9 March 1995): 6.

7. Laitin and Samatar (1987), cited in Bongartz, *The Civil War in Somalia*, p. 15.

8. The United Somali Congress (USC), a Hawiye-based political faction that drove Siad Barre out of Mogadishu, could not fill the power vacuum created in Somalia because it lacked a political programme and organization.

9. The notion of "Greater Somalia" drove successive Somalia governments into trying to unite all Somalis in the so-called five Somali regions. The failure of the unification efforts by the various Somalia governments led Siad Barre into a rapprochement with Ethiopia and Kenya in 1977. Somalia abrogated its treaty of friendship with the former USSR in November 1977 andexpelled 6,000 Soviet personnel from the country following promises of financing for military purchases from Saudi Arabia and indications of Western and U.S. support. However, the anticipated military assistance did not come.

10. UNOSOM I was established by Security Council Resolution 751 on 24 April 1992, and it requested the Secretary-General to immediately deploy 50 observers to monitor the cease-fire in Mogadishu. The council also agreed in principle to establish a security force to be deployed as soon as possible, and requested the Secretary-General to continue his consultations with the parties in Mogadishu in that regard. Resolution 751 called on the international community to provide financial assistance and support for the Secretary-General's 90-Day Plan of Action for Emergency Humanitarian Assistance to Somalia. The security personnel envisaged in the mandate were mainly to "provide protection and security for UN personnel, equipment and supplies at the seaports and airports in Mogadishu and escort deliveries of humanitarian supplies from there to their distribution centers in the city and its immediate environs." See Department of Public Information. *The United Nations and the Situation in Somalia—Reference Paper*. New York: UN, March 1993, pp. 2–3.

11. *Report of the Commission of Inquiry Established Pursuant to Security Council Resolution 885 (1993) to Investigate Armed Attacks on UNOSOM II Personnel which led to Casualties Among them*. New York: UN, 24 February 1994, p. 24. UNOSOM I troops were only mandated to "provide convoys of relief supplies with a sufficiently strong military escort to deter attacks and to fire effectively in self-defence if deterrence should not prove effective." See S/23829, 21 April 1992, para. 28.

12. For example, the port of Mogadishu remained closed for much of November 1992, and a World Food Programme ship that attempted to enter the port on 24 November 1992 was shelled and its bridge set on fire. Reported in SSC report S/24859 (Letter dated 24 November 1992 from the Secretary-General Addressed to the President of the Security Council 27/22/92).

13. On 3 December 1992, the Security Council adopted Resolution 794 establishing UNITAF with the principal goal of establishing a secure environment, including disarming Somali clans, in order to effectively deliver urgently needed humanitarian assistance.

UNITAF was authorized to use "all necessary means to establish as soon as possible a secure environment for humanitarian relief operations in Somalia." Acting under Chapter VII of the UN Charter, the council further authorized the Secretary-General and the participating member states to make arrangements for "the unified command and control" of the military forces that would be involved.

14. UNITAF did not muster the necessary capability to carry out the enforcement action that was anticipated by invoking Chapter VII. The U.S. maintained that force would be used only to remove obstructions to humanitarian relief and that if no such threats were posed and if the weapons of the militia were not menacing there would be no significant confrontation. *Report of the Commission of Inquiry*, p. 37.

15. UNOSOM II had a strength of 28,000 troops from 29 countries and about 2,800 civilians. The difference between the mandates of UNOSOM II and UNITAF was that the disarmament process of UNITAF derived from the cease-fire and disarmament agreements of 8 and 15 January 1993 between the warlords. This was not the case for UNOSOM II. UNOSOM II also had a broader mandate than UNITAF, since it was involved in all peace activities possible for a UN operation throughout Somalia. The newly created UNOSOM II interpreted its mandate as "not merely authorizing but requiring it to disarm the militia." *Report of the Commission of Inquiry*, p. 37.

16. The National Reconciliation Conference in Addis Ababa from 16 to 27 March 1993, with the participation of the main factions (except for the MNS of Somaliland) and of representatives of Somali civilian society as well as of regional organizations, produced a general agreement on cease-fire, disarmament modalities, and a transitional mechanism for the restoration of the Somali state. One of UNOSOM II's problems was that it was charged with the simultaneous performance of three tasks: peacemaking, peace enforcement, and peace building. These functions were carried out by distinct segments of UNOSOM II, and coordination was sometimes lacking. The aspect of UNOSOM II's mandate that required it to consolidate and expand the security in Somalia rested on its military forces. The second strand, which entailed nation-building responsibility, was the duty of the civilian component of UNOSOM II. The remaining provision in the mandate, humanitarian assistance, was undertaken by the Somali Aid Coordination Body (SACB). But "caught in a dilemma UNOSOM II was forced to erect a wall of separation between its peacekeeping and war-making *personae*-where its civilian authorities were often kept in the dark about military actions." This failure of coordination was a partial cause of the tragic events of 5 June 1993, when a confrontation between UNOSOM II and the United Somali Congress/Somali National Alliance (USC/SNA) left 25 Pakistani soldiers dead.

17. Resolution 837 adopted by the Security Council on 6 June 1993 reaffirmed among other things the authority of the Secretary-General to secure the investigation of the actions of those responsible for the armed attacks on UN peacekeepers in Mogadishu, including those responsible for publicly inciting such attacks.

18. On 26 March 1993, the Security Council, acting under Chapter VII of the Charter, adopted Resolution 814, thus expanding the size and mandate of UNOSOM I. The expanded UNOSOM I was called UNOSOM II. Resolution 814 demanded all Somali parties to comply fully with the commitments they had undertaken and in particular, with the Agreement on Implementing the Cease-fire and on Modalities of Disarmament, and ensure the safety of the personnel of all organizations engaged in humanitarian and other assistance to Somalia. See United Nations Department of Public Information, *The United Nations and the Situation in Somalia*, Reference Paper. (30 April 1993): pp. 2, 3, 7, and 10.

19. UNTAC (United Nations Transitional Authority in Cambodia) was the UN mission within which the 1993 elections were organized. ONUMOZ stands for the United Nations Operation in Mozambique, during which the 1994 Mozambique elections were conducted. "Second generation" peacekeeping operations (PKOs) have shifted significantly from classical peacekeeping operations, which used to involve the fielding of

troops and humanitarian relief monitors. The main characteristics of these "second generation" PKOs are that they are "endowed with prerogatives and functions of governments...." and also "... directed more at peace building than at a strict peacekeeping.... in fact, the operations would have to take place even if the 'settlements negotiated by peacemakers' have not obtained the full and serious cooperation of the parties." See Lalande, Serge. "Somalia: Major Issues for Future UN Peacekeeping." In: Warner, Daniel, ed. *New Dimensions of Peacekeeping*. Netherlands: Kluwer Academic Publishers, 1995, p. 96.

20. In *An Agenda for Peace*, the Secretary-General defines peacemaking "as an action to bring hostile parties to agreement, essentially through such peaceful means as those foreseen in Chapter VI of the Charter of the United Nations. *Peace enforcement ...* means restoring and maintaining cease-fire by force ... (with) more heavily armed ... forces placed under the command of the Secretary-General...." Cited in Bertrand, Maurice. "The Confusion Between Peacemaking and Peacekeeping." In: Warner, *New Dimensions of Peacekeeping*, pp. 163–164. Peacemaking, unlike peace enforcement, which is a police action, does not entail a mandate to stop an aggressor if one could be identified or impose a cessation of hostilities. *Peacekeeping*, on the other hand, "is the deployment of a United Nations presence in the field, hitherto with the consent of all parties concerned, normally involving United Nations military and/or police personnel and frequently civilians as well.... (while) *Post conflict Peace Building* is action to identify and support structures which will tend to strengthen and solidify peace in order to avoid a relapse into conflict." See Warner, *New Dimensions of Peacekeeping*.

21. Brian Urquhart, former United Nations under secretary-general for special political affairs, quoted by Cruickshank, John. "Our Last, Best Hope." *Globe and Mail Report* (Toronto) (January 1995): 1.

22. In June 1993, the former president of the Security Council, Professor Ibrahim Gambari, stated that there was no room for optimism about the success of UNOSOM II. According to Gambari, "... the situation in the country had deteriorated. The level of insecurity was unpredictable, and it might not be long before the mission was compelled to leave Somalia." Cited in *Somali News Up Date* 3 (7 June 1993), no. 17: p. 5.

23. The majority of UNOSOM international personnel lived at the former U.S. embassy compound, with the remaining living in the southern compound, a group of buildings along the airport road.

24. The UN Volunteers programme signed a Memorandum of Understanding with UNOSOM II in September 1993. The primary objective of the agreement was to "provide a flexible and rapidly responsive programming mechanism for the identification, selection, recruitment, orientation and administration of a contingent of 225 UNVs to support UNOSOM II operations in Somalia." UNV/PASU. *UNV Programme with UNOSOM: End of Mission Report*. Mogadishu, Somalia: January 1995, p. 27.

25. The zone offices were meant to reach out to the Somalis through political, social, religious, and professional groups and individuals, and to explain the mandate of UNOSOM in the context of Somali efforts to rebuild Somalia. These offices also were to report to the SRSG significant developments on security, justice, political, and humanitarian matters in the regions; to implement or with the relevant divisions assist in the implementation of the UNOSOM II mandate in the political, humanitarian, justice, and demobilization fields.

26. Out of 120 UN Volunteers who worked with UNOSOM II, 47 (39 per cent) were from Africa, 39 (33 per cent) from Asia and Pacific, 19 (16 per cent) from Europe, 13 (11 per cent) from America and the Caribbean, and 2 (2 per cent) from the Middle East. See UNV/PASU, *UNV Programme with UNOSOM*, p. 42.

27. At a workshop organized by the United Nations Volunteers Programme and Administrative Support Unit (UNV/PASU) in November 1994.

28. For example, local employees whose contracts were being terminated by Brown & Root, a firm contracted by UNOSOM, staged a demonstration in November 1994. Armed with

dangerous weapons, they entered the compound with their identity cards and blockaded the main entrances to the compound. Because they started the demonstration before 0800 hours, normal activities were disrupted for a half day. UNOSOM employees could not go out or come in, while those inside the compound were unable to move from one office to the other.

29. My assignment entailed "gathering information and drafting reports on various activities of political factions and modalities of governance and conflict resolution; consolidating information and data of major policy measures in Somalia with the view to developing appropriate resolutions, guidelines and recommendations; analyzing policy trends and updating implications for reference, policy and strategy formulation in accordance with UNOSOM's mandate; designing and developing methodologies for interpretation of information and data."

30. "The Prospects of Somali National Reconciliation Conference" and "An Assessment of SNA's Acceptance among the Somali People."

31. I wish to express my appreciation to M.A. Rao, former programme manager of the UNV programme in Somalia, for making vital UNV documents available to me. My appreciation also goes to Dr. Babafemi Badejo, my teacher and mentor, and Felix Nartey, a UNV colleague in Somalia, for their well-thought-out critiques that helped in shaping the article.

32. The Division for the Coordination of Humanitarian Affairs (DCHA) was created to coordinate the humanitarian relief assistance being provided for the Somalis, to assist in the repatriation of refugees and resettlement of internally displaced persons (IDPs), and to liaise with NGOs and UN agencies operating in Somalia.

33. UN Volunteers also helped to coordinate a UNESCO-sponsored tutor training workshop for camp schools. The workshop was part of a UNESCO effort to teach basic literacy to approximately 3,000 children and adults. Further, they collaborated with United Nations Development Office (UNDO) in producing regional profiles on Somalia's socioeconomic sectors and helped in the preparations for the launching by DCHA of a consolidated appeal of UN agencies aimed at facilitating continued relief and rehabilitation of Somali communities beyond UNOSOM's mandate.

34. The Secretary-General believed that the Somalis could assume full responsibility for law and order in their country if security and stability were restored through the reestablishment of the Somali police force, the judicial and penal systems. He was of the view that strengthening the legal system should take precedence over the police force. This is because the legal system would provide the basis and framework for police activities. The basic laws that the police would have to enforce, the judicial system to adjudicate the cases of those arrested by the police, and the penal system that could detain and punish offenders are all part of the legal system. See Secretary-General's Report to the Security Council, 17 August 1993, Annex 1, pp. 21–22.

35. Unfortunately, the UN Volunteers in this division were the worst hit by UNOSOM's draw-down situation and were repatriated just as they started initiating some constructive measures to re-establish and rehabilitate the criminal justice systems and structures in different parts of the country.

36. According to the UNV/PASU office, deployment and establishing posts was complicated because "... there was intense pressure from different sections to bring in UNV specialists quickly; UNV program with UNOSOM was only secondary for the program officer, as the main responsibility was to develop a new concept under a tight timeframe, involving UNDP and other UN agencies, NGOs and Somali communities; moreover, MOU did not offer guidance in terms of functional involvement of UNV with UNOSOM." UNV/PASU, *UNV Programme with UNOSOM*, p. 24.

37. *Ibid.*, p. 8.

38. This was part of the grassroots approach adopted by UNOSOM II in implementing the agreements reached by the Somali faction leaders on 27 March 1993 in Addis Ababa. Thus, when convening the regional peace conferences, which the Lower Juba Peace Conference was part of, UNOSOM II wanted to reinforce the process of national recon-

ciliation. It therefore undertook to help to resolve conflicts at the regional level and to assist in resolving intercommunal disputes. The Kismayo conference brought together 152 elders from the various parts that constitute the Juba Region to discuss issues crucial to the restoration of normalcy in the region, such as the reopening of all areas of the region for the free movement of people and commercial traffic, reunification of communities, settlement of property claims, cessation of hostilities and disarmament. Similar conferences were held in Mogadishu among the Hawiye clan families and in Boroma, north-west region.

39. Uncertainty over contracts and the termination of contracts on short notice were common. Those of us serving in areas related to national reconciliation went through tremors of abrupt termination and sudden renewal of contracts due to the piecemeal extensions of UNOSOM II mandates and its eventual winding-down process. My own four-month contract was cut short by one month, a common experience for most UN Volunteers and particularly those in the substantive divisions. Later, my contract was extended twice; however other UN Volunteers did not receive extensions.

40. United Nations Volunteers. *UNV News* (June 1993), no. 62: 7. UNV was created by the General Assembly of the UN in 1970 to serve as an operational partner in development cooperation at the request of UN member states. Since the inception of the programme, the UN Volunteers mainly have been working as volunteer specialists and field workers with community-based initiatives for self-reliance, and in humanitarian relief and rehabilitation.

41. UNV/PASU, *UNV Programme with UNOSOM*, p. 31.

42. There were 11 UN Volunteers with accommodation and catering unit, 18 with security, 25 with communication, 6 with building management services, 1 with electronic data processing unit, 1 with budget and cost control unit, 1 with property, control, and inventory unit, and 3 with UNV/PASU.

43. It was agreed in Addis Ababa that the 92 districts of Somalia would be those that were functioning as of 31 December 1990, that is, those created before the demise of the Somali state in 1991. The Transitional Charter Drafting Committee subsequently decided that each district council would have 21 members, selected in accordance with Somali tradition. Each district council was to select three of its members to serve on the regional council while each of the regional councils would have in turn selected three citizens of the region to serve on the Transitional National Council.

44. By November 1993, 38 district councils had been established and trained by UNOSOM II, and were running their own affairs. Similarly, 6 regional councils in Nugaal, Bakool, Bay, Galgaduud, Hiran, and Gedo (all around the Baidoa area) were functioning.

45. Among those challenges were facilitating the voluntary return of Somali refugees and internally displaced persons; providing jobs for unemployed Somalis; rebuilding the country's national capacity, and establishing education facilities. See Secretary-General's Report to the Security Council, 3 March 1993.

46. Sukehiro Hasegawa made it clear that the project was not a job-creation enterprise but an experiment aimed at encouraging Somali professionals to volunteer their services. He also stated that priority would be given to professionals inside the country as well as community leaders familiar with the problems in their respective areas. The professionals must be planners or technicians from the agricultural, medical, and related fields. See UNOSOM, *Weekly News Bulletin* (14 December 1993): 2–3. Additionally, the national volunteer scheme in Somalia was developed within the context of the Department of Humanitarian Affairs-led consolidated appeals process (CAP) for the funding of emergency relief and rehabilitation projects and as such was not initially associated with UNOSOM operations.

47. The project was aimed at enhancing the "spirit of self-reliance through the engagement of Somali technicians as volunteer workers and the use of an agricultural and development credit scheme which would make the people responsible for any funds they received." See *Soomaaliya MAANTA* (Somalia's Daily Newspaper) (29 November 1994): 1.

48. The UN Volunteers Programme management faced two problems: one, the programme coordinators were unable to withstand pressures by UNOSOM II officials to provide large numbers of support staff, and two, the deteriorating security situation under UNOSOM II meant the environment was too insecure for a revised course of action to materialize. UNV, as a volunteer programme, could be made more relevant to UN missions in the future by identifying and entering into collaborative ventures with the UN in particular areas where the expertise of the UN Volunteers could be used in ameliorating the problems of the local population.

49. The UN Volunteers programme works in partnership with governments, UN agencies, development banks, and non-governmental and community-based organizations in technical, economic, and social fields. In recruiting the UN Volunteers, three vital criteria, commitment, qualifications, and experience, are considered by the UNV office. Since half of the UN Volunteers work outside capital cities, in remote towns and villages in response to expressed needs, UNV emphasizes the commitment these volunteers show. Thus, interest is mainly in practitioners with excellent track records in village-level community work, exchange of skills, and knowledge.

50. See Ilsley, Paul J. *Enhancing the Volunteer Experience: New Insights on Strengthening Volunteer Participation, Learning and Commitment.* San Francisco: Jossey-Bass Publishers, 1990, p. 110.

8

PART OF THE SYSTEM: VARIETIES OF VOLUNTEER SUPPORT ROLES

Masako Yonekawa

IT WAS DURING my studies at the University of Kent in the United Kingdom in the early 1990s that my interest in development and humanitarian aid dramatically increased. I met a Jamaican man who taught me about racial discrimination and the psychological and social gap between whites and blacks. He totally changed my worldview, which had been limited to that of the Japanese and American cultures in which I had lived. I learned more from his stories about racial and cultural bias in the world than I did in my development coursework.

I began to ask myself: what can I do to lessen this inequality between these two distinct worlds and to help oppressed people obtain their rights? The answer was: if I really wished to be part of the solution of North-South issues, I should learn about the reality by meeting and working with the local people instead of trying to figure out these problems from the comfort of the Western world. In addition to my encounters with my Jamaican friend, I sought out non-governmental organizations

Masako Yonekawa, a Japanese national born in 1967 and a former reporter, graduated in sociology from the University of Kent, served as a UN Volunteer in various capacities with UNTAC (Cambodia), UNDP (Liberia), UNOMSA (South Africa), UNOSOM (Somalia), and WFP (Tanzania). She is now serving as a UNV Field Officer with the United Nations High Commissioner for Refugees in Rwanda.

in the United Kingdom, where they are numerous and vigorous, quite unlike in Japan, as I found myself drawn even further towards work in human development.

Shortly thereafter, I had the opportunity to live in the Golan Heights next to the Syrian and Lebanese borders and to see for the first time peacekeeping troops at work. I crossed back and forth between the politically sensitive areas of the West Bank and Jordan. Working during the summer of 1991 in Moshav, a farming community in Israel, gave me the opportunity to observe the strong tensions between some of the Jewish and Arab people. This experience aroused my concern about ethnic conflict and about peace and war and reconfirmed my belief that working in the field was the best way to learn about world issues.

As soon as I returned to Japan from Israel, I looked for NGOs that could send me overseas to do development and humanitarian aid work, preferably dealing with refugees. I believed that by standing on the same ground as those who are the most unprotected and vulnerable victims in the world, I could come to a deeper understanding of the difficult issues involved. Through my search, I learned about United Nations Volunteers (UNV).

In April 1992, I applied and was accepted for the position of UN Volunteer/District Electoral Supervisor in Cambodia. This mission, which was eventually a big success, relied on an unusually high number of UN Volunteer specialists to carry out electoral and humanitarian activities. Afterwards, many other UN Volunteer specialist posts opened up in other UN missions, such as in Mozambique and Somalia. Upon completing the Cambodian mission, I again applied to be a UN Volunteer, and emphasized my desire to work in Africa or the Middle East. Fortunately, successive missions in Liberia, South Africa, and Somalia came up one after another. Two of these missions, Cambodia and South Africa, had an electoral purpose, while Liberia and Somalia were humanitarian assistance missions.

In fact, it is not so common to sign up for several UN Volunteer assignments successively in a short period of time. If I keep on serving as a UN Volunteer specialist, it is not only because the assignments are regularly offered by UNV headquarters, but also because I believe that the capabilities of volunteers should be used. Compared to regular UN staff, some of whom are often most concerned with their careers and salaries, I found most UN Volunteers were motivated to work in challenging environments simply for the sake of what they could accomplish. They worked for satisfaction and job achievement, which harmonized with my own convictions. Although we are called "volunteers," a term that unfortunately leads some people to consider us second-class workers, volunteers prove most of the time to be extremely professional and are able to work both at the top and the grassroots levels. In this chapter, I will describe each of the assignments in which I participated and discuss the problems I faced and the lessons I learned.

CAMBODIA: WORKING AND LIVING IN LOCAL COMMUNITIES

In the United Nations Transitional Authority in Cambodia (UNTAC), the UNV Support Unit distinguished itself by organizing a six-week Khmer language course for arriving UN Volunteers. Although interpreters were recruited in the field, even a little knowledge of Khmer by the volunteers could make a big difference to the local people, and it demonstrated the volunteers' interest in the country.

After attending the course and election training in Phnom Penh, the 465 UN Volunteer district electoral supervisors, approximately half of us from Asia, were deployed in teams of two to every election district in the country. Because I was particularly interested in refugees, I asked to be fielded in the north-west region, where many Cambodian returnees tended to settle. Fortunately, I was assigned with a partner to Sisophon, the district capital of Banteay Meanchey Province, located next to the Thai border.

Upon arriving, we paid a visit to the district and provincial governors, political party members, and the local police to explain the purpose of our work. At the same time, we recruited Cambodian staff—two interpreters, a training assistant, and a clerk. We learned that Cambodians with management skills and fluent English could be found in Thai refugee camp, because of the extensive training provided there by NGOs. The district electoral supervisors in Banteay Meanchey Province obtained border passes and hired most of the local staff from across the border.

Our civic education efforts started in September 1992, when we began to visit all the villages in the district. We brought along television and video equipment to use as tools to teach about elections, democracy, human rights, and, particularly, the process of voter registration. The registration period began in November after we had recruited and trained additional staff. While some UN Volunteer district electoral supervisors were challenged by the task of registering Khmer Rouge in their territories, I found myself with the much easier job of "taxi driver," transporting the elderly and handicapped from their isolated villages to registration

UN Volunteer Masako Yonekawa, standing in the back of a UN truck, works to prepare the elections in Cambodia with her Cambodian counterparts, in her first UNV assignment. Photo: UNV

points. The overall effort of the UN Volunteer district electoral supervisors was so successful that 4.7 million voters were registered country-wide, meaning that 90 per cent of the population had a voter card and could vote.

The second round of civic education lasted for two months and centred on voter education. At the same time, we carried out the continual selection, recruitment, and management of nearly 50,000 Cambodian staff members all over the country. The two months prior to the election in May 1993 were spent training polling staff, establishing polling stations, and monitoring the activities of political parties during the campaign. During this period, we were under tremendous pressure because of the serious security problems in one of the most conflict-ridden provinces in Cambodia.

As part of a systematic and xenophobic Khmer Rouge strategy, ethnic Vietnamese living in Cambodia were repeatedly and violently attacked, and many eventually were forced to leave the country. Daily meetings with the Dutch military battalion, Civilian Police (CIVPOL), District Council members, and political parties were needed to discuss the security measures for the elections.

To the relief of all those working in the field, the long-expected five days of voting finally arrived, and during the election days there was no major violence in the country. In our district, more than 100 per cent of the eligible voters turned up; this percentage occurred because voters from other districts had been evacuated to our district for security reasons. Immediately after the voting, the manual counting of ballots was conducted for three consecutive days by UN Volunteer district electoral supervisors and International Polling Station Officers, and was observed by political party agents.

Besides living in the local communities we served, many UN Volunteer district electoral supervisors committed themselves to doing extra work, which provided another reason for local community acceptance. One UN Volunteer, a pharmacist, opened a clinic in his house and treated neighbours. Another UN Volunteer, a nurse, treated patients whenever she went to villages to conduct civic education. Other UN Volunteers helped rebuild village schools and bridges or coached local sports teams.

To help with education, I asked an NGO in a Thai refugee camp to donate Khmer books in order to establish small libraries in some pagodas in remote areas where there was no access to education materials. I also taught basic English to the children of my host landowner so they could get acquainted with the world through another language. Both of these activities were well appreciated by my community. These modest but significant acts brought UN Volunteer specialists closer to the communities in which we lived and worked.

UN Volunteers fostered the growth of local leadership by gradually giving our Cambodia staff more responsibility as the elections approached. Cambodians themselves conducted civic education and training throughout the country. This was not easy to develop in the beginning because most Cambodians were used to taking orders instead of acting on their own initiative. By inspiring the Cambodians to believe in efforts to build up their country, little by little we did our best to help them feel more confident. Because of my special concern about women, I tried to recruit as many women as possible and to give them more opportunities to participate in society; I tried to encourage them by talking to them about gender equality. While the informal training and civic education efforts were not likely to yield immediately visible results, these activities built into communities and people the potential for a better future.

Carrying out civic education in Cambodia was not without difficulties. The villagers' interests lay more in basic preoccupations such as housing, health, and food than in issues of democracy. How could one find interest in the ideals of democracy when one's basic needs are not fulfilled? I was sometimes afraid that UNTAC was trying to accomplish too many tasks simultaneously in too short a time: rehabilitation, repatriation, demobilization, and election. Could UNTAC have started first with rehabilitation and resettlement, and then consider organizing elections?

Just before the voter registration started in our province, some of the registration team members had not received their salaries. Therefore, paying local staff became a very serious issue for at least three months. Handling all financial matters from UNTAC headquarters in Phnom Penh proved to be a mistake. Most of the staff were returnees from Thai refugee camps and were starting all over in their homeland after a long absence. Obviously, they were in great need of money. It would have been tolerable if local and international staff also did not receive paychecks, but the fact that only local staff had not received payment could be seen as discrimination, which the UN should never practice. The UN Volunteers, working closely with the local staff, were probably the only people in UNTAC who could really understand and share the local staff's problems. As many UN Volunteers did, I lent money several times to our staff, although the lack of access to the remote Phnom Penh banks and my hectic work schedule meant I also faced financial difficulty from time to time.

Eventually, as the salary payment problem became unbearable, UNV district electoral supervisors and Cambodian staff planned a boycott during voter registration. Our supervisor, who opposed this idea, said that Cambodians could survive for three to four months without any pay after having painfully experienced 20 years of conflict. This inconsiderate attitude was unfortunately displayed by several UN staff who did not seem to realize the radical difference between the civil war and the present times. UNTAC, which had come to Cambodia to help, was creating by its own practices an opposite impression.

Although demobilization and disarmament were supposed to take place before the organization of democratic elections, UN Volunteers were deployed while civil war was still going on in certain areas. Initially, this odd situation did not significantly hamper UNTAC operations. But political violence and social tensions came to a climax as the election approached. One of the main factions, the Khmer Rouge, was openly hostile to both the electoral process and the UN staff.

UN Volunteers working at the grassroots were among the most exposed of UNTAC staff, at risk particularly because of our "political" role as symbols of the elections at the local level. Our recruitment of local staff, our possession of coveted equipment, and our handling of salaries of local staff also meant we were particularly vulnerable. One UNV district electoral supervisor was wounded in an ambush; another was injured in a mine accident; and a third was murdered. Three Cambodian electoral staff working with UN Volunteers were also killed. A number of UN personnel were detained, threatened (sometimes at gunpoint), and had their homes, offices, or vehicles broken into. Some were caught in cross-fire, were the direct target of armed attacks, or operated in areas under constant gunfire or shelling.

As the security situation deteriorated in several parts of the country, many UN Volunteers felt that the security measures taken by UNTAC did not keep pace with events. In April 1993, after the deaths of UNV district electoral supervisor Atsuhito Nakata and his Cambodian interpreter, UN Volunteers urged at a meeting in Phnom Penh with the representatives of the other UNTAC components that improved security arrangements and a review of the prospects for a "free and fair" election be undertaken.

It had been initially believed that the Khmer Rouge shot our colleagues dead. Then it was thought that a Cambodian who had applied to work in a polling station and had been rejected after an interview with Atsuhito might have ambushed him. Such news frightened many UN Volunteers, who were doing the same job as Atsu (as we called him) had been doing. Recruiting polling staff was arduous due to aggressive competition among Cambodians, including farmers, school teachers, students, housewives, public officials, and the unemployed. In my district alone, more than 1,000 applicants turned up for 250 polling staff positions. The salary was sometimes as much as US$200 a month. This is an extremely high amount of money when compared with the $10 to $20 a month salary of a Cambodian public official.

It may be worthwhile for the UN to carefully consider local standards before deciding on the salary of the locally recruited staff. UN Volunteers, who work closely with the community, could have been consulted before decisions were made regarding local personnel, especially because these decisions could have far-reaching consequences for volunteers' security in the field. UN Volunteers in the field often understood the local situation better than did headquarters personnel, who had little contact with local conditions. As later events proved, people in the field also would eventually pay the price.

Cambodia was also a challenge when it came to the distribution of any kinds of goods, including radios. Radio UNTAC was established to inform people about the upcoming elections, but many Cambodians did not own radios. The Special Representative of Secretary-General of UNTAC asked a Japanese organization to collect second-hand radios. These radios were to be distributed to Cambodians who could not afford to buy their own. Radios arrived throughout the country with this instruction: hand out the radios to people who could not afford to buy them. But how could we distinguish those who could afford to buy radios from those who could not? In fairness, shouldn't there be enough radios to give one to each family? Offering radios only to selected categories of people could be troublesome. Additionally, batteries were not always provided with the radios; these were essential in a country without regular electricity.

I decided to donate the radios one by one to each pagoda, school, and village centre, thereby giving villagers easy access to the news. However, some military observers gave out the radios randomly to the villagers. As could be expected, those who received small radios envied those who got big ones. The day after the distribution, some radios appeared on the shop shelves for sale. Soon after, our office and the Dutch military battalion base camp were surrounded by the people who had not received radios, shouting "I want radio!" Some UN Volunteers were threatened. It was a chaotic time!

This kind of incident could have had dangerous consequences. The impact on the community should be part of the planning of every activity. One way of doing this is to consult the people at the grassroots, i.e., those working in the field.

Security has been always the main issue for UN Volunteers working in the hazardous areas wherever I have served. As civilians, UN Volunteer specialists do not carry arms, but they are exposed to more danger due to their presence in the communities. This means precautionary measures need to be taken. Yet in Cambodia, despite the death of our colleague and the increase in violence before the election, most UN Volunteers were determined to continue and to see the job through. Even though I was advised by colleagues to leave the country, I refused to leave because of my desire to see the work finished.

Finally, UN Volunteer specialists have sometimes been perceived as cheap labour, and this perception has sometimes influenced their status or recognition in the operations. As a matter of fact, in UNTAC, it was estimated that the cost of fielding a UN Volunteer was about 75 per cent less than the cost for one regular UN staff member or for a consultant. Information needs to be carried out so that UN senior officials understand and recognize the special and unique role UN Volunteers play in UN operations.

LIBERIA: BEYOND ROUTINE ACTIVITIES

In December 1990, the United Nations Special Coordinator's Office in Liberia (UNSCOL) was established to organize delivery of emergency relief in Monrovia, the capital of the country, which was suffering from a bitter civil war. The work was later expanded throughout the country. The UN Volunteers serving with UNSCOL played important roles in logistics, food aid monitoring, and health and agricultural programmes.

In January 1992, UNV began its own programme of Multisectoral Technical Support for Emergency Relief Activities in Liberia. The aim was to ensure that emergency relief was effectively delivered to internally displaced people, and to encourage Liberians to grow their own food crops. More than one year later, in September 1993, the United Nations Observer Mission in Liberia (UNOMIL) was established to help implement the Cotonou Peace Agreement, which established guidelines for resolving the dispute between the warring sides. The creation of UNOMIL brought more UN Volunteers into Liberia.

Working as an information officer, first with UNSCOL and later with United Nations Development Programme (UNDP), I summarized weekly situation reports from all UN agencies, including United Nations Children's Fund (UNICEF), World Food Programme (WFP), World Health Organization (WHO), Food and Agriculture Organization (FAO), and United Nations High Commissioner for Refugees (UNHCR). I also recorded minutes of weekly meetings of heads of UN Agencies and UNOMIL, and disseminated to local organizations UN information received from the Division of Public Information. I also met with the UNOMIL Public Information Division staff to discuss the media promotion of UN activities, and I sometimes represented UNDP at ceremonies and local events.

Making the most of my previous field experience in Cambodia, I arranged information sessions on UN peace-related activities to be presented at elementary and secondary schools, and to university and government officials (such as the Ministry of Education), human rights groups, local journalists, and NGOs. Apart from my routine work, I also had the opportunity to participate in some humanitarian assistance activities by joining in food convoys or airdrops and other UNHCR field activities near the Sierra Leonean border.

Promoting International Volunteer Day, December 5, can be another means to strengthen volunteerism. To celebrate this special day with the local volunteers in Liberia, we collected financial donations from UN and local NGO staff to be used for vulnerable people all over the country. We distributed basic commodities to the aged, orphans, and women, and we built a home for a displaced family. Although it was only a one-day activity, events like this day help promote the ideals of volunteerism in the local population and can be followed up throughout the year by other voluntary action projects.

UN Volunteers had been working in Liberia even before the war, developing water projects and serving as aid coordinators. At the outbreak of the war in 1989, they were evacuated. Later, new requests were made for UN Volunteers who could work in emergency and logistical support. As of August 1994, 32 UN Volunteer specialists were serving in Liberia. They assisted Sierra Leonean refugees with the United Nations High Commissioner for Refugees; worked in multisectoral and emergency logistics support with United Nations Development Programme and United Nations Children's Fund; provided emergency relief to displaced persons; or helped the National AIDS Programme with the World Health Organization. Half of the UN Volunteers were from African countries, including Kenya, Sierra Leone, Somalia, Sudan, Tanzania, and Uganda. Other volunteers came from the United States, United Kingdom, Canada, Germany, India, Japan, and Sri Lanka. Most of my UN Volunteer colleagues were in their twenties or thirties.

The UNV Programme manager, who was from Germany, also served as programme coordinator for 45 small-scale businesses set up under the "Trickle-Up" project. This programme was a non-profit, private organization funded by UNDP. In conjunction with local NGOs, this German woman helped organize the "Partners in Development" project, which specifically targeted small-scale businesses and self-help initiatives for women in Liberia. UN Volunteers were involved in many small projects because more comprehensive programmes had not been developed due to the ongoing war. There will be expanded opportunities for UN Volunteers to assist Liberians in rebuilding their society and infrastructure, especially at the community level, when the country becomes more stable.

UN Volunteers also recruited national and regional volunteers in Liberia for humanitarian assistance. These volunteers were often the most effective at this work because of their understanding of local situations and their knowledge of the problems and what was needed to address them.

SOUTH AFRICA: SYMBOLS OF CHANGE WITHIN THE SOCIETY

In South Africa, I was one of the 200 UN Volunteer specialists deployed at the provincial level as Observation Support Officers within the United

Nations Observer Mission in South Africa (UNOMSA). We were given two main tasks: to prepare the logistics on the ground for the arrival of 1,600 UN International Election Observers (IEOs) just prior to the election, and to serve as observers during the election. Our duties included identifying the location of polling stations and local road conditions.

We also worked to reinforce peace activities by monitoring the last phase of the electoral campaign, and by observing party rallies and other political events. On the election days, we visited the voting stations and recorded the events. After the elections, we monitored the transportation of electoral material, as well as the counting and review of disputed ballots at the provincial and national levels.

I was deployed to a town called Beaufort West, in Western Cape, where the majority of the people were mixed-race South Africans, once designated as "coloured." The National Party dominated the area politically. Unlike Johannesburg and Natal provinces, the Western Cape was extremely peaceful, which made our work easier. I shared a house and worked in close cooperation with a UN Volunteer from Zambia. Almost all UN Volunteers teamed up in pairs of one black and one white volunteer. This startled the residents, who were unfamiliar with integrated work groups. It surely had a strong impact on the community by raising awareness of the radical changes taking place in the South African society.

However, apartheid still existed not only mentally but also physically in this conservative town. One of our colleagues was refused entrance to a hotel that had posted a sign saying "Whites Only." The daughter of parents from France and the Caribbean, she was identified in South Africa as "coloured." No matter how much she emphasized her French nationality, the hotel manager asserted that her skin colour was not white enough to stay at the hotel. As electoral observers, the only measure we could take was to report this incident to UNOMSA headquarters.

To my surprise, one Irish international observer had a bad reputation among the white South African voting staff for his "over-friendliness" to some of the mixed-race female staff. To the whites, it was unacceptable to see a white man with a mixed race or black woman. Though the election was successful, it will still take a long time for some South Africans to overcome these racial attitudes.

In South Africa, our work was mainly to observe the electoral process. UN Volunteers who had worked on the election in Cambodia may have felt at times that the limits placed on our activities were frustrating. Although our presence was necessary, I wish the assignment could have allowed us to participate more. I would have preferred to intervene more, rather than to just observe, which often meant simply reporting to UNOMSA what we saw.

Briefing manuals were essential to help us acquire a basic knowledge of the country and to learn about the people and their culture. In South Africa, the UNV orientation and briefing manual was so effective that it was eventually used as a model for training other observer groups. This kind of initiative can have a significant influence on missions. The duration of missions also is important. In South Africa, it would have been worthwhile for UN Volunteers to have arrived earlier before the elections and to have stayed on longer after the elections. By the time we were getting to understand the situation and to establish personal connections with the residents, we had to leave the country. The work of observing the elections process allowed us to become directly involved in communities throughout the country and to interact with the newborn political institutions. Because of the short duration of our mission, this potential could not be adequately exploited.

In Cambodia, although the mission had been much longer, some UN Volunteers felt this same frustration. The overwhelming attention had been given to preparation for and conducting of the elections, while the post-election nation-building seemed somehow to have been neglected. The opportunities UN Volunteers had in both of these missions to develop contacts within communities were extraordinarily valuable. Capitalizing on the experience of UN Volunteer specialists already in-country to build community projects would strengthen ties between local people and the UN. This is the unique grassroots contribution that UN Volunteers can make within the UN system. To better exploit this contribution it would be necessary to keep UN Volunteers in place, to allow them to contribute even more.

SOMALIA: ENHANCING LOCAL PARTICIPATION

I probably experienced the worst security situation, among my four UN Volunteer assignments, in Somalia. The United Nations Operation in Somalia (UNOSOM II) was established in an environment that was unstable and devoid of hope since the country collapsed into anarchy in January 1991. The UN mission itself was crumbling, both militarily and politically. The clan-based Somali factions were rearming rapidly; the kidnapping of foreigners was commonplace; and UN peacekeepers were being killed in record numbers, tolling the bell of UNOSOM's withdrawal.

Some Somali people seemed to perceive the whole international effort as something that was owed to them, and from which they should personally benefit. During my three-month stay, from July to October 1994, three UNOSOM zone offices outside Mogadishu closed down due to deteriorating security.

Most of the UN international staff based in Mogadishu, including UN Volunteers, stayed in the United States Embassy compound, where UNOSOM II's offices and residences were located. Movement outside the compound was restricted, and always under armed guard. Direct contact with the people, except for the locally recruited Somali staff working in the UNOSOM compound, was non-existent; shopping at local markets was forbidden.

Most of the 18,000 UNOSOM military troops were concentrated in the capital and were performing "force protection" roles, meaning they were mainly responsible for securing the UN staff's safety. Many unfortunate incidents occurred: a Zimbabwean unit of 168 men was robbed of its weapons, uniforms, and vehicles by General Mohammad Farah Aidid's militia and was forced to evacuate its base in Beletweyne; 25 Pakistani soldiers, including army doctors, were killed. UNOSOM had died much earlier in terms of its effectiveness. Some UN staff, including several UN Volunteers, were redeployed to Rwanda by the end of July 1994 to achieve more productive work. Many of the international staff had reached the conclusion that Somalia was likely to remain a country without a government for a long time to come. Finally, the Security Council made a decision to withdraw UNOSOM by the end of March 1995.

I had thought that UN Volunteer specialists were intended to provide technical development assistance to local people. In electoral missions, they were to manage and monitor politically sensitive activities, helped by their neutrality. In humanitarian missions, UN Volunteers were to help distribute humanitarian aid. However, in Somalia, UN Volunteers had become generalists. The UNV programme in Somalia started to expand in April 1994 with the signing of a Memorandum of Understanding for the fielding of 223 UN Volunteers to support the operations of UNOSOM II. UNV gave UNOSOM ample flexibility to determine the type of volunteer jobs that were needed.

Of the 213 posts established, 62 were in substantive divisions and were involved in formulating long-term development policies, providing humanitarian assistance to the Somali community, facilitating the resettlement of internally displaced persons, re-establishing the criminal justice system, and promoting the disarmament and demobilization of militia. Another 157 UN Volunteers were serving in administrative support areas.

The Memorandum of Understanding signed between UN and UNV left the door open for all types of positions with a singular objective—support to the UNOSOM operation. As a result, posts such as UN Volunteer switchboard operator and UN Volunteer accommodation officer were also created. UN Volunteers were being spread too thin and too wide, and they risked losing their identity while at the same time they were considered by some as unskilled cheap labour. This attitude raised levels of frustration and competition. Would it not have been better to identify a few visible and clearly distinct functions in substantive divisions?

I served as a UN Volunteer Orientation and Documentation Officer in the Policy and Planning Group (PPG) of UNOSOM. As an integral part of the office of the Special Representative of the Secretary-General in Somalia, the PPG developed strategies and policies, and planned for their implementation by undertaking research and analysis. It also carried out orientation and training of UNOSOM staff regarding the UNOSOM mission mandate, goals, roles, and activities. I was therefore involved in activities like following up political events, helping to conduct a Somali language course for UN Volunteers, meeting Japanese embassy officials to negotiate funds for the Somalia National Volunteer Program, and helping to organize a UN Volunteers workshop.

My main task was originally to gather relevant information for briefing and debriefing sessions and for training programmes for the newly arrived UNOSOM personnel. In fact, I ended up organizing these programmes only for UN Volunteers because in UNOSOM no orientation or training was given to any civilian or military staff except UN Volunteers. "The background of people must be taken into consideration; they have a strong nomadic tradition, they have fought over turf, watering holes.... If you are asking if they can run a (Western-style) government, the answer is no," the Special Representative of the Secretary-General once said. But at that time, when the UNOSOM operation was about to withdraw, and while I was conducting training, the environment was not very supportive of this kind of orientation exercise.

Besides administering international UN Volunteers serving in Somalia, the UNV Support Unit in Mogadishu also worked to implement an original Somali National Volunteer (SNV) Programme. The objective of this programme was to mobilize the constructive energy of youth and other people by engaging them on a volunteer basis in activities aimed at peace-building and capacity-building of communities, particularly at regional and district levels. This was to promote local participation in the management and ownership of rehabilitation, reconstruction, and development efforts undertaken in the country. The goal was the increased involvement of Somali professionals through expanded opportunities in project planning and implementation.

Together with a Somali officer of the Policy and Planning Group, I was given the responsibility to monitor one Somali National Volunteer project to rehabilitate an irrigation canal outside Mogadishu. The project aimed at enhancing the agricultural production through improved water flow, using the work of local volunteers. After assessing the situation at the site, the project was put into effect by the Nigerian military contingent, the implementing partner on the site.

One of the lessons from the Somali experience is that a too-high standard of living by international staff can deeply affect the relationship between this staff and the local communities. In Somalia, although some people considered the UN compound a "prison," life with 24-hour electricity, restaurant, bar, tennis court, and even a swimming pool was comparatively comfortable. At the end of the mission, each bedroom was equipped with a shower, refrigerator, and was air-conditioned.

Apart from the occasional shelling or stray bullets that reached the compound, it was a totally different world from the rest of Somalia. UNOSOM's efforts to improve the living conditions of hundreds of international civilian staff were somehow shocking for the Somalis. The international civilian staff appeared to have become a self-perpetuating bureaucracy of people biding their time, collecting their salaries in the relative safety of the UN compound, and waiting for the UN Security Council to pull the plug on a mission that was costing US$2.5 million a day. UNOSOM might have given the impression it spent more on renovation of the United States Embassy compound than on responding to the needs of the Somalis, and this image was one of the reasons many Somali people resented the UN's presence. This feeling contributed to the deterioration of the UN's relationship with the Somali society.

Another lesson from the mission is that projects that involve local people and resources, such as the Somalia National Volunteer Programme, should be enhanced in the future. These local programmes avoid dependency on external aid by receiving modest but sufficient support, and they can enhance the reallocation of human resources from unemployment or non-productive military activities to value-creating work. Particularly in a war-torn country, young people are drawn to violence and crime. Efforts to change that pattern require major incentives to lift them from the vicious cycle of conflict, deprivation, and poverty. Well-trained national volunteers can also be a "forecaster" of crisis, giving early warning of trouble so as to allow appropriate intervention.

One of the causes of the tension between UNOSOM and Somalia came from the misuse of military power. The show of international military strength not only scared the local people but also led to hostility towards the UN. This occurred despite the military contingents' great contribution to humanitarian assistance, including the assistance given to local NGOs for education and health services, which should not be ignored. To counter the effect of the heavy military presence, fielding UN Volunteers throughout the country to foster the recruitment of local volunteers from the beginning of UNOSOM's deployment could have helped forestall such a poisonous environment.

CONCLUSION

The expectation of close contact with the local people is often an important element in the decision to apply to become a UN Volunteer. The inherent value of making direct contact and assisting people who are experiencing distress or who have critical unmet needs is a fundamental part of the service-oriented motivation for many of us.

This is why my experience in UNTAC was probably the most rewarding. In Cambodia, UNV proved its potential to contribute significantly to peacekeeping and democratization. UN Volunteers lived and worked in the communities, but also took an active role by planning and implementing the election programmes along with the local Cambodian staff they had recruited. They had a widely recognized unique role as civic educators, electoral supervisors, and personnel and logistics officers at the grassroots level.

In my own experience in missions in Liberia, South Africa, and Somalia, this kind of social exchange with the community was almost impossible because of the lack of direct contact with people and the short duration of stay. In Somalia, the complexity and uncertainty of the UNOSOM mandates and operations, the sometimes low level of responsibility or required skills, and the lack of recognition eventually added to the UN Volunteers' frustration and affected their morale and identity.

The importance of proper orientation even for short-term assignments cannot be emphasized enough. Training, including language courses, can be crucial to helping people understand and integrate into local communities. Every effort should be undertaken to provide the best possible training, regardless of the time and expense it may take, especially when fielding a large group of people with different backgrounds, experiences, and assignment expectations, to ensure that all have a clear idea of what is expected from them as UN Volunteers. This was done successfully in

Cambodia and South Africa. Additionally, debriefing at the end of the mission is also necessary. It also gives the volunteers an opportunity to evaluate their assignment and avoids repetition of mistakes in future missions.

Technical cooperation, community development, environment, population, peace operations, democratization, and humanitarian relief and rehabilitation.... Since its establishment, and especially in recent years, the involvement of the UNV Programme is widening more and more. I think it is time for UNV to be an agency by itself, with its own autonomy, field infrastructure, and resources. Also, at the present time, the UN identification is the only official identification provided to UN Volunteers. This identification may lead to discrimination against them in their daily activities, and in certain circumstances it may hamper their work or put them in difficult situations. UN diplomatic passports should be provided to UN Volunteers for easy and fast access to mission countries.

At the same time, UNV needs to find ways of tapping its valuable network of "alumni" for its ongoing programmes, in the spirit of assisting volunteer networks worldwide. Establishing communication forums for UN Volunteers and developing channels for them to make contributions through means such as the UNV South Links project, a worldwide electronic networking effort, could be worthwhile. This kind of activity is especially important for Japan, where volunteerism is beginning to grow. Gradually, more Japanese people are showing interest in volunteering, particularly after the death of Atsuhito Nakata in Cambodia, which attracted wide media coverage in Japan. Atsuhito's father, Takehito Nakata, established a memorial fund in the memory of his son. As UNV honorary ambassador, he travels around the world, speaking about the importance of volunteering. However, many people in Japan and other countries may still feel as if volunteer development work is beyond their reach, done only by extraordinary people. It is part of our duty to erase this misconception.

I believe that UNV, a unique part of the UN, provides a specific and original kind of human resource. Many UN Volunteers are from Africa and Asia, whereas most international organizations are Western-dominated. By teaching and training, monitoring and managing, inspiring and motivating, UN volunteers are in the front line of the struggle against poverty and conflict.

9

THE ART OF BUILDING PEACE: ARTISAN SKILLS FOR DEVELOPMENT AND PEACE IN SOUTH ASIA

Shantum Seth

THE PRINCIPLES EMBODIED in the United Nations Charter[1] aim at saving succeeding generations from war, promoting social progress, and reaffirming faith in fundamental human rights. Yet today, 50 years after the UN was founded, the world situation is grim, especially from the perspective of the marginalized and dispossessed. Social disintegration, increasing militarization, lack of fulfillment of basic needs, and deprivation of fundamental rights are the stark reality for hundreds of millions of people around the globe.

With the rapid increase in industrialization and the recent trends of globalization of the economy, artisans[2] as a community are among the most adversely affected. They have become one of the poorest communities in the world. Continuing cycles of deprivation and unemployment have led to an increasing rise in the incidence of suicides, prostitution, and starvation[3] among artisan households of the South Asian region. The conflict is both economic and political. It pertains to access to raw mate-

Shantum Seth is United Nations Volunteer Programme Manager, for the Programme for Artisan Development in South Asia. An Indian-British national born in 1957, he is a graduate of the British Boot and Shoe Institute and holds a B.A. in development studies from the University of East Anglia.

rials, markets, credit, and policies that favour international capital and global markets, which, in turn, depend on sophisticated technologies. This global approach is the opposite of local, ecologically sustainable forms of economic production and marketing that support the poor majority and which are the strength of South Asia. This is a struggle between the voiceless, who have the knowledge and ability to sustain the Earth as a living planet, and the powerful, who are mortgaging and destroying its life support systems.

Additionally, in South Asia, the tensions between Hindus and Muslims brought on by religious intolerance easily flare up and consume thousands of innocent lives. Divisions of caste and class keep neighbours apart. The Aryan and Mongolian ethnic and racial groups have little understanding of each other, even though they inhabit some of the same countries. Tribal and non-tribal groups have a long history of fearing each other; conduct between hill people and people of the plains is often based on mistrust. Linguistic divisions have caused riots and deaths.

Increasing animosity between different groups within countries has led to alienation among nations as well. Religious and ethnic conflict thrive in an environment where there is often practically no communication, much less genuine sharing, between different communities. Nations in the region, with some of the largest standing armies in the world and equipped with the most sophisticated armaments, including nuclear capacity, are suspicious of each other. Past conflicts have produced waves of refugees.

Normally it is fear and ignorance that fuel conflicts, at both the personal and national levels. Accumulated experience has shown, however, that fear can be reduced, even eradicated, through processes to promote understanding and sharing. Bringing people together, especially those with a similar trade or skill and who are victims of marginalization as well as past or potential victims of open violence, can result in a healthy technical cooperation, sharing of information, and access to finance, raw materials, and markets. This bringing together also can yield practical lessons on how to ally with one another, to organize, to unite, and to voice alternatives relevant to their own condition and needs.

CONFLICT IN DEVELOPMENT

Mr. Sale is from a family of traditional shoemakers in the village of Chincholi, of the Maharastra region in western India. Until a few years ago, six shoemakers in the village handcrafted leather sandals for the local people.

But last year Mr. Sale joined the five other former shoemakers as daily wage labourers on the farms of the large landholders, because his footwear business had completely collapsed. Villagers were increasingly buying factory-made and plastic footwear, and he could no longer afford to buy the raw materials needed to make his shoes. The price for those raw materials had dramatically increased due to government incentives for export of leather goods by industrial corporations.

By Asian standards, he is rather lucky. Across South Asia, as local artisan-based economies collapse, horror stories abound: weavers in Andhra Pradesh in central India hanged themselves on their looms because they could no longer afford to buy yarn due to policies favouring exporters;[4] potters in Kerala in southern India encouraged their wives and daughters to become prostitutes when their earthen pots no longer could compete with aluminium and steel.[5] A leader among the carcass flayers was murdered by a local contractor for organizing a flayers' cooperative to demand their traditional rights and to bypass the contractor as a middleman.[6] Accompanying the tragic loss of these lives is the loss of centuries of accumulated human skills. Arts that have been handed down from generation to generation—in some cases for as long as 5,000 years—are vanishing over the course of a few decades.

Many of these dispossessed people join the growing ranks of the unemployed, living in unsanitary city slums and eking out an existence through begging and crime. This situation further waters the seeds for class, inter-religious, and ethnic violence. This is the plight of millions of people not only in Asia but in Africa and Latin America as well.

The situation epitomizes the escalating global conflict between industrial development and the traditional, indigenous ways of living in local, ecologically sustainable economies. This conflict results in profound human suffering at a physical, psychological, and spiritual level. Even artisans such as Mr. Sale who manage to find work to keep themselves and their families alive face the loss of their self respect and, indeed, of their very identity since their new employment is low-skilled, menial work.

In contrast to this bleak picture, traditional and appropriate technologies are decentralized and environmentally sustainable. They provide opportunities for individual creativity and community dignity while producing income. This alternative way of life, which supports livelihoods and provides a basis for the promotion of friendly relations, is the subject of this chapter and of a special United Nations Volunteers programme in South Asia.

THE UNV PROGRAMME FOR ARTISAN DEVELOPMENT IN SOUTH ASIA

The South Asian region has one of the largest resource pools of skilled crafts people in the world. After agriculture, the artisan sector provides the highest employment in the non-organized sector. At a conservative estimate there are 50 million artisans[7] in the region, a large number of whom are women and minorities. Most of the professional skills among artisans have been inherited and are fundamentally related to the culture of their host societies.

The United Nations Volunteers Programme for Artisan Development in South Asia (PADSA) began in 1992. Since then PADSA has been working over the past two and a half years with rural artisan communities in Nepal, Bhutan, Sri Lanka, and the five regions of India. The work has been concentrated in three sectors—bamboo, weaving (by women), and leather work.

PADSA takes the position that development work among the dispossessed contributes towards sustainable peace, and that the *Agenda for Peace*[8] and the *Agenda for Development*[9] complement each other. PADSA has developed a method to encourage mutual exchange and to build support systems among artisan groups, as well as with related non-governmental organizations (NGOs), community-based organizations (CBOs), and institutions. It has brought artisans together using "barefoot"[10] expertise to improve their livelihood, to gain a greater sense of self-esteem, and to influence policies that affect them. Artisan exchange is seen as helpful to the creation of peaceful environments, both immediately and in the longer term, in different communities. The objective is consonant with UNV's mandate to "promote peace, cultural exchange and understanding."[11] PADSA believes that in the long-term building equitable and sustainable economies motivated by volunteers using production and marketing methods harmonious with the culture of the host societies will lessen conflicts within and between societies.

PADSA has worked in both pre- and post-conflict situations. The pre-conflict work has centred on encouraging artisans with similar skills, but from different groups that often have traditional animosities towards each other and that are divided in many ways endemic to the subcontinent, to work together, share, teach, and learn from each other. The objective of these activities is to develop understanding and friendship and thereby to overcome potential conflicts. This mutual exchange is one method to lessen conflict and build peace within particular societies and between people from different countries.

Peace at a sensible price: "barefoot" artisans share their expertise in the UNV Programme for Artisan Development in South Asia. Photo: UNV/PADSU

One of the "barefoot" bamboo experts from Tripura in northeast India, Gita Bhowmick, is always accompanied by her young son, Biswajit. During many occasions he has broken the ice of social discomfort between people of different regions. The first time his mother came to Narendrapur in eastern India he was barely a year old. During the first hours the artisans were sitting in their own groups, based on their home regions. Brought together from four countries, they represented six regions, plains and hill people, tribal and non-tribal members, and various castes. Soon, Biswajit left his mother's lap and started crawling around, visiting all the participants; eventually he was adopted by everyone. He is an energetic boy, not shy, and always getting into some mischief. This creates ample opportunities for participants to keep a common eye on him as collective parents. It was touching for us to observe how Malati Hebram, a Santhal tribe member, overcame language and caste barriers to care for Biswajit as if he were her own grandchild. During these kinds of exchanges, I witnessed harmonious conditions subtly developing in a number of ways that encourage people of different groups to come together. This is done by artisans together buying raw materials, sharing space in dormitory rooms, and creating a common product.

I also introduced PADSA into post-conflict situations. When an exchange programme was being organized for bamboo artisans across South Asia, a possible venue was Tamil Gnat in South India. On hearing this a UN Volunteer from Sri Lanka suggested that an eastern India venue be chosen since it would not be possible for the Singhalese Sri Lankan artisans to attend if the venue was in the Tamil area of India, the homeland of their enemy. But the Tamil location was chosen, and when the Sri Lankan artisans, Mr. Hiratbanda, Mr. Bowathdeniya, and Mr. Sunil, arrived in the Tamil area, they settled down under a large tree where all the artisans were to meet and share their expertise with each other over the next ten days. It so happened that the Tamil artisans, Mr. Palaniswamy and Ms. Ambika, settled down next to the Singhalese Sri Lankans, and there they stayed for the whole period, and cultivated an ever increasing familiarity and friendship. The airline on which the Sri Lankans had flown did not allow them to carry their tools, which were perceived as a security risk. So the Sri Lankans needed to borrow and share tools of the other artisans, including the Tamils. As the days passed, a camaraderie developed within the group, exemplified by Mr. Sunil and Mr. Palaniswamy, Singhalese Sri Lankan and Tamil, walking together, arms across shoulders, after helping each other in the harvesting of bamboo.

Artisan work is also a means of occupying refugees in a creative way. Most often, even in a long-term refugee situation, there is not enough land to grow crops; this leads to cycles of dependence. Refugees, suffering from loss and displacement, can benefit from learning traditional skills, which then provide a basis for financial support. Refugees suffer from a lack of public recognition due to their temporary living situation, which can stretch over a lifetime in camps. Working together is the beginning of building a strong sense of identification; it also is a self-empowering tool for refugees to restore their confidence following flight and resettlement in another country.

I introduced PADSA into areas of work with Tibetan refugee communities located within India and appointed a National UN Volunteer who was a Tibetan refugee himself. Many of the artisans in this community, such as at Majnu ka Tila, near New Delhi in northern India, have given up their traditions and are selling food and Tibetan home-brewed beer. They reported they would be happy to return to craft work if they could market their products.[12]

I decided to concentrate on the Tibetan refugee communities in Karnataka in southern India. The refugee women weavers who participated in the programme from five refugee communities, Kollegal, Mundgod, Hunsur, and old and new Bylakuppe, were excited to meet weavers whose work they had heard about and to share weaving techniques and to feel a sense of solidarity in an alien land. They also started to help each other market their carpets, thus achieving recognition for their work. They organized an exhibition stall at the Kalachakra initiations given by the Dalai Lama, which many foreigners, the main group of buyers, visited. At the end of the exchanges, tears of gladness rolled down the cheeks of the participants.[13] In appreciation, the weavers wove some carpets incorporating the UNV logo. A number of them told me they were willing to volunteer and support PADSA to strengthen the artisan work in their own communities.

BAREFOOT DIPLOMACY

The *Agenda for Peace* put forward by the UN Secretary-General at the request of governments is being put into action by PADSA through practical skills exchange, cooperation, peacemaking, and preventive diplomacy by the people themselves. Often spanning communities with traditional animosities, these artisans commonly share the adverse effects of economic conflict arising from access to resources for livelihood.

The people of Nagaland in northeast India have been struggling for autonomy since India became independent in 1947. Phuden Phom, an artisan from Nagaland, found that by coming to the exchange workshop in Bengal, his prejudices about other people of India began to break down. Up until that time, he had been exposed only to army soldiers or business people from other parts of India. After meeting the artisans and volunteers, he said to me innocently, "I was not aware that there were such good people in India."

Nityanand Baishiya from Assam in northeast India made a similar comment about his visit to Bengal, with whom the people of Assam have had an ongoing cold war. He said it had been good for him to have had the opportunity to interact closely with the Bengalis and visit their homes. He was hoping that some of the artisans he had met in Bengal would visit him in his home in Assam. The artisans from Bengal wanted to study the bamboo species of Assam, which were better suited to their craftwork, and to find out if this bamboo could be cultivated in their own villages. I arranged such a visit.

The artisans of three villages of West Bengal visited four northeastern states to collect species of bamboo. At the same time they held discussions on how to jointly overcome the unfair pricing system of bamboo in India. An individual bamboo artisan buys one pole of bamboo for the equivalent of US$1 to US$2. However, the paper industry contracts to buy a ton of bamboo (approximately 700 bamboos) for seven cents (US), which works out to one one-hundredth of a cent for each bamboo, a ratio of 15,000 to 1 against members of one of the poorest communities in the world! Lawyers working with National UN Volunteer Gitanjali Varma, who is also a lawyer, volunteered to develop a case in support of the artisans.

It was fascinating to observe the satisfied smiles on the faces and hear the joyful laughter of many of the artisans, like Joydeb Pandit of Bengal, Subodh Roy of Tripura, and Niamon Phom of Nagaland, after they had shared some of their techniques with each other. This was possible even though these people did not speak a common language.[14] It was heartwarming for me to see artisans from different cultural and religious backgrounds who use different gestures and words of greeting making the effort to greet each other in the gesture and words of the others, thereby making efforts to communicate and appreciate each other.

It was during the informal moments that many of the friendships developed; these times were spent eating together, sharing each others' food, caring for each other at times of illness, shopping together, taking walks, and silently sharing the beauty of nature. While artisans with different racial features sat together at the base of a tree as friends, passers-by in the village stopped to wonder. On the other hand, working together with people of different races and gender was not easy in some of the more male-dominated communities of the subcontinent, where unkind and crude remarks were often made by passers-by, such as: "How much did you buy her for?"

Tolerance and mutual respect are the basis for diplomatic efforts. Not far from Nellie in Assam of north-east India, the site of a 1983 massacre among Muslims and Hindus, artisans from the two communities came together more than 10 years later for a sale and exhibition and an exchange, helping each other in techniques and methods of marketing. There were also many artisans from tribes in the area, for whom no feast would be complete without pork. During the exchange there was a special meal organized for the participants, and the Muslims, knowing the food habits of the others, were hospitably agreeable to having pork served for those who wanted it.[15]

Sometimes unexpected connections are discovered between commu-

Overcoming differences: music and dance help people from different regions to appreciate each other. Photo: UNV/PADSU

nities and nations that bring a sense of unity. When UNV Honorary Ambassador Takehito Nakata[16] visited our bamboo exchange in Bishnupur in eastern India, he shared his views on the importance of bamboo and artisanship in the culture of Japan. He encouraged the artisans to continue in their craft with pride. Birason Doley, a young flute maker from Assam and a participant at the exchange, played a few enchanting tunes on the flute on the pentatonic scale which were "remarkably similar to the Japanese folk songs which were mainly sung by the horsemen," the honorary ambassador told us.

In Japan, Ambassador Nakata explained, there were originally no horses. Horses and experienced horsemen were imported many years ago from the Asian continent. They brought with them their work songs, Mongolian melodies. "Listening to his melody, I felt as if I were in Japan. This is indeed a vast international cultural exchange, I believe," Mr. Nakata told us. This experience encouraged him to sing a song and the others to demonstrate their Bihu folk dances, since it was the celebration of Rangoli Bihu, the spring harvest festival and the start of the new year for some of the participants. At all of our exchanges, music and dance have created an atmosphere for sharing among people from diverse linguistic and cultural backgrounds and have helped to increase communication and the breaking down of barriers.

Niamon Phom of Nagaland spoke emotionally about how the opportunity to meet bamboo artisans from different states, whose work he had only heard about, gave him the same satisfaction as he felt after thoroughly enjoying a good meal with friends. It was "a God-sent opportunity, as the communities did not know much about each other" and "an opportunity to build peace through cultural exchange," Niamon Phom said.

VOLUNTEERISM

Caring, helping, sharing, creating alliances, and establishing cooperation on the basis of solidarity rather than competition or profit—these are the chief characteristics of volunteerism, expressed in a wide variety of situations and across barriers of class, ethnicity, community, and nation.

The spirit of selfless service runs highest in volunteers since their motivations are not for money, fame, power, or greed but are based on altruistic values. The motivation is the good of others, even though it may not serve the narrow conception of self-interest. It is based on love and non-violence and a desire to serve without reward and to bring about peace.

To be an effective volunteer requires a degree of commitment in which the volunteer extends to be of service to a wider cause. This means being willing to go beyond the call of duty and time, often at no remuneration or a remuneration that is below the market price for one's skill and expertise. Some of the volunteers in the PADSA team, including myself, used part of their living allowances to support artisans and develop programmes for artisan support.

Effective volunteering requires the ability to listen deeply to the people with whom one is working. Language skills are of great importance, but just as important is the ability to build understanding with the communities one is serving. The compassion that relieves the suffering of others and the loving kindness that provides joy to others are attributes of the volunteer. It helps if the volunteers are of a happy disposition so that their personal suffering does not burden others.

The process of becoming peaceful and building confidence can develop during social engagement. However, this requires occasionally taking time off for oneself, so as not to get "burned out," which is a bitter, common malady among peace activists. To be an effective volunteer, it is important to have a peacefulness within and a confidence in the knowledge of oneself.

THE SANGHA

Volunteers often work under trying conditions and for this reason it is particularly important for us to have a support group with which to work. The importance of this *sangha*,[17] or support team, cannot be overstated. It is to this community that a volunteer returns for the renewal of strength, assistance, and direction. The work of volunteers in conflict situations is hard and often lonely. Without a supportive situation, the struggle to build and use one's energy at times when the going is tough is most trying. A sangha of people who believe in themselves and share common goals can revive the personal strength necessary to face the rebuilding process with confidence. When decisions are made within the sangha itself, they are preferably worked out by consensus.

Each member of the PADSA team was encouraged to build up his or her own sangha of volunteers within the artisan community and outside of it. In the core team sangha, the day would start with a practice of sitting together quietly for 15 minutes. Then one of us would read an inspirational passage from a practical idealist such as Mahatma Gandhi, Rev. Martin Luther King, Swami Vivekananda, or Thich Nhat Hanh. The team had members of different religious backgrounds, and sometimes we read from the Gita, Koran, Bible, or Dhammapada. This helped in providing inspiration and strength for the work and a feeling of connectedness.[18]

PEACE-BUILDING IN AN ASIAN CONTEXT

It is through understanding and sharing that the fear at the origin of most conflicts and violence can be reduced to a level that allows a peaceful environment to develop. In Asia, there is a very specific conception of peace-building based on understanding and sharing. Over the last 2,500 years, Buddhist monasteries have developed special practices for settling disputes. This system of techniques was formulated to settle disputes within the circle of monks.[19]

Because conflicts between nations and within countries often arise from the same mechanisms as individual and interpersonal conflicts, lessons can be learned from the experience accumulated in small communities. The process of peace-building begins within the individual. Gradually, through observation and reflection, the interdependence of all phenomena becomes clear. One realizes that peace is not just an individual matter, but that it extends outward from the individual and is exercised by the individual in words and deeds that eventually extend to the world at large. In other words, people affect one another. If your loved ones are not happy and at peace, neither can you be; if a community's or country's neighbours are not at peace, then there can be no peace within the community or country.

There is potential for small conflicts within PADSA. These are the effects on people working across long distances and meeting after substantial periods of time have passed. Tensions and misunderstandings can arise and harm the work if they are not dealt with in timely way and in the right spirit. Such a situation occurred in the PADSA team when negative feelings and perceptions surfaced and the situation consequently became tense. I felt that a system of seven practices developed to settle disputes within the circle of monks as described by the Zen master Thich Nhat Hanh would be useful. These seven methods of settling disputes have been adopted by Buddhist monks and nuns in India, China, Vietnam, Japan, Korea, and many other countries. They can provide personal help to volunteers working in conflict situations to increase understanding and to promote peacefulness. These practices were used successfully in the context of the sangha to diffuse tensions and increase support within the group.[20]

PARTICIPATION OF NATIONAL UN VOLUNTEERS

The most valuable resource of a volunteer programme is people. PADSA has been a pioneering programme for recruiting National UN Volunteers (NUNVs), natives of the countries in which the work is taking place. For community-based initiatives to be encouraged, it is important to have volunteers from the community who can understand the subtleties of the local situations and who have access to local decision-making. This way there is more transparency; the volunteers are more accountable to the community; and they also have a long-term stake in the development and direction of the work. The concept of National UN Volunteers was developed by UNV, and received support from the governments of the countries involved after detailed meetings. This support came from the understanding that the knowledge and experience gained through the volunteer work would stay within the country in the persons of the NUNVs.

Additionally, being a UN Volunteer gave national volunteers access to persons at the highest decision-making levels in the state or country.

I used a number of methods for recruiting National UN Volunteers, such as advertising, letters to non-governmental and government organizations, word of mouth, and visits to Bhutan, Nepal, Sri Lanka, and the five regions of India. I spent a few days with each NUNV in the field, observing attitudes and behaviours in the context of volunteerism before recruiting them into the team. I also met the families of the volunteers to gauge and evoke their support.

National volunteers with different backgrounds and characteristics were selected in the experimental pilot phase to test the effectiveness of different types of people. I selected artisans with leadership or organizational abilities, a retired government servant, young professionals, social activists, and a civil servant on deputation. The common factor of the members of the volunteer team was their commitment to the artisan sector. The expertise was varied, including professional skills in areas such as technology, media, law, administration, computers, science, marketing, and finance.

Recruitment took place over a number of months, so not all of the areas of the programme started simultaneously. Also, the programme covered a large geographical area. A number of the communities in which the programme worked were marginalized in their own societies; some were indigenous tribes and some were classified as "untouchables." In fact, three of the eight National UN Volunteers and the video filmmaker in the programme were themselves from indigenous tribes. Many of the artisan communities in the subcontinent are considered "untouchable" by the caste system. However, National UN Volunteers from "higher castes" such as Ramlal Awale, a Newar from Nepal, mixed freely, working, eating, and sleeping in the homes of the untouchables such as the Saarkis leather workers.

I tried to ensure an equal balance of women and men among the National UN Volunteers. Women were deliberately recruited, even though in the South Asian context there is more pressure on a woman not to travel, especially in remote areas where it often takes many days and nights to reach the destination and by a variety of means of transport from boats to camels.

The National UN Volunteers have played many organizational roles, working among the people, not above them, working from within, not from the outside. The analysis, formulation of policy, and action were developed by the volunteers acting as catalysts, not as leaders. The

National UN Volunteers could see "both sides"—how the present systems affected artisans and how to solve their problems.

The volunteers lived in remote areas in the field in close contact with the artisan communities. Innovative methods of communication had to be developed, including the use of couriers. Some of the villages were more than a day's walk from a road, and over half the National UN Volunteers had no access to telephones. In some cases, as in eastern Bhutan, the closest telephone was five hours away at an army border barracks. In many areas, including my office, the supply of electricity was erratic at best. As I write this sentence, the electricity has been off for 38 hours!

The programme has built up a large database of contacts, volunteers, and resource people, along with information on their expertise. A number of different types of volunteers have been attracted to the programme from various strata of society, such as patrons (those who have financial resources, commitment, structures, and status), professionals, government civil servants, retired persons, housewives, and students. Within the community, volunteers have included farmers and other villagers, master artisans, enthusiastic young artisans, and children of artisans.

Right from the start the team tried to raise resources to match the UNV funds by stressing the volunteer nature of the programme and by giving institutions and individuals the opportunity to support the work and the team of committed people. The programme was able to get five members of the full-time team on deputation; the parent organization fully covered the cost of some, and in other cases the parent organization shared the cost. The value of infrastructure and human resources that PADSA attracted were considerable, including, for example, the use of free office space for nine offices across the region. Memoranda of Understanding were signed with the government of Maharastra, India, and other organizations, thereby initiating a programme to plant bamboo in 300 villages and to keep a close record of its progress. Small amounts of money were also raised, including voluntary contributions from artisans who had participated in the exchanges and workshops.

MUTUAL EXCHANGE

A bio-diversity study conducted from 1990 to 1991[21] in the north-eastern region of India made it clear that to protect the environment, especially forests, it was necessary to generate alternative sources of income. Instead of bringing in alien technology such as a micro-chip assembly plant,

I felt that encouraging traditional weaving skills would be the best way to generate local income. When the idea of a yarn bank developed, we decided to bring together Tibetan women, who had experience in purchasing and storing bulk yarn, with Naga women, who wanted to do the same. Following this, I did an exploratory study[22] enlisting artisans' views on mutual exchange and formulating a method using "barefoot" expertise, which UNV supported.

The programme has developed and tested a method of providing volunteer support to the artisan sector in the areas of need articulated by artisans themselves. The areas of intervention are marketing, finance and credit, organization of producer groups, design, materials, technology, government policy, and occupational health.

"Barefoot" artisan specialists—people from the community who have developed innovative and indigenous methods—shared their expertise with other artisan communities. They were identified by the National UN Volunteer programme facilitators, who collected and disseminated information to reach the appropriate experts, who were then invited to share their expertise with communities. Travel and other arrangements were organized and supported by the programme. Some of the experts had barely been out of their localities, and so the responsibilities were all the greater for the National UN Volunteer, who acted as a mediator of cultures. In some cases, artisans from the hills were seeing the sea for the first time, or artisans from a village were seeing high-rise buildings or travelling by air for the first time.

Despite the language differences, it was obvious that mutual exchange and learning were possible by sharing practical skills; as a weaver put it, "We spoke through the loom."[23] While we sometimes wondered whether artisans and experts would share their techniques with others, who could be perceived as potential competitors, there was, in fact, strong cooperation and sharing, quite different from the atmosphere of mutual distrust prevalent in the dominant market model of competition. As Subal Pramanik, an artisan from Midnapur in eastern India, said about sharing his skills, "To do something for others is the best religion. Peace originates only from a sympathetic mind."

The empowerment experienced by individuals ripened slowly, not only among the volunteer sangha but among the serving volunteers. Malati Hebram, a Santhal, was very shy and meek the first time she attended an exchange and was just starting to get interested in learning bamboo artisanship. "We are tribal (people), so we worship nature," she said. "We know that keeping the balance of nature is the best religion because nature is our only saviour." Over the past year she has gained tremendous confidence, especially after she was able to sell at a local crafts fair all the products she had made through the programme.

In PADSA, communication was encouraged from the traditionally more quiet group members, who were often women. Women sometimes needed the support of meeting among themselves before meeting with men and actively carrying on dialogue with them. "It is only by going out and seeing new places that our horizon will expand and we will get the confidence to speak boldly in front of the men," said Sushma Dattaray Karanjakar, a village woman from Shastabad, Maharastra, who led a group, as part of PADSA, to articulate their needs to government officials.

Villagers and volunteers were encouraged to share their opinions with government officials in open forums. Participatory planning was encouraged by getting villagers to articulate their needs and by providing estimates of costs and time frames for completion of work, including *shramdan* (voluntary labour).[24]

AN ALTERNATIVE APPROACH TO DEVELOPMENT AND PEACE

The Sustainable Human Development[25] agenda of the United Nations Development Programme has rightly put the emphasis on four pillars: women, nature, employment, and the poor. Household- and community-based impoverished artisans with their ecologically sustainable, labour intensive technologies can be a central focus in such a development agenda. To support these pillars, however, implicitly implies a stance against something else: the dominant economic industrial system, which is biased in favour of the 20 per cent of the world population that earns over 80 per cent of the world's income and holds access to nearly 95 per cent of commercial lending.[26] The challenge is how to move towards the development model that emphasizes peace and sustainability.

The dominant model of development emphasizes individualist market values of competition and self-interest, and the accumulation and speculation of capital and commodities at the expense of sharing and solidarity, where the means of production are within the control of the producer. The result is the replacement of diverse indigenous cultures and forms of social organization (which include a value for the aged and a place for the disabled) with unbridled universal consumerism. Among the communities of people that are most damaged by the present economic structures are those using traditional technologies, such as artisan communities. Marginal communities tend to be absorbed into a global system controlled by a small minority of governments, corporations, financiers, and media magnates.

Even in remote areas such as Nagaland, among the 18 indigenous tribes making up the population of the state, weaving skills, once a prerequisite for marriage, are fast disappearing. This is especially true among women under age 35 because of factory-made cloth imported into the state[27] and a devaluation of the local culture due to the influence of satellite-transmitted media.[28] Since factory-spun yarn dyed with chemicals is being brought in from outside the state, the cultivation of cotton and natural dyeing techniques have practically disappeared.[29] Meanwhile on the streets of the capital, Kohima, people dress in fashions influenced by MTV, including Michael Jackson-like styles. The conflict of cultures extends to home life, where there is an increasing incidence of alcoholism and drug addiction.[30]

In contrast, Niamon Phom, also from Nagaland, had never been out of his state before coming to a skills exchange in Bengal. In his village all the men do bamboo work; he explained how important this work was to the community. Even those who may be considered a burden in some societies, such as the mentally retarded, are included in the village society and contribute to their own livelihood through this craft. The person's formal education is immaterial in the arena of craft; for Mr. Phom's children, practicing and learning this craft was their essential education.[31]

THE ARTISAN CHALLENGE

Artisans today are powerless in their own countries and have no voice at a global level. Most artisans in the South Asian region are landless, so when their traditional means of livelihood disappear they become unemployed slum dwellers and we all lose the accumulated wisdom of a sustainable economic system. Most of these inherited skills are fundamentally related to the culture of their host societies and are fast disappearing due to changes in the economic system.

In India alone, an estimated 21 per cent decrease in the number of artisans occurred between 1961 and 1981.[32] Such statistics are necessarily rough because artisans belong to the dispersed and unorganized sector of the population. They are among the poorest people, with no political power, little public recognition, and a diminished sense of themselves as a group. In my view there is a need for institutional forms of linkage in order to break political weakness and voicelessness.

The problem of these voiceless people is aggravated by debt and the consequent structural adjustment measures often imposed as the price for external loans by the International Monetary Fund and the World Bank. For example, leather artisans in Rajasthan and many other parts of India are increasingly unable to buy their raw materials.[33] This is because tax-free incentives are being given to exporters to produce cash income that contributes to the national economy; this cash is then used largely for petroleum and the acquisition of advanced technology.[34]

The dominant system of development uses an accounting system that is essentially short-term in outlook and not economical in ecological terms. This system subsidizes petroleum, the transportation infrastructure, and even the wars to keep control of global resources that are needed to maintain this system. The war in the Persian Gulf, which cost billions of US dollars, was primarily a war over the control of petroleum, the fuel that lubricates the dominant industrial economic system. With increasing industrialization, chemicalization, and nuclearization, greater dependency is placed on scarce resources across the earth. An alternative model would evaluate economic decisions in terms of their environmental, cultural, and intergenerational costs. Comparative analyses of energy consumption and accounting that actually count the environmental costs of products produced by the industrial and artisan sectors need to be attempted.

"Industrialize and perish"[35] was one of Mahatma Gandhi's slogans as he popularized the *charkha* (spinning wheel) to emphasize self-reliance and decentralized cottage industries. His *swadeshi*[36] concept of economic development included loyalty to one's neighbours; a duty to patronize goods produced in one's neighbourhood. Gandhi believed that the focus should be on "production by the masses instead of mass production." He said that "the character of production should be determined by social necessity and not by personal whim or greed."[37] "True economics," Ghandi said, "never militate against the highest ethical standard, just as all true ethics to be worth its name must, at the same time be good economics. An economic (system) which inculcates Mammon worship and enables the strong to amass wealth at the expense of the weak is a dismal science. True economics on the other hand stands for social justice, promotes the good of all equally, including the weakest and is indispensable for a decent life."[38]

Today his message and thoughts on the subject of an economy of "peace and permanence" still hold true for Southern societies whose strengths lie in human skills and labour. The time is ripe for the message to be heard and acted upon before we continue on a path that exacerbates the growing social, environmental, and political problems that arise mainly from the dominant development model.

According to the Rio Declaration on Environment and Development, "Peace, development and environmental protection are interdependent and indivisible."[39] Concerned people the world over are searching for ecologically sustainable methods of production while artisan systems, developed and sustained over thousands of years, continue to be used by millions. The term "artisan system" can, in my opinion, be broadened to include indigenous socio-political-economic systems that have developed through the understanding and genius of accumulated local wisdom and in keeping with the psyche of local communities. It is a locally-based system that values time-tested skills and methods of production and marketing that are environmentally sound and encourage self-sustaining communities.

Different countries have various policies for artisans, and there is still great scope for learning and collaboration. Many countries do not even recognize their artisan potential. Many Northern countries are not doing as much to preserve and promote artisanship as some Southern countries, and could learn from them.

Keeping up communication by linking artisan communities and volunteer forces, and by building up alliances among existing interregional networks, can help develop a virtual institution to support the growth of such a movement. Information can be shared among artisan volunteer representatives and community leaders, and between them and policy- and opinion-makers at the national and international levels.

ANOTHER WAY TO PEACE

Interestingly, hope for an alternative approach sometimes springs from those who benefit least from the global system, and whose survival depends on volunteer efforts by the local community. In the short-term, such an approach can help improve livelihood and self-esteem at the micro level, and it can also bring together people who have little understanding or even traditional animosity towards each other. They can join to share and learn from each other, as has happened in PADSA.

In the longer term perspective, the hope is to have an increasingly equitable and sustainable "economy of permanence"[40] motivated by service, that uses production and marketing methods in keeping with the nature, rhythm, and culture of the host societies. This would help create "conditions of stability and well-being which are necessary for peaceful and friendly relations," by attaining "full employment, and conditions of economic and social progress and development."[41]

The United Nations Volunteers Programme for Artisan Development in South Asia is only a small attempt to foster genuine sharing and communication through common skills, while trying to improve livelihoods. With its agenda of skills exchange, the programme has tried consciously to bring communities with animosities together and in some cases has also worked among refugees. PADSA has helped to foster understanding between these communities, and also has enhanced self-dignity among the marginalized artisans. "These exchanges are one way of keeping our traditions and cultures alive," one artisan said.[42]

At its most radical, the programme mounts a challenge—or at least presents an alternative—to the sort of industrialization that is destroying our environment and our traditional communities as it widens the gap between the rich and the poor. The programme presents from within the United Nations an alternative model of economic and cultural development. Such an illustrative effort can be reproduced. The success of trust and sharing that is built up, even over a few days, can have lessons for wider application.

Equally important is the recognition of a common fate of powerlessness and in some cases hopelessness that faces traditional artisans, even while they are the holders of a rich human heritage that has value for the future. This coming together can build a movement of artisans for a common cause, cutting across traditionally hostile lines (as the programme has illustrated in a small way) through shared understanding. The focus is to bring pressure to bear on the powers that determine economic and political policies that affect these workers. The confidence gained by working side by side with artisans of a similar profession but from different geographical areas and cultural backgrounds must not be underestimated.

Through the exchange mode of intervention I have witnessed, artisans have benefited from not only improved livelihood, but from broadened life experience and horizons of the mind that go towards dissolving barriers of race, religion, nation, language, ethnicity, caste, class, and region, while gaining a stronger sense of community and self respect. The *Agenda for Peace* seems daunting in the South Asian context. Since peace is the path that we have chosen to tread, and since it is a process rather than a product, we have to accept that the results will emerge gradually and will come only with small improvements, step by step, stitch by stitch, moment by moment.

NOTES

1. *Charter of the United Nations*. New York: UN Department of Public Information, 1993 reprint, p. 1.

2. Artisans are people who work primarily with their hands, using traditional skills and implements and locally available natural resources for making products of utilitarian and decorative value. They are largely self-employed, functioning at the household and community levels.

3. Dogra, Bharat. "Weavers Struggle to No Avail." *National Herald* (15 July 1994): 2.

4. Srinivasulu, K. "Handloom Weavers' Struggle for Survival." *Economic and Political Weekly* (3 September 1994).

5. Prasad, Swati. "A Better Future Emerges from Muddied Waters." *Economic Times* (19 February 1995).

6. Joshi, Deep. "The Plight of Flayers." *The Pioneer* (4 May 1995): 10.

7. This is an estimate derived from census records in India and discussions with government and non-government personnel working in the artisan sector.

8. Boutros-Ghali, Boutros. *An Agenda for Peace 1995*. New York: UN Department of Public Information, 1995, p. 1; or UN Doc. A/47/277-S/2411, 1992.

9. Boutros-Ghali, Boutros. *An Agenda for Development 1995*. New York: United Nations, 1995.

10. "Barefoot" denotes local grassroots leadership and expertise. *UNV News* 65 (March 1994): 2.

11. General Assembly Resolution 2659 (XXV), 7 December 1970.

12. Dorjee, Tenzin. *Monthly Programme Report* (November 1994).

13. Video report of PADSA women weavers exchange held at Bylakuppe refugee settlement, Karnataka, India, August 1994.

14. Nandi, Robi. *Report on Bamboo Artisans Exchange at Bishnupur*. West Bengal, India, April 1995.

15. As related by Kiron Ayengia, a National UN Volunteer in north-east India.

16. Takehito Nakata is the father of Atsuhito Nakata, who was killed in Cambodia while serving as a UNV district electoral officer in April 1993. Since then, Mr. Nakata has dedicated himself to the cause of volunteerism as honorary ambassador for United Nations Volunteers.

17. Support team. In Buddhist terminology it denotes a Community of Practice.

18. It helps to have some ground rules or a code of conduct to provide a basis for the community to develop understanding and overcome differences. In the *sanghas*, codes were developed to set boundaries on irritation, anger, and greed. The attempt was to be non-hierarchical in the management of PADSA and to come to decisions by consensus, using the "council process." Adapted from a Native American tradition in which each person in the circle puts forward a view on the matter being discussed or tells a relevant story, the meeting continues until a consensus emerges. In PADSA, some decisions on communication and expenditure matters were made, such as communicating with each other at least once a week and using the cheapest option on all activities unless limited by time. Codes were developed to keep harmony in the team, such as the signing of a Peace Treaty (a treaty developed in Plum Village, a Buddhist community in France to keep harmony in the community), and "Beginning Anew" (a practice developed at the time of the Buddha, for communities of monks and nuns to de-escalate underlying conflicts). This practice consists of sharing openly what one may have felt was unskillful behaviour of oneself or others. Some practices were developed in sanghas to keep one's own cool, such as breathing and smiling through anger and irritation, while others existed simply for joy, such as walking meditation. See Hanh, Thich Nhat. *A Guide to Walking Meditation*. Nyack, N.Y.: The Fellowship of Reconciliation, 1985; and Hanh, Thich Nhat. *Being Peace*. Berkeley, Calif.: Parallax Press, 1987, pp. 74–79.

19. The Community of Practice includes methods for resolving conflicts between individuals. For example, the two persons in conflict know that the others of the community expect them to make peace, so they try to remember the history of the conflict. Non-stubbornness is very important. The fact that each person does his or her best to show the willingness to reconcile and understand is even more important than the outcome.

The senior member of the group of monks tries by words to de-escalate the feelings of anger and resistance between the two persons in conflict. Known as "covering the mud with straw," this method is simply explained: when we walk in the countryside after a rain, it is very muddy. If we have straw to spread over the mud, we can walk safely.

20. This was difficult to put into practice, since one of the parties in a dispute only very reluctantly agreed to even sit face to face, which is a basic exercise. Through the mediation of another volunteer, the meeting did take place and both parties sat together with the group, in an atmosphere of confidence and peace with the willingness to help and not to fight. Through voluntary confession each one revealed his own shortcomings, without waiting for others to say them. Even though it was a very minor confession, it helped the other person feel better. It encouraged a confession of something of the same magnitude by the other person. Decision by consensus and acceptance of the decision were the final steps. It was agreed in advance that the two persons experiencing conflict with each other would accept whatever decision is made by the group.

21. Reflected in a study I carried out, which was sponsored by the Worldwide Fund for Nature (India) and Indo-German Social Service Society on "Conservation of Dzukou Valley—A Unique Eco-system."

22. UNV Programme for Artisan Sector in South Asia, Phase I, an exploratory report, April 1992.

23. Choeki Ongmo, a weaver and National UN Volunteer in Bhutan, as recorded on the video "Speaking Hands," directed by Bano Haralu and produced by PADSA.

24. Voluntary labour is a tradition in the sub-continent, especially for community projects.

25. Speth, James Gustave. "Building a New UNDP, Agenda for Change." A presentation to the UNDP Executive Board, 17 February 1994.

26. *Human Development Report 1992*. New York: UNDP, 1992.

27. Personal communication with Mene Chandola, a weaver and Delhi convener of the Naga Mother's Association.

28. Personal communication with Bano Haralu, national television correspondent from Nagaland.

29. Personal communication with Metsi Iralu, a weaving expert from Nagaland, India.

30. Personal communication with Ricky Medom, pastor, Nagaland Baptist church.

31. Bishnupur Exchange speech by Niamon Phom, a bamboo "barefoot" expert from Nagaland, India, 12 April 1995.

32. Society for Rural Urban and Tribal Initiative. *Statistical Overview of the Artisan Sector*. New Delhi, 1988, p. 4.

33. Personal communication with William Bissel, owner of Fab India, a shop selling traditionally handcrafted footwear made in villages of Rajasthan, India.

34. Ministry of Finance, Government of India, *Economic Survey 1994–95*.

35. Gandhi, Mohandas Karamchand. *Industrialize and Perish*. Ahmedabad: Navajivan Publishing House, 1966.

36. Kumarappa, J.C. *Swadeshi, The Moral Law of Self-Reliance*. Delhi: Rajesh Press, 1968.

37. Narayan, Shriman. *Relevance of Gandhian Economics*. Ahmedabad: Navajivan Publishing House, 1970, p. 224.

38. Gandhi, Mohandas Karamchand. *Harijan* (9 October 1937).

39. United Nations Conference on Environment and Development, Rio Declaration on Environment and Development, 1992.

40. Kumarappa, J. C. *Economy of Permanence*. Varanasi: Sarva Seva Sangh Prakashan, 1984.

41. Article 55 of the *Charter of the United Nations*, Chapter IX, International Economic and Social Co-operation, p. 30.

42. Ongmo Dazer, a "barefoot" expert weaver, as recorded on the video "Speaking Hands," directed by Bano Haralu and produced by PADSA.

CONCLUSION

UN VOLUNTEERS AND THE UNITED NATIONS SYSTEM

Larry Minear and Thomas G. Weiss

THE ACCOUNTS BY UN Volunteers of their experiences in recent assignments on the front lines of armed conflicts provide glimpses of the United Nations system responding to complex emergencies and of the contributions made by committed individuals to that response. Just as the UN Volunteers Programme provided a point of entry for these nine individuals into the global effort to meet urgent human needs, so, too, the experiences described here bring alive for readers the challenges faced by the international community as it confronts civil strife, ethnic tension, and endemic poverty and powerlessness.

At a time of growing doubt that an "international community" really exists, these UN Volunteers and other concerned individuals like them within and outside the United Nations system affirm by their activities that a caring community remains within reach. They also validate the important roles that outsiders may play in expressing solidarity and providing assistance and protection to imperiled populations. Accomplishments of UN Volunteers—and their frustrations as well—illuminate the problems confronted by the UN system—and suggest some creative solutions.

THREE PROBLEMS

Three problems faced by the United Nations system in this first decade of the post-Cold War era are evident from these first-person accounts. Varying a bit from country to country and conflict to conflict, the problems form something of a *leitmotiv* throughout. The first tension is between humanitarian activities and the political-military side of the United Nations. The second is between the grassroots orientation of assistance and the headquarters orientation of the UN bureaucracy. The third is between the UN system that frequently takes the lead in complex emergencies and those outside of it with skills and energy to contribute. Each of these problems deserves examination.

Tensions at the Political-Military Interface

As noted in the Introduction, the complex emergencies that increasingly provide the setting for UNV work involve almost inevitably the political-military side of the United Nations. UN Volunteers and UN staff with mandates in the humanitarian, human rights, and development arenas share the terrain with personnel having mandates in conflict resolution, consensual peacekeeping, and more coercive peace-enforcement duties.

The identification of UN Volunteers and their activities with the UN system has proved a great asset for many volunteers. In places like Cambodia, Mozambique, and South Africa, it was the United Nations that had helped set the stage for the resolution of the conflicts and for the reconciliation and reconstruction of which the volunteers would be a part. UN and associated diplomatic efforts had drawn down the curtain on past armed conflicts and opened up new vistas.

For certain other volunteers, the UN connection has been a definite liability. The UN Volunteers were fully integrated into the second UN Operation in Somalia, with three-quarters of the volunteers assigned—in effect, confined—to UNOSOM headquarters, as Anthony Nweke notes in "Behind the Compound Wall." The observations by other UN Volunteers confirm that their association with UNOSOM II created problems in terms of local perception and access. Similarly, in the former Yugoslavia, Benny Ben Otim found that the "lack of a coherent political strategy" complicated and ultimately undercut the best efforts of UN and other humanitarian organizations.

The interface between the "sides" of the UN was on occasion more ambiguous than positive or negative. In Cambodia, association with the United Nations Transitional Authority, initially an asset, became less so as UNTAC's authority was undermined by the country's political factions and by the behaviour of some UN troops. "The same staff who at one time had taken so much pride in being part of UNTAC," writes Nandini Srinivasan, later "had to conceal their identity cards." UN soldiers would do well to take seriously the observation of one UN Volunteer that "[O]ur own conduct was as important as the duties we were assigned."

The accounts highlight the struggle of individual volunteers with how the interface between their work and that of the political-military UN should be managed. For Stephen Kinloch, the credibility of the United Nations as a humanitarian agent suffered from its ineffectual response to Rwanda's genocide, leading him to recommend the creation of a permanent UN ready-response force. His view is echoed by his counterpart in the former Yugoslavia, who calls for greater UN military muscle and a clearer distinction between humanitarian and political-military roles on the one hand and a more determined search for lasting political solutions to conflicts on the other.

While some volunteers view the tension between political-military strategies and their own work in terms of philosophy and values, others take a more pragmatic approach. For them, the issue seems to be not the appropriateness or legitimacy of peacekeeping or peace-enforcement but the professionalism with which these undertakings are implemented.

One of the specific areas in which tensions come to a head concerns the different timetables for action. A recurring theme is the sense among the UN Volunteers that their activities were concluded too soon—and, in some cases, initiated too late—to accomplish durable results. Had they been able to remain longer in Mozambique and Cambodia, they say, the durability of the political as well as the humanitarian accomplishments of the UN would have been consolidated. This plea represents not simply the logical and laudable desire of committed professionals to see a job through but also the underlying need for more continuity of international presence and resources than is typically provided by the political-military side of the United Nations. The composite picture that emerges is of the UN tackling the essential tasks, but failing to be provided with adequate resources and appropriate time frames to succeed.[1]

As of mid-1995, the proper balance has yet to be struck. Finding the proper balance preoccupies Under-Secretaries-General at the United Nations in New York, who are seeking ways to achieve more coherence between and among their respective duties in humanitarian affairs, political affairs, and peacekeeping operations. It also concerns Governments— Australia and the Netherlands have recently done major studies on the subject. It animates discussions among non-governmental organizations

(NGOs). Some private relief groups have emerged from the latest round of complex emergencies more committed to cooperate closely with the political-military UN, while others are convinced that independent rather than integrated activities are more likely to be effective.

The international community is seeking ways to conceptualize and capture the potential synergism between political-military and humanitarian, human rights, and development concerns.[2] Particularly noteworthy are the benefits to political-military interests of well-managed humanitarian activities. Thus, the work of UN Volunteers in Mozambique in the areas of demobilization made a positive contribution to what UNOMOZ was able to accomplish in a broad range of sectors. The need flagged by UN Volunteers for increased security in Cambodia brought overdue attention to the electoral component by the larger UN peacekeeping operation and augmented UNTAC's broader chances of success.

UN Volunteers also sought, and brought about, institutional changes in the ways that humanitarian organizations themselves functioned, as the account of protection activities by UNHCR in the former Yugoslavia illustrates. Institutional change is envisioned by the suggestion from Rwanda that, in order to avoid some of the dependency-producing effects of emergency assistance, UN Volunteers be deployed "to encourage community-based activities and to facilitate the recruitment and training of local volunteers." The experiences of UN Volunteers related in this volume thus deserve examination as the UN system in all of its facets seeks to enhance its effectiveness in war zones.

Tensions between Grassroots and Headquarters

A consistent theme throughout this volume has been the tensions arising from the grassroots orientation of UN Volunteers. In Cambodia, South Africa, Mozambique, the former Yugoslavia, Rwanda, and South Asia, the volunteers were working in their assigned tasks in local communities. Conspicuous by its exceptional nature was Somalia, where, we are told, "Most of the UN Volunteers were deployed to administrative and technical support units, where their responsibilities did not make use of the professionalism for which the UN Volunteers are known." In what clearly was an aberration, three-quarters of the UNV complement worked at UNOSOM headquarters.

By and large, UN Volunteers bring a critical dimension to the field presence of the UN system. In some instances, they join with personnel from other Agencies such as UNHCR and UNICEF posted in the hinterlands. At the same time, UN Volunteers greatly augment the human resources that other organizations, including NGOs, are able to post. In fact, the numbers of UN Volunteers mentioned in this volume—465 in Cambodia, 200 in South Africa, 120 in Somalia—are unusual in their magnitude. Even where UNV complements were more modest in size—initially 32 in Liberia, 26 in Rwanda, 18 in former Yugoslavia—those numbers frequently overshadowed the international personnel resources available to other Agencies. Taking into account national staffs trained by UN Volunteers, the extent of UNV presence in the countryside becomes more impressive still. Deployment in the hundreds rather than the dozens offers leveraging and outreach possibilities that often elude other Agencies, even those that pride themselves on maintaining grassroots profiles.

The importance of a genuine UN presence throughout a country in conflict can hardly be overstated. In the words of one volunteer, "The contribution that UN Volunteers bring to UN efforts may be squandered if this resource is not recognized for what it is: a powerful alliance at the grassroots by and for people of the country with the United Nations." The observation made in Cambodia has been equally true in other settings: "[W]hat made UN Volunteers different was our daily contact with the population, which was our own distinct advantage."

Without UN Volunteers, the United Nations in these various settings would have been far too thinly represented on the front lines, if represented there at all. The 465 volunteers who functioned as election supervisors, two in each of the country's districts, where few of UNTAC's 20,000 personnel were in evidence, made a demonstrable contribution to the successful conduct of the elections. Without the 49 technical unit camp officers, one for each of Mozambique's assembly areas, the UN would have been hard-pressed to carry out the demobilization of soldiers, on which its other many activities depended.

The frustration of volunteers with the lack of adequate support for their efforts from the UN system is apparent throughout, although it is balanced by their appreciation for the difficulties the system itself is facing. Examples abound of the creaking and groaning of the UN system in the face of the needs of those staff working in isolated areas at the community level.

The idea that what happens at the grassroots level is important—often even decisive—comes as no secret to the managers of the UN system and its various component parts. The make-or-break aspect of what happens in local communities is acknowledged in UN Secretary-General Boutros Boutros-Ghali's *An Agenda for Peace: Preventive Diplomacy, Peacemaking and Peace-keeping*. Unveiled in early 1992, the *Agenda* staked out what the Secretary-General envisioned as the future directions of the world body. Drawing linkages between high-level political-military activities and the reinforcing changes needed at the local level, he observed that "The focus of the United Nations should be on the 'field', the locations where economic, social and political decisions take effect."[3] This theme has been reiterated and emphasized more recently in *An Agenda for Development*.[4]

The UN system has yet to take up the Secretary-General's challenge. Doing so would require a fundamental reconfiguring of the system and of the interrelationships of its component parts. In fact, one of the currently unresolved policy issues pertains to which actors have a comparative advantage in particular areas—for example, at the grassroots—and at particular points in the spectrum of violence and armed conflicts. The experience recounted here suggests that UN Volunteers have the community-level contacts and expertise normally associated with NGOs but with greater national and local outreach than most NGOs can muster. With respect to the effectiveness of various actors at different points in the conflict spectrum—pre-conflict, active conflict, post-conflict—the experience narrated here is too limited and too particularistic for much generalization.

Tensions between the UN System and Those Outside

Given the demonstrable contributions by UN Volunteers to the UN system, the recurrent tensions between volunteers in the field and various responses from the UN bureaucracy are troubling. In several conflict zones, UN Volunteers describe frictions between themselves and UN colleagues, on both the political-military and the humanitarian sides. While some of the tensions are natural products of normal interactions in tense and even life-threatening circumstances, structural issues are also involved.

The identification as "volunteers," reports Masako Yonekawa after four back-to-back UNV assignments, "unfortunately leads some people to consider us second-class workers." The fact that the cost of a UN Volunteer was about one-quarter of the cost of a regular staff member or consultant led to the perception that UN Volunteers were "cheap labour." One setting in which serious frictions did not seem to develop was South Africa, where UN Volunteers, perhaps because the UNOMSA operation itself was new, were "on equal ground with the international UN staff." Even there, however, the distinction that those who were paid more did the more valuable work proved divisive.

Some of the tension is understandable since many UN Volunteers are new to the UN system. Many are initially unfamiliar with the policies and procedures of the particular organization to which they are assigned or with the culture of the international civil service more generally. Yet that is hardly a satisfactory explanation for what is clearly a more generic problem. In the words of one, "Though UN Volunteers often had little or no previous UNHCR experience, they brought with them maturity and flexibility, in addition to their own specialized experience in their respective fields."

The need for ensuring fuller and more creative use of volunteer resources is self-evident. The UN system is overwhelmed by the current spate of conflicts and desperately in need of help from the outside. UN Volunteers themselves represent an enormous reservoir of skills, experience, and energy. Not only can they extend the effectiveness of the UN system; they can also help to offset some of its acknowledged shortcomings. "Volunteers can help improve the image of the UN, which is too often perceived as a stiff bureaucracy perpetuating the interests of a few civil servants pursuing career strategies," says a volunteer in Rwanda.

An underlying policy issue involved concerns the need for a fundamental rethinking of the meaning of the term "volunteer." The UN Volunteers provide their own understandings and personifications of that concept. Anthony Nweke is quite typical of his colleagues in identifying motivation, commitment, and dedication as "the basic elements of volunteerism." In a larger sense, however, these are also the desirable characteristics of international civil servants with whom UN Volunteers work on a daily basis. Nor is the distinguishing factor that one group is "professional" or "more professional" than the other. Perhaps the difference lies not in motivation or skills but rather in relationship to the UN system itself.

The broader issue for the international community concerns how to structure institutions in ways that take fuller advantage of the resources coming from outside the UN system proper.

UNV CONTRIBUTIONS

In addition to their grassroots connections and their critical mass, UN Volunteers bring five special, if not altogether unique, attributes to the work of the United Nations system and of the international community in conflict settings.

First, volunteers *address some of the root causes of conflict*. In chapter after chapter, UN Volunteers attempt to tackle problems at their source. In South Asia, nurturing the skills of artisans is approached as an exercise in bridge-building across divided communities. In Mozambique, the target of demobilization programmes is the social alienation that had contributed to the conflict and the reincorporation of people into productive roles. The UNV approach provides an instructive contrast to much humanitarian action, which is frequently—and often rightly—criticized for attending to immediate and urgent needs while leaving root causes unaddressed.

Second, UN Volunteers *support change rather than leading or coercing it.* The UNV approach is suggested in microcosm by an incident at an organizational meeting of a peace committee in South Africa in which local leaders turned to the UN Volunteers and UNOMSA staff for actual decisions. "While we were there to support the process, we were not there to lead it," Diane Conklin recalled in passing the baton deftly back to the group. The emphasis on enabling rather than doing was appropriate in view of the fact that UN Volunteers were on hand for the final phase in a complex transformation and would leave before the transformation process was completed. The narratives in this volume provide countless other vignettes of international personnel facilitating rather than manipulating. While conflict resolution may be encouraged from outside, the process to be sustainable and effective must be led by local people themselves.

In this context, one of the attributes cultivated by UN Volunteers is what Shantum Seth calls "to listen deeply." Many volunteers convey their sense that as outsiders they must work long and hard at understanding the complex processes of social change. Seeking to direct or orchestrate such change would be risky and ultimately counterproductive. The value of listening to local voices, even when doing so requires sitting patiently through endless diatribes, is dramatized in the former Yugoslavia. There, trust built up over time by UN Volunteers enabled the successful negotiation with local authorities of safe passage for minority populations.

Third, *the composition, skills, and training of UNV contingents is distinctive.* A recurring theme throughout the accounts has been the multinational and multiethnic makeup of UNV country teams. The UN Volunteers in Cambodia were drawn from 65 countries. Half of the UN Volunteers in Liberia were African, with Kenya, Sierra Leone, Somalia, Sudan, Tanzania, and Uganda represented. The fact that UNV Observation Support Officers in South Africa came from 39 countries, with more than half of the volunteers of African origin, had far more than cosmetic value. It affected the perceptions not only of local communities but also of the non-African UN Volunteers themselves. A larger cross-section of

UNV experience than recounted here might even establish a positive correlation between the inclusiveness of UNV teams and their successes.

The skills that the volunteers brought with them were impressive. Descriptions of tasks—from demobilizing soldiers to setting up electoral processes to training artisans—provide fascinating glimpses of the demands of their jobs. What emerges from these various accounts is a picture of an organization that provides a point of entry into the UN system for skilled professionals from around the world. Moreover, at a time when the humanitarian enterprise has primarily a Western and developed country flavour, the inclusiveness of the UNV Programme is noteworthy.

The accounts provide a picture of volunteers who have received careful training for their tasks, although it is clear from other settings that trade-offs exist between posting personnel on short notice and providing the requisite orientation. As one of the volunteers involved with training notes, placing large groups of people "with different backgrounds, experiences, and assignment expectations" into insecure settings on difficult missions requires the best possible training. Quality briefing and support services are needed to avoid the ravages of "depression, burnout, and high turnover of staff."

Fourth, UN Volunteers *focus on the pragmatic*. A recurrent theme throughout is their results-oriented approach. Among the accomplishments described in this volume were the conduct of elections in which more than four million Cambodians voted in 1,400 polling stations; the demobilization of some 78,000 government and insurgent soldiers in Mozambique; the facilitation of talks among faction leaders in Somalia; the negotiation of safe passage for Muslims from Banja Luka; the arranging of trucks in Tanzania for use by relief organizations in Rwanda; and problem-solving and the building of solidarity among artisans in South Asia.

Finally, UN Volunteers *put people at the centre of their work*. "People and their well-being are what really matter," noted Gláucia Vaz Yoshiura from her Mozambique experience. While the comment seems axiomatic for humanitarian professionals, the international machinery for responding to armed conflicts is often less focused and more cumbersome. Putting human well-being at the centre sometimes requires playing an advocacy role on their behalf within the UN system, with other international actors, and with host political-military authorities. Examples recur through/out this volume of UN Volunteers pressuring their own Agencies to meet their responsibilities more adequately.

Keeping the needs of people first and foremost also involves taking personal and professional risks. The work of most volunteers meant physical hardship, personal inconvenience, and, in some cases, insecurity and risk. In Cambodia, one UN Volunteer, to whom this volume is dedicated, was killed in the line of duty; two other UN Volunteer electoral supervisors were wounded; and three national staff were killed. As the insecurity increased with the approach of the elections, the wonder is not that 60 UN Volunteers opted not to return to their districts but that 405 went back to their posts.

The picture that emerges is of volunteers who "care passionately," to use the words of one, "about the welfare of people." In fact, two mention additional activities undertaken on their own time to extend what they could accomplish as UN Volunteers. Yet their idealism is not starry-eyed. Their accounts are characterized by a sense of tough-mindedness, balancing what volunteers would like to do against what can reasonably be accomplished in the circumstances.

PARTICIPATION IN "HISTORY IN THE MAKING"

The UN Volunteers Programme has given persons outside the United Nations system a point of entry onto the front lines in major international crises. "From my deployment in the Far Northern Transvaal," recalls one, "I was able to witness and to be part of this truly extraordinary historical event." Other volunteers communicate that same sense of excitement from their own geographic locations. "It was clear," recalls one from Mozambique, "that we were witnessing the birth of a unified effort by people of different political convictions to attain a common goal."

The history into which this volume provides a glimpse is chaotic and the experience of the UN Volunteers contains contradictions. Many obstacles are encountered and few of the initiatives—the South African and South Asian experiences are perhaps exceptions—are unalloyed successes. In places such as Cambodia, Mozambique, the former Yugoslavia, Rwanda, and Somalia, talk of enduring success is premature, notwithstanding the real contribution by UN Volunteers and others to reducing life-threatening suffering, and setting the stage for a fresh start.

It is almost a truism of volunteer activity that volunteers benefit as much as, and frequently more than, those assisted. Volunteers come to their task with what one calls "curiosity mixed with compassion" and often come away with a satisfying sense of what they have learned along the way. It may be unusual to have direct displays of gratitude, such as the weaving of the UNV logo into rugs made in South Asia. However, all of the volunteers reflect a positive sense of purposefulness and accomplishment. At the same time, they carry with them sharp and sometimes painful images of injustices and unaddressed business. Their own sense of values and their own professional goals and directions have also been affected.

Emerging from the volume is also the sense that international activity undertaken in a spirit of solidarity is rewarded less by the success of specific activities by outsiders than by what people are able to accomplish for themselves. This insight is particularly helpful at a time when the international community is suffering from a failure of nerve. The UNV experience reminds us that what is needed is not first and foremost a global bureaucracy to mitigate human suffering and manage social change. The future demands instead a more creative, extensive, and inclusive network of relationships and resources geared towards facilitating and enabling the efforts of people and societies themselves to shape their own futures. This insight from the UNV experience deserves a more prominent place among recommendations being made for fundamental changes in the UN system.

In that broader context, the experience of these volunteers takes on additional importance. As one of them points out, the determination and resilience of countries and communities that have been assisted should now provide reassurance to those on the outside who question the value and the urgency of international humanitarian action and development cooperation. The challenge of the United Nations is to find ways of making even better use of UN Volunteers and their efforts.

NOTES

1. For an elaboration of the issue of the differential timetables of political-military and humanitarian action, see Donini, Antonio. *UN Coordination in Complex Emergencies: Lessons from Afghanistan, Mozambique, and Rwanda.* Occasional Paper #22. Providence, R.I.: Watson Institute, forthcoming; and Equizábal, Cristina, David Lewis, Larry Minear, Peter Sollis, and Thomas G. Weiss. *Humanitarian Challenges in Central America: Lessons from Recent Armed Conflicts.* Occasional Paper #13. Providence, R.I.: Watson Institute, 1993.
2. For one recent elaboration of the issue and of three approaches to resolving interface tensions, see Minear, Larry and Thomas G. Weiss. *Humanitarian Politics.* New York: Foreign Policy Association, 1995.
3. Boutros-Ghali, Boutros. *An Agenda for Peace 1992.* New York: United Nations, 1992, para. 81.
4. Boutros-Ghali, Boutros. *An Agenda for Development 1995.* New York: United Nations, 1995.

POSTSCRIPT

ONE OF THE basic assumptions underlying our work at the United Nations University (UNU) is that all members of the global community must be aware of the far-reaching effects of their individual actions. We all influence the course of human events beyond our immediate neighbourhoods and we must be responsible for the consequences of those actions. We need to improve our understanding of the ways in which individuals can respond to the changing world around them. Our participation and involvement are crucial. This is a role in which UN Volunteers obviously have great experience—both by their individual acts as well as in their stimulation of the involvement of others. We have much to learn from the experiences of the United Nations Volunteers in fashioning new responses to pressing global problems, that are the concern of the United Nations and the United Nations University.

In this context, it is my hope that this book has provided the reader with an overview of some of the most ambitious and ground-breaking missions of the UN. The strength of this volume lies in the first-hand accounts of people who volunteered to serve in these missions and I am sure that it will contribute not only to a wider awareness of UNVs' roles and volunteerism, but also to a fuller understanding of the role of the international community in addressing complex emergencies.

Postscript

The United Nations University is happy to contribute to the further dissemination of the important work of United Nations Volunteers to the world community.

HEITOR GURGULINO DE SOUZA
Rector
United Nations University

ACRONYMS

ANC	African National Congress
AWB	Afrikaanse Weerstandsbeweging
BLDP	Buddhist Liberation Democratic Party
CAP	consolidated appeals process
CBO	community-based organization
CDE	District Electoral Commission
CIVPOL	Civilian Police
CODESA	Convention for a Democratic South Africa
CORE	Reintegration Commission
CPAF	Cambodian People's Armed Forces
CPP	Cambodian People's Party
CSCE	Conference on Security and Cooperation in Europe
DCHA	Division for the Coordination of Humanitarian Affairs
DEO	District Electoral Officer

DHA	Department for Humanitarian Affairs
DPA	Division for Political Affairs
DPI	Policy, Planning and Information Division
FADM	Mozambique Defence Forces
FAM	Forças Armadas de Moçambique
FAO	Food and Agriculture Organization
FRELIMO	Mozambique Liberation Front
FUNCINPEC	United National Front for an Independent, Neutral, Peaceful and Cooperative Cambodia
GPA	General Peace Agreement
HRU	Humanitarian Relief Unit
ICRC	International Committee of the Red Cross
IDP	internally displaced persons
IEC	Independent Electoral Commission
IEO	International Election Observer
IFP	Inkatha Freedom Party
ILO	International Labour Organization
IOM	International Organization for Migration
IRS	Information and Reference Service
JNA	Yugoslav People's Army
KPNLF	Khmer People's National Liberation Front
LDP	Liberation Democratic Party
MPNC	Multi-party Negotiating Council
MSF	Médecins Sans Frontières
NATO	North Atlantic Treaty Organization
NDF	National Defence Force
NGO	Non-governmental Organization
OIC	Organization of the Islamic Conference

ONUMOZ	United Nations Operation in Mozambique
PAC	Pan African Congress
PADSA	Programme for Artisan Development in South Asia
PASU	Programme and Administrative Support Unit
PDK	Party of Democratic Kampuchea
PKO	Peace-keeping Operation
PPG	Policy and Planning Group
PRK	People's Republic of Kampuchea
RAF	Rwanda Army Forces
RENAMO	Mozambique National Resistance
RPA	Rwandan Patriotic Army
RPF	Rwandan Patriotic Front
RSK	Republic of Serb Krajina
RSS	Reintegration Support Scheme
SACB	Somali Aid Coordination Body
SADF	South African Defence Force
SIOC	Special Representative's Information and Operations Center
SNA	Somali National Alliance
SNV	Somali National Volunteer
SRC	Supreme Revolutionary Council
SRSG	Special Representative of the Secretary-General
SSA	Somali Salvation Alliance
STAE	Technical Secretariats for the Administration of the Elections
TEC	Transitional Executive Council
TUCO	Technical Unit Camp Officer
TVC	temporary voting card
UN	United Nations

UNAMIR	United Nations Assistance Mission in Rwanda
UNCHR	United Nations Centre for Human Rights
UNCRO	United Nations Confidence Restoration Operation in Croatia
UNDO	United Nations Development Office
UNDP	United Nations Development Programme
UNHCR	United Nations High Commissioner for Refugees
UNICEF	United Nations Children's Fund
UNITA	National Union for the Total Independence of Angola
UNITAF	Unified Task Force
UNOHAC	United Nations Office for Humanitarian Assistance Coordination
UNOMIL	United Nations Observer Mission in Liberia
UNOMSA	United Nations Observer Mission in South Africa
UNOMUR	United Nations Observer Mission in Uganda-Rwanda
UNOSOM	United Nations Operation in Somalia
UNPA	United Nations Protected Area
UNPREDEP	United Nations Preventive Deployment Force
UNPROFOR	United Nations Protection Force
UNREO	United Nations Rwanda Emergency Office
UNRISD	United Nations Research Institute for Social Development
UNSCOL	United Nations Special Coordinator's Office in Liberia
UNTAC	United Nations Transitional Authority in Cambodia
UNV	United Nations Volunteers
USC	United Somali Congress
WFP	World Food Programme
WHO	World Health Organization
ZANU	Zimbabwean African National Union